AIGA
Professional
Practices in
Graphic Design

Second Edition

AIGA
Professional Practices in Graphic Design

Second Edition

ALLWORTH PRESS
NEW YORK

the professional association for design

12   11   10   09   08   5   4   3   2   1

Published by Allworth Press
An imprint of Allworth Communications, Inc.
10 East 23rd Street, New York, NY 10010

Cover design by James Victore
Interior design by The Roberts Group
Page composition/typography by Integra Software Services, Pvt., Ltd.,
Puducherry, India

Library of Congress Cataloging-in-Publication Data

AIGA professional practices in graphic design / edited by Tad Crawford.—2nd ed.
   p. cm.
 Includes bibliographical references and index.
 ISBN-13: 978-1-58115-509-9 (pbk.)
 ISBN-10: 1-58115-509-3
1. Commercial art—United States—Management.   2. Commercial art—United States—Marketing.   I. Crawford, Tad, 1946-   II. American Institute of Graphic Arts.   III. Title: American Institute of Graphic Arts professional practices in graphic design.   IV. Title: Professional practices in graphic design.

NC1001.6.A44 2008
741.6068—dc22

                                                                    2007047113

Printed in the United States of America

TABLE OF CONTENTS

PREFACE

RICHARD GREFÉ,
Executive Director, AIGA,
The Professional Association For Design

AIGA, the professional association for design, is dedicated to advancing designing as a professional craft, strategic tool, and vital cultural force. It is committed to leadership in the exchange of ideas and information, the encouragement of critical analysis and research, and the advancement of education and ethical practice.

This book is a comprehensive guide on professional practices for designers at all stages of their careers. The contents were developed in response to questions raised regularly by our members—working professionals. The authors, in turn, have each worked regularly with practicing designers, so that their solutions to the challenges they address are based on both principle and pragmatism.

As a young profession, both in terms of the age of many practitioners and the history of the profession, it is important that designers begin to address challenges in their relationships with clients that develop a set of norms for professional practice. Only as designers reflect a consistent, responsive, and businesslike tenor in relations with their clients will an expected set of norms define an established ethos for the profession.

The practices described in this guide will help designers in managing their practices—whether in a studio, agency, or corporate design department. They will also help to develop respect and trust for the designer in the business environment. Designers play an increasingly important role in creating value in a post-industrial society and information economy. AIGA and the advice contained here will help in assuring designers' success as professionals, leaders, and a creative force.

Part **1**

Relationships

1

Short History and the Longer View

MILTON GLASER

So many legends, so little time. Ric Grefé has asked me to speak briefly on the value of continuity in our profession. Of course one could take that charge to mean the short history of design, perhaps beginning with Peter Behrens, who is credited with the invention of identity programs and coordinating graphic and industrial design activities. Or one might consider our history as beginning with the first cave paintings at the dawn of history.

I prefer the longer view that relates our activity to the fundamental needs of the human species—a species whose most distinctive characteristic is making things for a purpose, which turns out to be the actual description of what we do.

Any grandiosity or self-importance that this cosmic description of our activity creates in us will be quickly erased by the discovery that in a typical design class, only 30 percent of the students will have any idea who Paul Rand is and will not be able to identify Eric Nitsche or Lester Beall, let alone Joseph Hoffman, Edward Penfield, or Gustav Jensen. Incidentally, Jensen was a mentor to Paul Rand and, Cassandre aside, perhaps the designer he most admired, but I would not be at all surprised if most of us have never heard of him—so much for understanding our own history.

I have always believed that there is a psychological and ethical difference between those who make things and those who control things. If form making is intrinsic to human beings and has a social benefit, then we can think of the "good" in good design having more than a stylistic meaning. Linking beauty and purpose can create a sense of communal agreement that helps diminish the sense of disorder and incoherence that life creates.

The part of design that is involved in fashion and marketing has the least need to examine and understand our history. Examining what has happened over twenty years seems to provide enough information to meet professional requirements, but, if our field aspires to be significant and worthy of respect, it must stand for something beyond salesmanship. Being a legend is an accomplishment that is hard won and sadly ephemeral, but being part of humankind's desire to make useful and beautiful things links us to a glorious history.

Two weeks ago I developed a sudden, painful wrist condition. I went to a fancy hand doctor who told me I probably had a "gouty" incident. That's not "Gaudi" the Barcelonian designer and architect. It's gout, as in those eighteenth century engravings of rich, fat men with inflamed big toes. My wrist is fine, but while I was in the doctor's office I noticed a document on his wall called "What a Surgeon Ought to Be" written in the fourteenth century. I've changed a word or two but it seems like good advice for our profession.

What a Designer Ought to Be

Let the designer be bold in all sure things, and fearful in dangerous things; let him avoid all faulty treatments and practices. He ought to be gracious to the client, considerate to his associates, cautious in his prognostication. Let him be modest, dignified, gentle, pitiful, and merciful; not covetous nor an extortionist of money; but rather let his reward be according to his work, to the means of the client, to the quality of the issue, and to his own dignity.

2

Standards of Professional Practice

RICHARD GREFÉ

A PROFESSIONAL DESIGNER adheres to principles of integrity that demonstrate respect for the profession, for colleagues, for clients, for audiences or consumers, and for society as a whole.

These standards define the expectations of a professional designer and represent the distinction of an AIGA member in the practice of design.

THE DESIGNER'S RESPONSIBILITY TO CLIENTS

1.1 A professional designer shall acquaint himself or herself with a client's business and design standards, and shall act in the client's best interest within the limits of professional responsibility.

1.2 A professional designer shall not work simultaneously on assignments that create a conflict of interest without agreement of the clients or employers concerned, except in specific cases where it is the convention of a particular trade for a designer to work at the same time for various competitors.

1.3 A professional designer shall treat all work in progress prior to the completion of a project and all knowledge of a client's intentions, production methods, and business organization as confidential and shall not divulge such information in any manner whatsoever without the consent of the client. It is the designer's responsibility to ensure that all staff members act accordingly.

1.4 If a professional designer accepts instructions from a client or employer that involve violation of the designer's ethical standards, these violations should be corrected by the designer, or the designer should refuse the assignment.

THE DESIGNER'S RESPONSIBILITY TO OTHER DESIGNERS

2.1 Designers in pursuit of business opportunities should support fair and open competition.

2.2 A professional designer shall not knowingly accept any professional assignment on which another designer has been or is working without notifying the other designer or until he or she is satisfied that any previous appointments have been properly terminated and that all materials relevant to the continuation of the project are the clear property of the client.

2.3 A professional designer must not attempt, directly or indirectly, to supplant or compete with another designer by means of unethical inducements.

2.4 A professional designer shall be objective and balanced in criticizing another designer's work and shall not denigrate the work or reputation of a fellow designer.

2.5 A professional designer shall not accept instructions from a client that involve infringement of another person's property rights without permission, or consciously act in any manner involving any such infringement.

2.6 A professional designer working in a country other than his or her own shall observe the relevant Code of Conduct of the national society concerned.

FEES

3.1 A professional designer shall work only for a fee, a royalty, salary, or other agreed-upon form of compensation. A professional designer shall not retain any kickbacks, hidden discounts, commission, allowances, or payment in kind from contractors or suppliers. Clients should be made aware of markups.

3.2 A reasonable handling and administration charge may be added, with the knowledge and understanding of the client, as a percentage to all reimbursable items, billable to a client, that pass through the designer's account.

3.3 A professional designer who has a financial interest in any suppliers who may benefit from a recommendation made by the designer in the course of a project will inform the client or employer of this fact in advance of the recommendation.

3.4 A professional designer who is asked to advise on the selection of designers or the consultants shall not base such advice in the receipt of payment from the designer or consultants recommended.

PUBLICITY

4.1 Any self-promotion, advertising, or publicity must not contain deliberate misstatements of competence, experience, or professional capabilities. It must be fair both to clients and other designers.

4.2 A professional designer may allow a client to use his or her name for the promotion of work designed or services provided in a manner that is rightful and appropriate.

AUTHORSHIP

5.1 A professional designer shall not claim sole credit for a design on which other designers have collaborated.

5.2 When not the sole author of a design, it is incumbent upon a professional designer to clearly identify his or her specific responsibilities or involvement with the design. Examples of such work may not be used for publicity, display, or portfolio samples without clear identification of precise areas of authorship.

THE DESIGNER'S RESPONSIBILITY TO THE PUBLIC

6.1 A professional designer shall avoid projects that will result in harm to the public.

6.2 A professional designer shall communicate the truth in all situations and at all times; his or her work shall not make false claims nor knowingly misinform. A professional designer shall represent messages in a clear manner in all forms of communication design and avoid false, misleading, and deceptive promotion.

6.3 A professional designer shall respect the dignity of all audiences and shall value individual differences, always avoiding the depiction or stereotyping of people or groups of people in a negative or dehumanizing way. A professional designer shall strive to be sensitive to cultural values and beliefs, and engage in fair and balanced communication design that fosters and encourages mutual understanding.

THE DESIGNER'S RESPONSIBILITY TO SOCIETY AND THE ENVIRONMENT

7.1 A professional designer, while engaged in the practice or instruction of design, shall not knowingly do or fail to do anything that constitutes a deliberate or reckless disregard for the health and safety of the communities in which he or she lives and practices or the privacy of the individuals and businesses therein. A professional designer shall take a responsible role in the visual portrayal of people, the consumption of natural resources, and the protection of animals and the environment.

7.2 A professional designer shall not knowingly accept instructions from a client or employer that involve infringement of another person's or group's human rights or property rights without permission of such other person or group, or consciously act in any manner involving any such infringement.

7.3 A professional designer shall not knowingly make use of goods or services offered by manufacturers, suppliers, or contractors that are accompanied by an obligation that is substantively detrimental to the best interests of his or her client, society, or the environment.

7.4 A professional designer shall refuse to engage in or countenance discrimination on the basis of race, sex, age, religion, national origin, sexual orientation, or disability.

7.5 A professional designer shall strive to understand and support the principles of free speech, freedom of assembly, and access to an open marketplace of ideas, and shall act accordingly.

3

How Clients Want to Be Treated

DAVID C. BAKER

DEPENDING ON WHICH survey you read, the average client relationship in this field lasts twenty-three or twenty-nine months. That's a number that probably strikes you as low, though truth be told you've never actually measured the average length of a client relationship at your firm. Your instincts are more weighted toward clients who have stayed, writing off those that left early on, figuring that they weren't a good fit anyway. They slide from your consciousness and don't inform the average.

The reason clients leave, however, is more important than how long they stay. As we'll explore later in the article, there are definite advantages to cycling your client base (provided that you lose them in the right way). Regardless of what happens, you should seek to be in control. In other words, clients should stay because you've screened them well in the first place, treated them as they'd like, and checked in frequently.

Keeping clients long-term will enable you to do more effective work for them. It will also contribute to increased profitability, as well as reduce the acquisition costs of new clients.

FOUR COMPONENTS OF RELATIONSHIP MANAGEMENT

Treating clients well includes four elements—it's not as simple as merely good customer service. For example, no amount of great customer service will save a client relationship that wasn't well-suited for your firm in the first place. It involves screening them carefully in the marketing process, formalizing the relationship carefully, treating the client well, and then closing the feedback loop by asking the client for advice.

#1: **Marketing.** Clients come to you for specific reasons. The safest reasons are your focus, specialization, or category experience. But if you've been trying to attract clients with your "cost effectiveness" or "responsiveness" or other unproven, unsustainable gibberish, you'll attract clients for the wrong reasons and will face an uphill battle pleasing them. Better to attract them for the right reasons (you know what you are doing), and then keep them for other reasons (you know how to treat them).

#2: **Formalizing.** Once clients come to you, consider defining the relationship carefully to cause "service" issues to surface early. The very "definition" process itself is more important than any document that might be formulated as a result of the process. That process will surface issues before they arise. In fact, think of any written agreement as a "discussion outline" to help both parties address their perspectives on key points.

#3: **Servicing.** This article is mostly about this component of relationship management, and the information found here is based on hundreds of conversations with principals, account people, and their clients.

#4: **Listening.** A good starting place is noting that it's critical to know what your clients think about you and, even more important, what they say about you, since this will inevitably spread to prospects and other clients. The American Marketing Association says that only 4 percent of customers who are dissatisfied enough to switch to a competitor take the time to complain. And a complaint, as the management book says, can be a gift. To encourage these gifts, a company should undertake a consistent, systematic program of gathering feedback from clients.

TAILORING CLIENT TREATMENT

Treating clients well does not mean treating them identically. The better your customer service program, the more distinctly clients will be treated.

This usually depends on a "customer information file" (CIF for short), a repository of information on how a specific client defines a good relationship. It might include information on the best means of contacting that client (phone, fax, email, etc.); how frequently he wants an update on projects (usually weekly); when budgets are decided; and anything else that would allow exceptional customer service. It also includes purchasing patterns to begin to unearth trends in the relationship.

The data collecting for this CIF begins during the marketing phase, where little hints are put to paper for later use. Your sales person might ask who the potential client has been using, followed with a query about what he liked and didn't like in that relationship. The data collection continues when the account person interviews the client and discusses typical procedures.

While maintaining a CIF in a consumer setting can be difficult because of the number of customers and the variables that are created, the well-managed firm has eight to twelve clients and the data is manageable, particularly if it is stored in a digital, database driven environment.

KEEPING CLIENTS HAPPY

The following suggestions are compiled from working with hundreds of firms, conducting scores of end-client interviews, poring through client surveys, and devouring patterns in client relationships. Some are suggestions to implement, and others are things you might want to avoid.

Communication Elements

- ❏ Create an orientation kit that includes contact information, sample forms, places to store project updates, and typical procedures.

- ❏ Provide the client with proactive updates (as in "unprompted"). Preferably these will occur weekly, in writing, and will emerge from management software.

- ❏ Watch for information in the news that would interest your client and send an occasional fax or email to demonstrate that you are thinking on his behalf.

- ❏ Be sure that the client has ready access to someone who knows the status of his projects. If that person is not available, indicate when she will be and provide a backup contact if the client can't wait.

- ❏ Conduct organized, agenda driven meetings that indicate a sensitivity to the client's busy schedule.

- ❏ Confirm the results of those meetings in writing. This will preserve organization and communicate that the details are being handled.

- ❏ Manage deadlines and budgets. That doesn't necessarily mean meeting them, but rather anticipating which ones will be met, and then arriving at a plan suitable to the client for those that will not be met.

- ❏ If you use an auto attendant for your phone system, make sure that calling for the operator (pressing "zero") always results in someone answering the phone. The caller may not be able to talk to her first choice, but she should always get a real person if she wants to.

- ❏ Keep the client's work confidential.

Leadership Elements

- ❏ Know the client's field. If somehow you slipped into the relationship because he didn't ask too many questions, do your homework and catch up with the rest of the class.

- ❏ Do zero-based work. In other words, don't just build on the status quo. Instead, start from scratch without making too many assumptions. Pretend it's a new client every year.

- ❏ Have an opinion. Express your point of view. Don't just take orders.

- ❏ On the other hand, be collaborative. Let the client win whenever he should.

- ❏ Surprise clients by doing more than you promise. Then let them discover what you have done rather than trumpeting it.

- ❏ Do your own homework instead of expecting the client to do it for you.

- ❏ Take advantage of your role in providing more brand continuity than the company itself, particularly if your contact point keeps rotating.

- ❏ Do effective work. It is not required all the time, but eventually not doing so will catch up with you.

Personal Elements

- ❏ Treat the account as important. This means that you'll talk about it and proudly show what you are doing. It also means rotating the spotlight for public relations announcements so that every client has a turn.

- ❏ If great results do ensue, share the credit with the client. Invite him to an awards ceremony, write an article together, speak together, etc.

- ❏ Support client causes, even if only to a limited extent.

- ❏ Ask the client how you are doing. Your performance is not as important as your interest in getting the client's perspective.

- ❏ Be human, but not too human. Be vulnerable with personal stories, dress comfortably, and use first names. But don't share more than clients need to know, and don't pursue client friendships.

- ❏ Be likable. No client will tolerate an unusually difficult person unless there is no other choice. Even beyond this, clients should feel that you enjoy the relationship.

- ❏ Stay sober at any function where there is alcohol present. A client will quickly lose confidence when control is absent. It's not cute.

- ❏ Don't hire employees from the client side except in rare circumstances, particularly if the potential employee is high on the food chain. In many cases no ramifications ensue, but it's difficult to predict the downside.

- ❏ Don't get involved in client politics. Listen, seek the truth, be fair, and communicate in turn as if your client's enemy is listening. If you choose sides, you forsake the independence that makes your firm so valuable.

- Don't keep switching the client's contact point at your firm. And if you do, give the client some input as to whom he will be working with.

- Be passionate about the client brand, contributing enthusiastically for great collaborative results (thus the importance of choosing the brand carefully).

- Don't neglect out of town clients, assuming that in person visits are not expected.

- Pay your bills so that word of your financial difficulty doesn't work its way back to the client. There are no good explanations in the client's eyes.

LARGER SERVICE ISSUES

Since the 1980s, very specific studies of service quality have been undertaken (see Terry G. Vavra's *Aftermarketing*). Over that period of time, consumers have changed their definition of what constitutes "quality" in a product, but their beliefs about the "quality" of a service have not changed substantially. There are consistently five aspects of quality service that appear in unprompted discussions, and these five aspects have retained their relative importance over the years.

#1: **Reliability.** On average reliability is deemed most important by respondents. This describes your firm's ability to perform the promised service dependably and accurately. It means doing what you say you'll do, fixing things right the first time, minimizing errors on invoices, not forgetting meetings, etc.

#2: **Responsiveness.** On average responsiveness is deemed the second most important component of quality service. This would include your willingness to help customers, the level of promptness clients can expect, the degree to which phone calls and e-mails are answered within a reasonable period of time, and the overall helpfulness they sense.

#3: **Assurance.** On average assurance is deemed the third most important component of quality service. Within this category, four phrases surface repeatedly.

The first is competence, or your possession of the required skills and knowledge to perform the service. In other words, do you know what you are doing.

The second is courtesy, or your politeness, respectful treatment, consideration, and overall friendliness.

The third is credibility, or your trustworthiness, believability, and honesty as a service provider. Put simply, how good is your reputation.

The fourth is security, or the confidence that your exchanges will remain confidential.

#4: **Empathy.** On average empathy is deemed the fourth most important component of quality service. Within this category, three phrases surface repeatedly.

The first is access, which would include the ease of contacting you and then how easily clients can hold your attention once contact has been made.

The second is communication, which includes both listening to the client and keeping the client informed in language he can understand.

The third is understanding the customer, which relates to knowing the customer and his needs.

#5: **Tangibles.** On average tangibles are deemed the fifth most important component of quality service. These tangibles include the general appearance of your facilities, equipment, personnel, and communication materials.

PROSPERING FROM LOSING CLIENTS

If your prospect screening and customer service skills were perfect, and if nothing changed at the client level, client cycling wouldn't happen. While most of our customer service efforts are designed to prevent this cycling, there are times when client cycling is good. There is a therapeutic side effect of "firing" clients, but it should be a business driven exercise.

Cycling your client base is especially useful when you are growing quickly, adding capabilities quicker than the typical client perception can keep pace. With new clients you'll be able to inform their perceptions from the outset, which is always easier than changing them.

If you are restructuring your role as the principal too, new clients will not have the same expectation of principal involvement that your current clients do. And growing—if you are managing the transition with dignity—absolutely will mean less direct client involvement on your part.

If the average firm replaces one-third of its clients every year, you might want to aim for less turnover. But when turnover occurs, use it to your advantage. Start fresh and align new client expectations more closely with what you can actually deliver. Re-educating clients is only slightly more enjoyable than doing your own dental work at home. It takes the fight right out of you.

Losing Clients Well

In working with hundreds of firms, I have never heard a principal express regret for making a courageous client decision. But in spite of the underlying frustration that might be prompting your decision, don't make it a personal quest. Keep the focus on business reasons, either for them or for you. It is a small world, and you might have to walk back through it.

First, indicate that this is not personal. And, if it's true, tell the client that on a personal level you would like to continue the relationship, but that there are business reasons for severing it. These might include a change of direction on your firm's part, the discovery that only a relationship of certain depth will allow you to be profitable and effective, or that the situation has not allowed you to really use your strengths well.

Second, give clients an option. Don't present the decision as final. Instead, present your perspective and then see if they see any other options that work for both of you. From your perspective this might mean access to a more strategic, planning role; a minimum monthly fee; or better, more timely information.

Third, consider referring them to a provider more suited to their needs once the decision has been made, even if that means feathering a competitor's nest. The goal is for them to find great solutions within their budget. There is boundless opportunity, and your competitor doesn't have to lose for you to win. (Besides, they might lie awake at night wondering why you did it!)

This will be an especially difficult process if the client has been with you since the firm's early days. The natural growth process makes early clients suspicious anyway, as the time you spend with them declines as a percentage of the whole. They (rightly) feel partly responsible for your success, and having less access to you doesn't seem like a fair return to them.

Whenever possible, try to conduct an exit interview. If you don't want to keep the relationship, you'll still glean valuable insights into how to keep your remaining clients. If you do want to keep the relationship, it may be possible to save it. Either way, expect 35 to 50 percent of exiting clients to be willing to sit down for a candid discussion. The longer they have been clients, the more willing they'll be to sit with you. And this is not the time to be defensive. Just listen and be kind.

AFTERMARKETING TO NEW CLIENTS

Marketing has a role in customer service, not just client acquisition. Studies show that the most attentive audience for your marketing is a recent buyer, not a potential one. Recent buyers want to reinforce internally the decision they have just made. And "aftermarketing" can prepare them for the onslaught of questions that detractors might pose about any given decision to use you.

As it relates to keeping clients happy, keep new ones content by (1) marketing to them in order to reduce the "cognitive dissonance" that any buyer struggles with (popularly known as "buyer's remorse") and (2) rewarding their decision with a simple show of gratitude. When you reward specific behavior (like a decision to accept your proposal), that exact behavior is likely to be repeated. (If this were not such an upstanding topic, we'd talk about dog tricks and little treats.)

Assuming, then, that you will intentionally and unintentionally lose clients, keep marketing in mind. It will make it easier to find new ones to replace the losses, and it will aid in keeping the ones you have. (This is one of the very few reasons you might do your own newsletter, which will have a much greater impact on existing clients than prospective ones.)

SUMMARY

Keeping your clients happy depends on an orchestrated approach with several components. These include:

- Specialization, without which it is difficult to be competent. Focus ensures sufficient experience to do great work.

- Honesty about your abilities, eliminating bad surprises for the client.

- A good customer fit, which will prime clients to let you be a great partner.

- Defined relationships, which will surface the issues that should be discussed in advance.

- Frequent monitoring, which will provide an early warning for fixable tensions.

- Avoiding the hot buttons, of which there are many.

- Hiring the right people, who will think like owners and create a customer centered environment.

- Setting standards for that customer service, so that employees have measurable goals.

- Empowering employees to reach those goals, trusting in their ability to manage client relationships.

- Structuring roles carefully, eliminating employee turf wars that might catch clients in the cross fire.

- Training employees regularly, adding to their knowledge as they delve deeper into client relationships.

- Rewarding employees who contribute to the right environment.

If your clients get these things from you, they'll let you fail once in a large way, but probably only that one time.

4

Marketing the Design Firm

MARIA PISCOPO

DESIGN FIRMS—LIKE ANY business—need to create a marketing plan and target a market; they need techniques and tips for getting the work they want. This will involve both personal and non-personal promotion. Personal promotion involves identifying the prospective clients for sales calls. Non-personal promotion supports selling and includes Web sites, publicity, and networking. Together, these techniques increase sales success and decrease sales rejection. Clients get to know designers through their Web sites, publicity, and networking. Then, direct sales contact is "warm calling" as opposed to "cold calling."

PERSONAL PROMOTION
Sales Strategy

A computer database is required for the maximum effectiveness and efficiency in the search for new business. Selecting the best program is not as easy as finding out what is on sale this week at the local software warehouse. Many designers use the database in their existing project management programs, such as FileMaker Pro, for managing client data. Some word processing programs come with their own database programs. There are two basic directions one can go with database software, and understanding the difference will help designers decide what to buy.

One choice is to buy a program that has a preexisting client profile form and fields of information. This works great if it is the first database the designer has used, as it is simple to input client profile information from index cards into existing fields. (A field of information is anything a designer will want to retrieve later, such as addresses, phone numbers, or dates of client contacts.) This type of database is quick to set up, but generally not flexible in terms of setting up data fields.

The other choice is to buy a program that requires designing client profile form fields, also called records, and laying out the form. This type takes more time to set up, but it will be exactly what the designer needs, especially if he or she changes to a different database program. Designing the form for this client profile is critically important for sales follow-up. Selling design services can be as simple as managing the information on what clients and prospective clients need and when they need it!

For example, designers can imagine the following situations using database information. First, they can call prospective clients, sorted by zip code, so that when they make appointments they're not driving from one end of town to the other. Second, they can sort clients by date of contact, in order to call all current clients they talked to in March who said to call back in June. Third, they can mail new promo pieces to all prospective clients to whom they presented a food packaging portfolio in the previous month. Fourth, they can mail a different promo piece to magazines and manufacturers. Information management is the key to successful selling.

Researching New Clients

The more designers know about prospective clients, the better presentation they can make. The better the presentation, the more likely they will get work! Because they research their target market, designers know what kind of client they are looking for. There are six areas of research to find new clients.

1. The daily newspaper business section always has information on new products, services, expansions, and personnel changes that provide opportunities to get in the door. For example, a news item that is headlined, "XYZ Food Company Launches Six New Products" can be translated into a lead for food packaging design!

2. The office or industrial park where the studio is located will give the names and types of tenants. These may make a great bread-and-butter client base to launch a sales strategy.

3. Magazines designers want to work with have editorial calendars that list the theme for each issue. This information is valuable when approaching the publication for appointments. Instead of being just another designer who wants to show a portfolio, the designer can discuss how he or she can meet the magazine's needs on a specific topic in an upcoming issue.

4. Trade shows are still one of the best sources for new business. Not every company exhibits in its own industry trade show. The ones that do are always going to need more promotion, design, production, and printing services than the ones that stay home!

5. Awards annuals are good for clients that have a strong sense of style and are willing to take creative risks. These best of the best annual awards

programs recognize clients that take chances. If a client used highly creative and stylish design once, he or she would probably do it again.

6.   The bulk of the database of prospective clients will probably come from your own Web site searches. Though these are also printed directories available in the local library reference section, you will find using the Internet a faster (and more comfortable!) research tool. As much as clients are looking for designers via the Internet, the same tools are available to you! Many of these online databases are now available on CD and make the entire process of setting up a file much easier—no keyboard work required.

Turning Information into Prospects

Once designers have the basic information on the prospective client they want to work with, the next step is to identify the true client, the individual with the responsibility and authority to hire designers. The best way to approach this step is to write a script for the phone call, almost as a preproduction step. Scripts are simply preparation for any interaction with a client or potential client where there is a specific objective. The interaction must be accomplished with confidence and efficiency, and the objective is to get the name of the individual that purchases design services. A typical script might read, "Hello, this is (name) from (firm) and I'm updating the information we have on your company. Who is the person in charge of (name a specific type of design or service)?"

Getting the Portfolio Appointment

If the clients do not contact you first from an online search for design services, you can always consider trying to get your portfolio in the door by appointment. Today, because many clients prescreen designers' Web sites before calling them, portfolio reviews may be less common. Still, if you identify clients based on their need for your specific services, you may be able to convince potential clients to let you present your portfolio.

A script for a portfolio appointment might read, "Hello, this is (name) from (firm), and I am calling in regard to your service provider for (type of services). When would be a good time for us to meet?"

This script prompts the prospective client to decide whether or not there is a need to meet with you. The approach allows a client to make an informed and efficient choice, and can save you a lot of time and energy. If the client decides not to meet, the script reads, "When should I check back with you?" allowing you an opportunity to schedule the next call.

The Portfolio Presentation

The problem with the use of the term "portfolio presentation" is that it implies a one-way flow of information. To simply present the portfolio will not give enough information for follow-up and will probably waste the client's time. The better approach is a consultation to discuss the client's needs and the designer's ability to meet those needs.

Since this makes each appointment with a prospective client completely unique, a script isn't possible, but preparing an agenda is a great idea! Following is a checklist for a client consultation including sample scripts:

- ❏ Prepare an introduction. Even though this appointment was made the day before, the client has had many distractions since the call. While settling in for the meeting, review the agenda with the client. Is this meeting from a referral or listing in a directory or an item in the newspaper? State what items will be discussed in the meeting. This gives the client an opportunity to mention any changes in his or her needs, or the meeting's agenda.

- ❏ Go behind the scenes. When presenting work from the portfolio, be sure to discuss the who, how, and why and not the what. The client can clearly see whether it is an annual report, packaging, or a newsletter. It is the creative process and problem solving that went into the work he or she needs to hear about. Discuss who the work was for, how the client's problem was solved, and why this was the best solution. Design clients are hiring for what designers can do for them or what problems they can solve!

- ❏ What happens next? Probably the biggest mistake designers make when presenting a portfolio is not connecting the meeting or consultation with the follow-up steps. The follow-up to this appointment begins now, in the meeting, not after. The key to being persistent and not a pest is coming to an agreement as to what happens next while still in the meeting. There are three different agreements the designer and the client can choose from: first, meeting again within a specified time (usually this is when the consultation has stimulated the prospect of a job); second, a call to the client regarding follow-up on a specific project or need; and third, mail the client updated promotion material as it becomes available (usually this is the lowest level of follow-up). All of the above options are decided on within a timeframe to update the database for both the type of contact and the date of next contact.

- ❏ Ask for a referral. Before leaving the meeting, ask the prospect for a recommendation for a referral. Be sure to ask an open-ended question and not a yes or no question. For example, "Do you know anyone that should see my portfolio?" does not allow the client to take the time to think about the question. A better approach would be, "Who do you know that should see my portfolio?"

NON-PERSONAL PROMOTION

Internet Marketing

Most designers have learned how to use their Web site as an advertising tool, a portfolio, and even as a project management tool, but the Web site has become a primary non-personal marketing tool and is more like a showroom where clients can visit and be enticed to stay and "shop," or leave.

Therefore, your emphasis should be on getting clients to "shop" or stay on your site, by supplying easy navigation and useful information. The most common client negative feedback today on designers' Web sites is that they are "too busy, take too long to load, and have annoying sound and animation effects."

Your home page is the entrance to your Web site, so it should be designed to make a strong impression and encourage the client to search for more information. Clients stopping at your home page will look for navigational guidance, introduction copy, who you are, what you do, how to contact you, and evidence that other clients have found you and your site worth visiting.

Graphic design is a business of relationships, and your Web site is now often "first contact." Your goal is to drive traffic to your site and then drive those visitors to your door.

Find ways to add interesting content to your site. By using "editorial" with your promotion copy, clients have the potential to visit your site during their own research, and another reason to revisit your site later. Identify pro bono work you are doing, industry-meeting announcements, or interesting trade news items, upcoming industry conferences, a discussion thread, a survey or a contest. Obtain links from other Web sites that relate to your marketing message. Use any technique to create interest and interaction. This requires a lot of maintenance but will build reputation, recognition, and loyalty to your site.

Use the unique speed factor of electronic response time to test different page designs. Ask for feedback and be open to learning. Faster than any print promotions, you can quickly turn around a test, get feedback, and make changes.

Remember that your Web site must be integrated and work with all your personal and non-personal marketing. The best reference I have found for an archive of tips, techniques, and actual examples of Web sites that work can be found by researching on the DMA Web site, *www.targetmarketingmag.com.*

Publicity Strategy

Submitting press releases is probably the most overlooked area of self-promotion, yet for the low cost, it has high return. Like direct mail and advertising, the goal of publicity is not to sell. Only selling can sell! Press releases support the sales strategy and bring the designer name recognition. There is no guarantee of publication; however, publicity carries tremendous credibility because information must be submitted and accepted for publication. Also, the reprints of any publicity make wonderful promo pieces!

Here is a five point checklist to start or improve publicity strategy:

1. Research trade and design industry publications that hold annual creative awards. Designers get the immediate exposure on entering when, quite often, their potential clients are the jurors. When they win, they get publication exposure and get to write their own press release, further expanding on the equity earned from the entry fee.

2. Submit work to book publishers to try and be included in their compilations. NorthLight Books, for example, published *Fresh Ideas In Promotion*. If your "fresh idea" is accepted, you have a newsworthy event ready for a press release.

3. Identify the appropriate media contacts to which you can submit press releases and build a mailing list database. Unlike advertising, where designers would only buy space where clients can see the ad, it is appropriate to submit publicity as broadly as possible. Research magazines, newspapers, and newsletters of the three major media: clients, designers, and the community.

4. A newsworthy item to submit to the media can be generated at anytime! In addition to submitting book publication and magazine awards, here is a list of what to look for:

    ❑ Recently opened or moved a business?

    ❑ Added (even part time) any staff or a rep?

    ❑ Included any new or expanded services?

    ❑ Been in a juried show or exhibit?

    ❑ Completed an interesting project?

    ❑ Involved in any public service projects?

    ❑ Been elected to an association board or committee?

5. Use a standard format press release to submit the news to the media. Editors receive hundreds of press releases a week, so be sure to conform to the standard format to avoid having the release thrown away! Always enclose samples or photos whenever possible to increase the media interest and the chances of being published. Be sure to print the release on letterhead—it looks more professional than a photocopy of the letterhead.

Networking Strategy

Getting the marketing message broadcasted should also be done by the traditional word of mouth method. Joining trade associations in which your clients are members will gain their attention. This will also provide opportunities to buy mailing lists, advertise, submit press releases to a pre-qualified audience in association newsletters, and participate in public service projects. Peer association membership such as AIGA is also important to any self-promotion plan. Other designers offer professional support, industry information, and referrals. In addition, the membership is a professional credential in advertising and direct mail promotions.

Community association networking gives great access to public service projects. These projects make wonderful promo pieces, can be used for press releases, and can be satisfying to give back to the community!

CONCLUSION

Ultimately, the best design clients come from an effective plan to get the work a designer really wants. This plan includes a top-rate Web site, effective portfolio consultations, follow-up deadlines, and networking support. No waiting for the phone to ring. Do the homework, update your Web site, write those press releases, plan the networking, and follow up to get the jobs. Always do good work to keep the client coming back for more!

5

Negotiating: Lessons From a Caveman

ED GOLD

I WAS SITTING at home the other night watching, with some envy, I must admit, several very erudite and sophisticated cavemen whose visages were being used to sell insurance.

I couldn't quite understand the connection, but I was reminded of a play that I had seen several years ago. It was another of those traveling one-actor shows that producers turn to when Andrew Lloyd Webber stops returning their calls. This one happened to be Rob Becker's show *Defending the Caveman*.

In the show, Becker drew parallels between the behavior of modern men and women and that of cavemen and cavewomen. I have to say that he was very good at doing this, although I, myself, am well past the age of "guyhood" and have a difficult time identifying with most of the "guy" attitudes and behaviors he was describing.

As I sat there watching Becker, however, I began to realize that much of what he was saying on stage could easily apply to designers and how they try to get what they want.

For example, Becker described a scene in which four men are sitting around a coffee table watching a football game when they realize that the chip bowl needs to be refilled. They begin the process of trying to identify which of them will have to get off his butt, go into the kitchen, and refill the bowl.

"I bought the chips," says the first.

"I put the bowl on the table," says the second.

"I filled the bowl," says the third.

The fourth man kind of sheepishly says, "I did all I could do. I ate the chips."

The others all look at him accusingly until he finally gets up and trudges off to the kitchen, chip bowl in hand.

According to Becker, what they've been doing has been searching for the one with the weakest excuse, who is then tagged as the loser in the game and sent off to their personal Siberia, the kitchen, to refill the bowl.

In other words, they are "negotiating."

According to Becker, modern men negotiate almost all the time, over practically everything, because negotiating allows them metaphorically to focus on a specific target, hunt it down, kill it, and drag its carcass back to their cave to be presented as proof of their skill as hunters, just as their cavemen ancestors did.

I agree with Becker. Negotiating is all about winning and losing.

It would be nice to think that the secret handshake admitting a designer to the exclusive club of successful designers is the ability to orchestrate mutual cooperation and satisfaction between designer and client. After all, it seems obvious that, in any relationship, both parties have to feel satisfied with whatever they are getting from each other or the relationship can't last.

The problem is, when it comes to conflicts between designers and their clients, seldom are both sides really seeking cooperation; they are seeking a win. They are not looking for mutual satisfaction; they are trying to get whatever it is they want, and, whatever it is they want, they want it all. They are willing to settle for less, if necessary, but not without a fight. We call this battle "negotiating," and like all battles, if one wants to come away with all of one's body parts intact, there are certain rules to follow and tactics to employ.

Most designers I've met are already convinced that they are great negotiators. After all, that's practically all they've been doing ever since they began to design. But, if designers are so good at negotiating, why do they complain so often that their clients don't respect them, don't listen to them, don't understand design, and almost always screw up their jobs?

The sad fact is that most designers are actually pretty bad at getting what they want from a client. Here are what I believe to be the ten most common reasons why they don't.

Lesson 1

Sharpening the spear: they don't know what they want.

The most important part of the process of negotiating takes place long before the negotiating begins. It begins when the parties figure out what they are really trying to come away with. For most designers the answer to the question "What are you trying to get from your client?" is easy. "Whatever it is I'm asking for." Sometimes it's a job, sometimes it's a price, sometimes it's the freedom to do things their way.

But most of the time, it's not that simple. If all the designer wanted was just to be given the job, then all he or she would have to do would be to find out what the client was looking for and provide it. But we know that "Tell me what you want and how much you're willing to pay for it" seldom works, and when it does, both parties feel cheated and suspicious of the other. The relationship is shaky at best.

When closely examined, the answer to the question "What does 'getting what you want from a client' really mean to you?" can be very complex. It could mean achieving a short-term goal such as making a sale, or getting a particular design approved, or getting paid the price you asked for. But it could also mean establishing a long-term relationship or getting the client to trust your advice.

Each of these goals requires a different strategy, and, since no two clients are exactly alike, each client requires that a different strategy be employed to accomplish the same goal. Furthermore, each designer is different, with a different set of values and limits. While one designer couldn't care less if a client wanted to use a snapshot of his five-year-old grandchild holding a bowling ball on the cover of the client's annual report, as I once was asked to do, another might have picked up the nearest sharp instrument and thrown it at the client, as I once also did. Luckily, my aim is so bad that I didn't come close to hitting the client.

The fact is, we all have individual goals and limits. Before a designer can complete a negotiation successfully, he or she must have a clear idea of precisely what his or her goals and limits are. A designer needs to identify precisely the least that he or she would be willing to accept, as well as know when to walk away from the table. If the client won't give a designer the least that designer will take, the designer hasn't lost anything by walking.

Lesson 2

Tracking the raptor: they don't know what the other guy wants.

Human nature dictates that, when it comes to conflicts, we tend to think more about what we want than what the other party wants. This might explain why everyone who argues with us seems to be so damn hardheaded, stubborn, or just plain stupid. The fact of the matter is that it doesn't make any difference how dumb other people's ideas may be or why they believe these ideas will work. They happen to be their beliefs, like it or not, and these beliefs will drive them forward relentlessly, regardless of whether or not you agree with them. In fact, the more you attack these beliefs, the more they will dig their heels in and defend them.

But people are not made of cardboard. They are multidimensional and have many beliefs and needs, some stronger than others, some in great conflict with each other. If the purpose of any negotiation is to get the other person to give you what you want, then the fastest way to do this, other than pulling out an Uzi, is not to try to change the other person's mind about one strongly held belief, but to search for another that allows the other person to cooperate more willingly.

Several years ago I was asked to design an annual report for a new client. The report was one I really wanted to work on, since the budget was good and the quality of the report over the years had consistently been very high. But the CEO of the company had a reputation for mistrusting the advice of everyone when it came to running his business. This was especially true of designers, whom he placed, in terms of pecking order and behavior, on the same level as his chiropodist. . . . someone he knows he needs once in a while, but who is quite below him and has to be watched carefully.

The person I was working with was convinced that the CEO always wanted his people to present him with a completed design that they had all agreed upon, which he then proceeded to reject because it didn't express exactly what he wanted to say. Of course, he didn't know what he wanted to say until he had some ideas to react to. Based on the CEO's new directions, everyone went back to the drawing board and started over. Eventually, after several false starts, deadlines began to dictate that one of the designs already created be approved. A report was finally printed, having gone way over budget, and having brought everyone involved to the point of near panic and frustration.

I was quite certain that the CEO would not let me proceed with the job until he had satisfied his need to show me how much more he knew about his business than I or anyone else did. Until he got this out of his system, it would make no difference what I said, how good the work I showed was, or how many different designs I did.

I knew that a pre-planning session was probably going to be useless because the CEO's normal way of working was to wait until he was presented with various options, which would then suggest other possibilities to his mind. But I also knew that the CEO was very proud of his company's reputation for promoting teamwork and group cooperation. I decided that I might be able to use these two beliefs to help me avoid the hassle of doing dozens of different designs.

Rather than just producing lots of alternative designs, I asked my contact to set up two formal brainstorming sessions to which the CEO would be invited. I would serve as the facilitator at the session. The first would explore lots of possible options; the second would try to choose one of these options to proceed with. I thought this might give the CEO lots of concepts to choose from, give us all his input, and, at the same time, satisfy his sense that this was a true team effort.

It worked. By the end of the second session we had made a choice. The work proceeded smoothly and effortlessly. The job was finished on time, well under budget, and was a design I was very satisfied to put in my portfolio. Furthermore, from then on, the CEO's perceptions of the value of a designer changed completely. I was no longer just another in a string of difficult prima donnas, but a real member of his corporate team.

In any negotiating exchange, the person with the most knowledge of the other is usually the one who wins. If you hope to be successful in a negotiation, you must shift your focus from you to your client. You must know who the client is, what he or she expects to get out of the negotiations, where the bottom line is, and what ingrained attitudes and beliefs he or she holds. This information can only come from asking lots of questions of the client and of those who know him or her, and from listening very carefully to the answers you get and the statements that are made.

A few weeks ago I was having lunch with a very good designer. He was telling me how difficult it is to find good clients. I asked him to tell me what his definition of a good client was. He told me that a good client is one who allows him to do great work and pays him a lot of money to do it.

I agreed that this sounds like a pretty good client to have. I then asked him how many clients he had had that fit this description. He replied, "Not enough to live on."

The fact is that most clients have the potential to fit this description. While all of us will encounter a few unscrupulous people in the course of our professional careers, most of the clients that hire us are honest and fair. They do not enter into a relationship with a designer with the intention of destroying the relationship and coming out of it with a bad job and an unpleasant experience. The problem is that both parties in the relationship see things only from their own perspectives and are interested only in achieving their own objectives.

It would be wise for the designer to recognize that the client usually doesn't understand the process of design very well, often views the relationship as if contracting to have a house painted, couldn't care less about what the designer will be getting out of the relationship, and really has only one interest, "What can you do for me?"

Lesson 3

When attacking the beast, it's not a good idea to look at your own feet: they think too much about themselves and not enough about the other guy.

In the midst of a heated negotiating session, most designers' minds are totally focused on what their next move will be. This gets in the way of where their minds should be, on the ultimate result they are looking for. The ultimate result will be determined more by what their clients are willing to give them at the moment than it is by what the designers want or what the clients might give them in the long run. As a matter of fact, most clients probably have no idea at that point how much they really are willing to give. They might be persuaded to move a little from their established position, but probably not much.

In order for designers to get what they want, they will have to stop trying to change their clients' minds and focus on trying to figure out what other strategy to adopt that will get their clients to cooperate. Sometimes it means doing some research in order to validate claims and opinions. At other times it means trying to win a small concession from the client based on something the designer knows the client would be willing to agree to, and, in a series of small steps, gradually move the client closer and closer to your position.

Lesson 4

Sometimes retreat is the best attack: they think "compromising" is a dirty word.

No one likes to compromise. There's something so wimpy about compromising. Our nation was built on a tradition of going for it. We celebrate examples of our refusal to compromise or surrender. Remember the Alamo! Remember McAuliffe's "Nuts!" at Bastogne? We seem to think that anything less than "Unconditional Surrender" somehow translates into a loss. Which is why we fight so hard to hold our positions at all costs, even if it may be absolutely the wrong thing to do.

The truth is that "compromise" is just one of many tactics used in the process of negotiating. Use it when it is appropriate to do so, in order to arrive at the position, after the difference has been split, where you were willing to be before the negotiations began.

Lesson 5

No two dinos are alike: they use the same negotiating technique again and again.

It goes without saying that every client is different, just as every person is different. This may seem obvious, but it affects every aspect of the negotiating process. Unless a designer has done some homework on how a client has responded in similar situations, has really studied the client's personality, is listening for conversational cues that can tip a designer off to a client's attitudes and perceptions, and is consciously planning and adjusting a strategy that fits the characteristics of the client, negotiation might not work with that particular client at that particular time.

Lesson 6

A knife is no match for a raptor: they try to solve the wrong problem.

Let's say a designer is hired to produce a capabilities brochure. The designer designs the best damn capabilities brochure in history. When the design is presented to the client it is obvious that the client has had second thoughts. "Maybe we don't really need a capabilities brochure. Maybe what we really need is a whole new look. Maybe what we really need is an 'Identity Program!'" Warning bells start going off in the mind of the designer. He or she knows that, sooner or later, this will end up as a problem, and it usually does, in the form of disputed bills, finger-pointing, and blaming.

Clients are notorious for coming to designers with requests to help solve the wrong problems. If designers aren't on their toes, they can find themselves the messenger who has to be killed.

The best way to avoid a sticky negotiation is often to be alert to the kinds of situations that cause the need for a negotiation in the first place. If, right at the outset, the designer had dug deep enough to uncover the real problem the client faced, not only would there be no need to negotiate the extra time and costs, but the designer would have been transformed from a mere puppet who moves when a string is pulled by the client to someone who stands beside the client helping to pull the strings.

Lesson 7

There's more of them in the bushes: they don't recognize the hidden agendas.

Sometimes a designer will be negotiating with one person, sometimes with more than one. The designer should always be aware that the people sitting across from him or her, whether one person or many, have their own agendas. These agendas aren't always easy to recognize.

Sometimes a client's agenda has to do with getting Brownie points from the Big Kahuna. Sometimes it has to do with undermining someone else in the company. Sometimes there's an internal struggle for power going on that has absolutely nothing to do with the ongoing negotiations. Any of these hidden agendas can end up affecting those negotiations dramatically.

It pays for designers to try to find out as much as possible about who they will be dealing with and to be alert to the various agendas that may be driving their negotiating counterparts' arguments. These may have a greater impact on the negotiations than the stated issues themselves.

Lesson 8

A T-Rex can smell fear: they let their emotions get in the way of their goals.

A lot of designers approach the negotiating process prepared for a calm, logical exchange of positions, leading to a friendly resolution sealed with a handshake and a glass of wine.

In your dreams.

The negotiating process, by its very nature, means giving and taking. Expect the client to try to move you from your stated position. Sometimes you will be pushed very hard by some tough and experienced negotiators, who will be searching desperately to find just the buttons that will set you off and make you lose it.

Don't cooperate. They want you to lose your cool and force a deadlock. When you do this, they achieve their goals. The status remains unchanged. They don't have to give an inch. Result: you lose, they win.

No matter what your adversaries are doing or saying, never forget that your ultimate purpose in negotiating at all is to get them to do something that is to your benefit, not theirs. At the same time, you should recognize that you won't get anything if they don't think they have benefited as well. Although this often means getting less than you want, it should always mean getting at least as much as you think is fair.

Lesson 9

When a raptor shows you its belly, you better not miss: they don't recognize an opportunity for closure when they're given it.

Don't forget that the whole purpose of beginning the negotiating process at all is to close it as fast as possible. Be alert. When the opportunity for closure presents itself, grab it. Otherwise, you may lose it forever.

Lesson 10

It's OK to look back—they're gone: they don't spend enough time reviewing results.

It wouldn't make much sense for a designer to go through hours of negotiating without having learned something from the experience, and we know that the only way to learn anything is to consciously study the subject. After each negotiating session designers should take time to reflect on what went right and what went wrong. They should try to figure out why things worked or didn't and make plans to use the information the next time they run into a similar situation.

Unlike the caveman, if we lose a battle, we can always hunt again tomorrow.

6

The Process
of Setting Fees

EVA DOMAN BRUCK

THERE ARE THREE fundamental conditions to consider during the process of
setting fees. One is the cost of staying in business (overhead), second is a best estimate of the nature and complexity of the proposed project (variable costs), and
third is knowing the intrinsic value of the final product (market conditions).

No matter the size of the organization, it is most likely to enjoy long-term
success when there is detailed, up-to-date information available on its consumption
of resources translated into financial terms. Resources may be staff and freelance
personnel, supplies and materials, and outside services. Therefore, it is imperative
to set up a record keeping system that tracks time, payables, and income. Record
keeping can be approached in a variety of ways. An experienced accountant should
be retained in helping to determine whether the business requires a customized
bookkeeping system or whether off-the-shelf software may be suitable.

OVERHEAD AND SETTING THE HOURLY RATE

Start the fee setting process by examining in detail the constant costs of the business, or in bookkeeping parlance what is called the overhead. Included in the
overhead category are rent, utilities, equipment leases, office supplies, business
insurance, salaries, taxes and benefits, accounting and legal services, and the cost
of nonbillable time devoted to self-promotion and administrative chores. Don't
forget to include profit in this equation; a healthy business should aim to generate about 20 percent of annual profit after all expenses have been paid. For the
purpose of determining your hourly rate, these costs are calculated on an annual
basis. The total dollar amount is divided by the total number of hours you have
estimated are available for billing to clients for the year. The best way to learn

how much of your time is available to devote to paying projects is to gain some experience in tracking actual time spent on billable versus nonbillable work. You should be able to bill out at least 50 to 80 percent of your time. If you find you have less time than this for project work, take a hard look at your daily activities and see how you can gain some efficiencies and free up more time for billable activities.

To calculate the hourly rate:

Annual Overhead (including salary + profit) / Annual Billable Hours = Hourly Rate

Unless you are being hired on an hourly basis, your hourly rate should be relevant only to you; for most pricing situations the hourly rate should be transparent in the fee structure. Studio members also need to understand how to control and keep track of time, not only to meet project deadlines, but also to allow for administrative, marketing, and maintenance chores. It helps to inform everyone from the beginning why this information is needed (cost control, client billing, and staffing information), and that disciplined time management allows for significantly more time for creative work.

Studio members should transfer pertinent aspects of this information to standardized time sheets. They should track time spent on active assignments regardless of whether such time is directly billable. In flat fee situations, the information is used periodically to calculate how much budget is left to work with and finally, how profitable the job was or wasn't.

How detailed should a time sheet be? It depends on management's need to know and client requirements. Some design companies want to know how much time is spent on every aspect of an assignment, from briefing meetings to print/fabrication supervision. This information is useful in tracing the relative levels of job costs phase by phase and can also be used to help price similar assignments in the future. Unfortunately, it's also a large inputting headache for this level of detail and many smaller companies avoid excessive subcoding. There are intranet programs that make it possible for each employee to enter information on an electronic time sheet that then is transferred to a database for tracking and report generation. Agencies and design companies also track time spent preparing presentation materials used to pitch accounts; they may also want to see how long administrative and studio maintenance takes. This information is used to monitor studio staff's productivity, that is, how much of a person's time is billable, how much is used to bring in future income, and how much is simply downtime.

MATERIALS

Supplies that are routinely a part of the studio's activities are part of the overhead, while materials that are billable back to projects must be accounted for in such a way that you can show evidence of the purchase. Code these invoices with the project number and keep a set of copies to back up bills to clients. It is best for one person to be in charge of ordering general supplies and shared equipment, while individuals requisition what they need only for their own projects. Naturally, there has to be a purchase order system for items over some specified amount, and a trusted staff person should be authorized to approve these orders.

SERVICES

All outside services need to be documented. Whether it's for retouching, illustration and photography, model making, outputting, slide production, or independent contractors and freelance personnel, there has to be a written record of what is being requested, by when, at what price, and for illustration, photography, and copywriting, under what kind of terms (copyright, usage rights, credit lines, etc.). The purchase order system for materials is just as useful for outside services. However, remember that a purchase order is a legal commitment to pay, so don't issue any purchase orders if you are only intending to evaluate a product or service. It is also useful to include standardized terms and conditions that are part of each purchase order regarding such issues as ownership, copyright, payment terms, confidentiality, and any other items you consider important to the protection of your interests. Included in payment terms can be the payment schedule, which is generally one-third in advance to begin work, one-third upon approval of design drawings, and one-third upon completion.

PROJECT ESTIMATING

The difference between a good estimate and a bad estimate is the difference between profit and loss. The key to an accurate estimate is a thorough understanding of the project specifications as well as the production process. Make sure you have an opportunity to see firsthand what the project looks like, either from prior examples, or competitive ones. If you know what is being requested and also know how to produce it, and build in a certain amount of safety, you have an excellent chance of setting an accurate fee.

Most professionals break down a project into phases: preproduction for initial client briefings, competitive research, and concept development; design development, which begins with refinements to the concept sketches based on client input, followed by the application of the approved concept to the project's main components; next is the production of finished art and design; and finally, printing and/or fabrication of all the project elements. Phases are further classified into tasks, which then can be analyzed in terms of duration. An important element of successful estimating is knowing approximately how long it takes to do specific tasks and adding on just enough to allow for hitches and breakdowns in the process. Certain contingencies, such as delayed client approvals, can be covered in the project agreement, but delayed delivery of outside elements, such as photography or copy, is the designer's headache and requires an allowance to be built into the production process.

Once you have outlined all of the elements and their production requirements, attach to each step the number of different personnel, their hourly rates, and how long it will take each of them to carry out the necessary steps. Some firms calculate rates per each individual, other firms have a tiered system of rates. A tiered system is preferred, especially in instances where it is necessary to reveal to clients what the firm's hourly rates are. In this way, different levels of personnel are grouped by levels of rates. Generally, the categories are: principals, senior designers, junior designers, and production personnel. In this way, you also avoid revealing salary information to anyone within your organization, as well as to your clients. Add up the personnel hours/days, making sure to account for time to prepare for presentations and client approvals as well as the delivery of those elements they are supposed to provide. Count in responsibilities for art direction, print supervision and fabrication of three-dimensional elements. Multiply the final total by approximately 15 percent for contingencies. For well-defined projects of a simple nature, the contingency allowance can be smaller; for large, complicated, vaguely defined projects, the contingency allowance should be greater. You now have your design fee.

OUT-OF-POCKET EXPENSES

Estimate all of the out-of-pocket expenses that are reimbursable. These items are usually standard, but with some clients they may have to be negotiated. Generally, the following items are included in this category: outside services, such as illustration, photography, copywriting, prototyping, and outputting; delivery services; and items such as models, props, and unique references. Most often, these are expenses that the designer may mark up in order to cover the administrative expenses of researching, bidding, and supervising, as well as for laying out and carrying their costs. Some designers mark up printing and fabrication. Others prefer to have clients pay for them directly. This is a negotiable matter. In the event the client is going to pay directly but the designer is still responsible for supervision, the fee for supervision needs to be built into the estimate.

CHANGES AND ADDITIONS

The tiered system of staff rates is especially useful when clients request changes and additions to their original project specifications. Changes and additions should be considered separately in the project agreement. A brief statement, which describes what is considered outside of the project's scope of work, followed by the tiered rates will take care of this thorny, but frequent, contingency. It is especially useful to document such additions and changes in advance of doing them and have the client sign off, in writing if possible.

MARKET CONDITIONS

Aside from the actual time and expense it takes to create something, there is another critical factor to consider: the inherent worth of that particular item. Inherent worth isn't the same as actual cost. Inherent worth has to do with how much someone is willing to pay to have something, or its market value. An annual report for a Fortune 500 corporation is going to have a much greater inherent worth than an in-house newsletter for a small regional trade association. Not because the large corporation is necessarily better, but because it has a more urgent need to communicate effectively with a greater number of people and because it has far more money to pay for what it wants. There is no social or moral value involved. A bottle that holds $100 per ounce perfume may have the same market value as a bottle that holds $1.29 dishwashing soap. A two-page, full-color spread that appears in a minor, local newspaper may pay the same as a quarter-page, black and white insert in a national consumer magazine. Value has to do with distribution, exposure, and the kind of industry being served. Advertising and corporate clients tend to pay the higher rates, but they are also the most sought after and, usually, the most demanding to service.

USAGE RIGHTS

Always remember to consider future uses of your work. The prospect of building future "passive" income is not only attractive financially, but important in terms of professional prestige. If you designed a two-color poster for an off-Broadway play that then became a huge Broadway hit, but did not reserve the right to your artwork for collateral uses, it could happen that your artwork could be used on book covers, posters, movie ads, and billboards, and possibly even for promotional items, and none of these would carry your credit line.

Do designers have the same rights issues as photographers, illustrators, and artists? Yes and no. Corporate identity is a nonissue. Annual reports and time or event-based materials have limited life spans. On the other hand, cover designs for books, posters, product literature, advertisements, and other items which may be expanded in terms of media, print-run, and time, should be considered as more open-ended opportunities for future use and future income. Therefore, a general rule of thumb is to limit usage rights and pricing to only those media and applications that the client is requesting, and reserve all other rights. And always do so in writing. A complete buy out requires a significantly higher fee. Consider what the compensation might be for future uses of the design. In the event you are sharing copyrights with other artists for the same item, try to coordinate your efforts. Either make sure you own all rights to the various design elements, or carry separate agreements that specify future compensation for them. Avoid making the client have to think about negotiating with a group of different artists for one design.

NEGOTIATIONS

While checking with colleagues and other sources (such as pricing guidelines) can be useful, it is usually best to find out directly from clients how much they have budgeted for the project. This information is helpful for the designer to gauge the client's expectations. There may be an opportunity to expand a project, or if necessary, to walk away from it in the event the designer believes it is not possible to do justice to it for the level of remuneration.

In most instances of business life, negotiation is a key activity. In the course of normal operations, you will be negotiating with clients, employers, partners, suppliers, landlords, among many others. Negotiation is an important skill, and one that can be learned and improved continually. Fundamentally, it is necessary to understand the goal of productive negotiations—that both parties must feel that they have gotten a fair value and can proceed in good faith. Good relations rarely follow horrible negotiations. There must be the transmission of a certain level of trust and good will on both sides. Neither side should be made to feel like a loser. Neither side should feel that it has been unfairly coerced.

Once you have identified what you are seeking—whether it is a higher fee, a more prominent credit line, or free portfolio samples—identify those areas upon which you are willing to trade a smaller markup on out-of-pocket expenses, additional sketches, changes at no cost, or print supervision at a lower rate, the choices may be quite extensive. Also, always ask for a little more and know the point below which you will not proceed. Negotiation is an ancient human activity (hobby to some people) and the nature of it is such that one always expects to get a little more for a little less. As long as you know your upper and lower ranges, finding the comfortable medium is a matter of building your case to support your demands. Be prepared, know what you are talking about, and never feel obliged to commit to a number on the spot if you are not sure it is the right number. It is always possible to stall in order to give yourself a chance to make new calculations or just simply weigh the advantages and disadvantages of the proposition. Naturally, in instances where fees are fixed, or in a competitive situation where the lowest bidder wins automatically, there is little opportunity for discussion. The opportunity afforded by the work, whether monetary or otherwise, is the only basis on which to make a final decision. In such cases, you may decide a lower fee is worth the widespread exposure a project offers; or the prospect of a longer term commitment for additional work outweighs the limitations of an uninspiring project. Many designers take on bread and butter assignments to cover their overhead and let high fee projects support those in which they have a personal interest, but may pay little or nothing.

There are many opportunities and many trade-offs. The trick is to balance them well enough to have an overall sense of satisfaction and progress, which, ultimately, is further promoted when you have mastered the technique of setting fees accurately.

7

Standard Form of Agreement for Design Services

JIM FARIS AND SHEL PERKINS

Reprinted from *AIGA Design Business and Ethics*,
"Chapter 9: Standard Form of Agreement for Design Services."

WELCOME TO THE latest version of the *AIGA Standard Form of Agreement for Design Services*. If you're familiar with the previous versions, you'll notice that this one is quite different. It does not take a one-size-fits-all approach, and it is not an extensive pre-printed document where you simply fill in the blanks. Instead, it acknowledges that most design firms develop their own custom proposal document for each project and are looking for an appropriate set of terms and conditions to attach to it. When put together and signed, the custom proposal document and its attached terms and conditions comprise the binding agreement with the client.

With this in mind, the new focus of the *AIGA Standard Form of Agreement* is on those terms and conditions. AIGA members are involved in many different design disciplines. Because of this, the recommended terms and conditions have been prepared in a modular format. This also helps to keep individual agreements down to a more manageable size. The first two modules, *Basic Terms & Conditions* and *Intellectual Property Provisions*, should be used for all design assignments. An additional three modules are provided as supplements that can be added to the agreement as needed: *Print-Specific Terms & Conditions, Interactive-Specific Terms & Conditions*, and *Environmental-Specific Terms & Conditions*.

This new format for the *AIGA Standard Form of Agreement for Design Services* was developed by a team of industry experts: Don Brunsten (intellectual property attorney, Don Brunsten & Associates), Jim Faris (co-founder of The Management Innovation Group and current AIGA national board member), Linda Joy Kattwinkel (intellectual property attorney, Owen, Wickersham & Erickson), Frank Martinez (intellectual property attorney, The Martinez Group) and Shel Perkins (design management consultant and past president of AIGA San Francisco). It is being provided as a reference to all AIGA members. However, this information is not a substitute for personalized professional advice from an attorney. If you have specific legal questions, you should always seek the services of appropriate legal counsel.

HOW TO USE IT

In general, the process of drafting, negotiating, and finalizing an agreement with a client will follow this sequence of activities:

- ❏ Advance preparation and information gathering about the client and the potential project
- ❏ Internal planning of budget and schedule
- ❏ Drafting a custom proposal document that the client will see
- ❏ Attaching these AIGA modules for all design projects: *Basic Terms & Conditions* and *Schedule A: Intellectual Property Provisions*
- ❏ Adding these AIGA supplements as needed: *Print-Specific Terms & Conditions, Interactive-Specific Terms & Conditions, Environmental-Specific Terms & Conditions*
- ❏ Reviewing the final AIGA checklist of options in the terms and conditions
- ❏ Presenting the agreement to the client and answering any questions
- ❏ Negotiating any modifications requested by the client
- ❏ Finalizing the agreement with authorized signatures

The following pages offer practical advice on the overall process and discuss the important legal and financial issues to be addressed in the "fine print" of any agreement. To help you with the jargon involved, basic explanations of legal terms are included. However, these notes can only serve as a brief introduction to the issues involved. Depending on the type of work that you do and the size of your projects, some of the contractual issues can become rather complex. When finalizing an agreement with a client, you will of course want to have it reviewed by your attorney. With that in mind, these notes end with some pointers on how to find the right attorney and make the best use of his or her time and expertise.

ADVANCE PREPARATION AND PROJECT PLANNING

A proposal is a detailed project document that defines the scope of work, the process, the schedule, and the total price (usually in the form of a fixed fee). It is a discussion document where the designer puts forward a recommended course of action for the client to consider. Many proposals go through several rounds of changes and negotiations before they are finalized. Some negotiations with the client may relate to project specifications while other discussions might focus on the legal terms and conditions. The final goal is to have one comprehensive document that, when accompanied by an appropriate set of terms and conditions and signed by both parties, serves as your agreement for the project.

Initial Steps for You

Start with some general preparation that is relevant to all of the work done by your firm:

- ❏ Think about your creative process. Write down the ideal sequence of activities—phases, steps and milestones—that allows you to produce your best work. If you are active in more than one practice area, you may have several variations. Your own creative process should be the framework that you use for planning and managing projects.

- ❏ Calculate a standard hourly rate. This is an important internal tool that you need in order to sketch out initial budgets. Rates vary from firm to firm based on the amount of overhead being carried, the number of hours available to devote to client projects, and the target profit margin included in the calculation. (A sample format for calculating an hourly rate can be found in chapter 6 of this book.)

- ❏ Become familiar with standard terms and conditions appropriate to the type of work that you are selling.

Now you can zero in on the particular project that you are bidding on:

- ❏ Gather as much information as possible on the potential project. If the client has provided you with an RFP document (a request for proposal), review all of the details carefully. Beyond this, you may want to complete your own form of project questionnaire to make sure that no important details are overlooked. This may involve additional discussions with your client contact and possibly others at the client company in order to learn more.

- ❏ Now you're ready to prepare a preliminary project plan and budget. Even though you may be allergic to spreadsheets, it's important to get in the habit of using an internal planning worksheet to calculate a "suggested retail" price for the project. This ballpark number has to be based on the scope of work required, your own step-by-step design and implementation process, the size of the team that will be required, an estimated number of hours for each team member (valued at your standard hourly rate), and estimated outside purchases (including a standard markup). Now you have to make a judgment call: adjust the totals as needed in order to reflect market conditions and the ultimate value of the work to the client.

❑ You'll also need to draft a preliminary work schedule that shows the number of work days or work weeks required (don't forget to factor in your prior commitments to other clients). A good approach is to do this as a Gantt chart that shows blocks of time and indicates project activities that can happen concurrently. Whenever possible, it's best to avoid locking in specific start dates, approval dates, or completion deadlines, because all of them are sure to change. It's better to plan the schedule in terms of the elapsed time necessary.

This internal preparation and planning has been just for you. The next step is to begin drafting a document that the client will see.

PROPOSAL DOCUMENT

Information that Is Sent to the Client

Written proposals include specific details, which vary quite a bit based on the individual project and the creative firm. However, there is a fairly standard structure for the proposal document itself. Typical components include:

❑ An overview of the client situation (its industry and competitive challenges)

❑ A description of the scope of work and specific objectives for this project (the immediate need that must be addressed and the specific targets that must be achieved)

❑ The process that you are recommending (for each individual phase, spell out what is included and what is not—describe the sequence of steps, the deliverables and milestones, the number of creative directions that you will be showing, the number of revisions or refinements that are included, the format for delivery, the necessary timeframe and a subtotal of fees and expenses; along the way, be sure to clarify the client's responsibilities and explain how the client will be integrated into the process)

❑ A recap of the total timeframe, total fees, and total expenses (plus any applicable taxes)

❑ A billing plan (a simple list of invoice amounts and when they will occur during the project—the payment terms will be explained in the terms and conditions)

- ❏ Appropriate terms and conditions (discussed in detail below)
- ❏ Two lines for authorized signatures at the end of the document (submitted by and accepted by)

You may want to include some extra items, particularly if the client's approval process involves routing the proposal to an executive who has not met you:

- ❏ Capsule bios of senior team members
- ❏ Background information on your design firm's capabilities and your credentials

When finalizing a proposal package, always include a cover letter. It will be written last. Keep it short, professional, and enthusiastic. Don't repeat any of the details that are in the proposal itself. The letter is simply an invitation for a follow-up conversation and it should indicate your willingness to update or revise the scope of work if necessary.

Next, consider the best way of getting the proposal package to the client. Whenever possible, present it in person. This allows you to explain the contents, to address any concerns that the client might have, and to begin building a positive professional relationship.

NOTES ON BASIC TERMS AND CONDITIONS

This first module of the AIGA system includes general terms and conditions that apply to all creative disciplines, addressing such essential issues as payment terms, client changes, and portfolio usage. These shared issues are discussed in detail below. Some descriptions of related concepts are included as well in order to provide additional context.

Definitions

Important terms such as "Agreement" and "Deliverables" need to be used in a consistent way in both the proposal document and the attached terms and conditions. Internal conflicts in terminology will cause confusion and weaken the agreement from a legal standpoint. After a term has been defined, it will be capitalized each time that it is used.

Proposal

The terms and conditions should not restate any of the project specifications already included in the body of your proposal document, but they should include an expiration clause. This is a statement of how long the unsigned offer will remain valid. If the client sits on the proposal for a month or two, you may need to update the document to reflect changes in your pricing or availability.

Fees

If you are charging for your services on a fixed-fee basis, the total amount will be specified in the body of the proposal.

Taxes

It's a good idea to state that the client is responsible for any applicable sales or use taxes, even if they are calculated after the fact (for example, during a subsequent audit of the designer's tax returns).

Expenses and Additional Costs

Every project will involve at least a few expenses. They may be small like reimbursements for photocopies or taxi rides, or they may be large like the purchase of photography. You should spell out for the client exactly how project expenses will be handled and whether or not estimated amounts for those expenses have been included in your proposal. Some clients may want to receive photocopies of receipts for reimbursable expenses while others may simply request the right to audit your project records if they ever feel it's necessary to do so. It's not unusual for a client to require pre-approval if a purchase exceeds a certain amount. If you are requesting a mileage reimbursement for automobile use, you may want to use the standard rate published each year by the Internal Revenue Service (available on *www.irs.gov*). In most design firms, out-of-pocket travel expenses for projects are passed through at cost but all other expenses are subject to a markup. State what percentage you use for your standard markup (20 percent is common). If a client wants to avoid a markup on a large expense, consider allowing the client to purchase it directly. However, your fee for services must cover the time that you put into vendor sourcing and quality control. Many design firms do not want to take on the potential legal liabilities of brokering expensive third-party services. If something goes wrong with a third-party service, such as printing, it's much safer for the designer if the client made the purchase directly.

Invoices

Your schedule for project billings should be stated in the body of the proposal. Progress billings can be based on phases or milestones, or they can be weekly or monthly. You might also want to specify that you will print hard copies in duplicate and send them via regular mail to the accounts payable address given to you by the client.

Payment Terms

When you send an invoice to a client, full payment is due within a certain number of days, counting from the day that the invoice was issued. For example "Net 30" means that the client must get full payment to you within thirty days. Some corporate clients stretch this a bit by saying that the days should be counted from the date they receive the invoice. It's common for design firms to establish client payment terms of "Net 15" because client cash must be received in time for the design firm to pay for related project supplies purchased from vendors on terms of "Net 30." Related to this, you may want to put a limit on the amount of credit that you are willing to extend to a new client. This would be a judgment call based on the client's credit history and your own financial needs. You should state that a project may be put on credit hold if required payments are not made.

Late Payment Penalties

Most design firms charge clients a late fee on overdue payments. The standard rate tends to be 1.5 percent per month (which is the equivalent of 18 percent per year), but there are legal limits to the rate in some states. Separate invoices are not generated for the penalty amounts. Instead, they appear as line items on monthly statements sent to clients to remind them of unpaid invoices. When client payments are received, the funds are applied first to the penalty charges, and then to the unpaid balance on each open invoice, starting with the oldest.

Full Payment

If you have agreed that you will be transferring some or all rights to your client, you should definitely make any transfer of rights contingent upon receipt of full payment from the client for your services.

Changes

It's fairly common for minor client changes to be billed on a time-and-materials basis, so your standard hourly rate(s) will be listed here. You might also want to state that your standard rates will not change without thirty days advance notice to the client. When a client requests additions or modifications, you should respond with a change order form. A change order is a document drafted by the designer to acknowledge a client request that is outside of the original scope for the project. The designer describes the amount of additional time and money required and sends the change order to the client for review and an authorized signature. It is essentially a mini-proposal. You'll want to reference the original proposal and state that the same terms and conditions will apply. Compensation for a change order can be calculated on a time-and-materials basis or as a fixed fee. As the work involved is completed, each change order should be invoiced separately. If a client requests substantial changes, however, it's sometimes cleaner and less confusing to start all over with a new proposal for the entire project. You may want to define a substantive change as anything that exceeds a certain percentage of the original schedule or budget (such as 10 percent) or a certain dollar amount (such as $1,000)—whichever is greater.

Timing

It's paradoxical that the typical client will negotiate for a very tight schedule, yet in the middle of the project, that same client may cause serious delays by failing to provide necessary information, materials, or approvals. Most design firms specify that if a client causes a lengthy delay it will result in a day-for-day extension of the project's final deadline. During that client delay, you may also have to reassign some of your resources to other projects, if you have any. You might have cleared the decks for the fast-track project by delaying or turning down other assignments. The danger for you as a businessperson is that an unexpected delay could mean that you're temporarily unable to produce billable hours. To offset this risk, some creative firms attempt to charge a delay penalty or a restart fee. You may want to raise this issue as a negotiating point. However, most clients are not very receptive to the idea.

Testing and Acceptance

All work that you deliver to the client should be considered accepted unless the client notifies you to the contrary within a specified period of time (usually five or ten days).

Cure

Related to testing and acceptance is the concept of cure. If the client notifies you that the work is not acceptable, you should have the opportunity to effect a cure. This means to repair, correct, or re-design any work that does not conform to the project specifications in order to make it acceptable to the client.

Client Responsibilities

If clients have never purchased creative services before, they may not be aware of how extensive and important their own involvement in the process will be. You'll want to point out what is required of them in terms of information, content, schedules, decision-making, and approvals.

Accreditation/Promotions

This has to do with receiving proper credit for the work and being able to add it to your design portfolio. You should ask for a credit line to be included in the work itself. You should state that, once the project has been completed and introduced to the public, you will have the right to add the client's name to your client list and the right to enter the work into design competitions. You'll also want to be able to show and explain portions of the completed project to other companies when you are pitching new business. Sometimes clients who are in highly competitive industries have concerns about this. They may ask for the right to review and approve such promotional activity on a case-by-case basis. If you have licensed the final art to the client rather than making a full assignment of rights, and the work does not fall within the category of work-for-hire (defined below), you are legally entitled to show the work in your portfolio. As a professional courtesy, however, you will want to be sensitive to client concerns. (For more information about ownership and licensing, see *Schedule A: Intellectual Property Provisions.*)

Confidential Information

In order for these terms and conditions to be complete and comprehensive, confidentiality should be included here even if you've already signed a separate confidentiality and non-disclosure agreement (perhaps during your very first meeting with the client). Depending on the type of work that you do, you may want confidentiality and non-disclosure to be mutual so that your own proprietary information is protected as well.

Relationship of the Parties

Your agreement should reiterate the fact that you are not an employee of your client and you are not forming a joint venture or partnership with them. As an outside supplier of services, you are functioning as an independent contractor. You will also want the ability to bring in your own assistants or agents as needed.

Work Made for Hire

Discussions with your client about independent contractor status and about ownership and use of project deliverables are sometimes complicated by confusion over the related concept of work-for-hire. This phrase comes from U.S. copyright law. It refers to original work made by an employee within the scope of his or her job, in which copyright ownership automatically belongs to the employer. However, it can also refer to original work made by an independent contractor or a design firm, in which copyright ownership might automatically belong to the client. This is only true if the work meets very specific criteria—it must be specially ordered or commissioned, and it must fall within one of nine categories:

- ❏ A contribution to a collective work (such as a magazine, an anthology, or an encyclopedia)

- ❏ A work that is part of a motion picture or other audiovisual work (such as a Web site or multimedia project)

- ❏ A translation

- ❏ A supplement prepared as an adjunct to a work created by another author (such as a foreword, an appendix, or charts)

- ❏ A compilation (a new arrangement of pre-existing works, such as a catalog)

- ❏ An instructional text (whether it is literary, pictorial, or graphic)

❑ A test

❑ Answer material for a test

❑ An atlas

Also, a written agreement must be signed by both parties saying that it is a work made for hire. If the project doesn't meet all of these criteria, work-for-hire does not apply. Copyright will belong to you unless you assign it to your client. (More information about copyright is available in the AIGA publication *Guide to Copyright* and directly from the U.S. Copyright Office at *www.copyright.gov*.)

No Solicitation

It doesn't happen very often, but sometimes a client is so pleased with the work of a particular member of the designer's team that he or she will seek to establish a direct relationship with him or her. Some people refer to this as "cherry picking." If a client recruits one of your team members away from you, you should at least be entitled to a placement fee for having made the introduction. Beyond that, you should also consider the impact on your operations. If your most experienced and productive team member is no longer available, your business may be damaged by the unexpected interruption to your activities.

No Exclusivity

You may want to add that the relationship between you and the client is not an exclusive one. You sell services to a range of clients and some of them may be competitors. If a company wants to be your only client in a particular category, your pricing will have to reflect that. An exclusive relationship would require you to turn down projects from similar firms. Higher rates are necessary in order to offset that lost business.

Warranties and Representations

A warranty is a promise in a contract. It is a written guarantee that the subject of the agreement is as represented. As a designer, you might warrant that your work is free from defective workmanship or that it is original and does not infringe the intellectual property of others. If some portion of the work turns out to be defective (for example, a problem with some line of custom computer code in an interactive project), then it is your responsibility to repair or replace it. Legal issues related to originality can be a bit more challenging. You can only infringe a copyright if you knowingly copy someone else's work. However, trademark, trade dress, and patent rights can be infringed even if you create your work independently. Thus, it's best to limit your warranty of non-infringement to "the best of your knowledge." If you are going to provide a guarantee of non-infringement without such limitation, then at some time before the end of the project a formal search should be conducted to determine whether or not your work inadvertently resembles a third party's trademark or patent ("prior art"). It's best to place responsibility for this type of prior art search on the client. If you agree to arrange for the search, then your schedule and budget for the project must include the hiring of an attorney or legal service to actually carry it out. It's best for warranties and representations to be reciprocal. The client should make the same promises to you for any project components that they supply.

Infringement

Infringement is the unauthorized use of someone else's intellectual property. It is the opposite of seeking and receiving permission, using correct notice of ownership, and contracting for payment of a royalty or fee. Even though the infringement may be accidental (you may independently create a logo for your client that looks like someone else's trademark), there may be infringement liability, and the infringer may be responsible for paying substantial damages and stopping the use of the infringing work.

Disclaimer of Warranties and Use of ALL CAPS

If an agreement includes a disclaimer of any warranty, many states require by law that the disclaimer language be sufficiently "conspicuous" in the document. It needs to stand out in such a way that any reasonable consumer would notice it. This usually means that the disclaimer must be printed in all capital letters, or in type that is larger or in a contrasting color. If you do not follow these guidelines, you run the risk of making the disclaimer invalid.

Indemnification

In the event that you breach any warranty that you have given, you agree to provide security against any hurt, loss, or damage that might occur. You would have to make the client "whole" by giving it something equal to what it has lost or protecting it from any judgments or damages that might have to be paid to third parties, along with attorney's fees. For example, you might be asked to provide indemnity against third party infringement claims. At the same time, however, you need to have the client indemnify you against any breach of warranties that it has made. Indemnification is a very important issue for designers because the scope of potential liability can be considerable.

Liability

Liability means legal responsibility for the consequences of your acts or omissions. Your accountability to the client may be enforced by civil remedies or criminal penalties. For example, a Web developer who has agreed in writing to complete an e-commerce site by a specific date will have liability to the client if the project is not completed on time.

Limitations on Liability and Use of ALL CAPS

Again, if an agreement includes a limitation on liability, many states require by law that the limitation language be sufficiently "conspicuous" in the document. It needs to stand out in such a way that any reasonable consumer would notice it. This usually means that the limitation must be printed in all capital letters, or in type that is larger or in a contrasting color. If you do not follow these guidelines, you run the risk of making the limitation invalid. It's smart for a designer to ask a client to agree that it may not recover any damages from you in excess of the total amount of money agreed to in the proposal. While it's possible for you to limit the amount that each of you might owe to the other in this way, you should keep in mind that you cannot contract away the rights of any third party to make a claim.

Remedy

A remedy is the legal recourse available to an injured party. It may be stipulated in an agreement or a court may order it. A remedy might require that a certain act be performed or prohibited, or it might involve the payment of money.

Damages

Damages are financial compensation for loss or injury suffered by a plaintiff (the person suing). The amount of money awarded in a lawsuit can vary greatly. There are several different categories of damages, including the following: actual damages, such as loss of money due on a contract; general damages, which are more subjective and might relate to loss of reputation or anticipated business; and punitive damages, which may be awarded if the defendant acted in a fraudulent way.

Term and Termination

The normal term of a project will begin with the signing of a written agreement and end with the client's acceptance of your completed services. If something happens in the meantime to make cancellation necessary, the agreement must describe in advance the process for doing that, from notification through calculation of your final invoice. That final billing might cover time and materials for actual services performed through the date of cancellation, or it might be a lump-sum cancellation fee, or perhaps a combination of the two. Cancellation also raises questions about ownership of the unfinished work. Typically the designer will retain all preliminary art, including any studies and comps already rejected by the client, while the client might receive the most recent approved version of the work in process.

GENERAL ITEMS

Most of the legal issues addressed in this section of the terms and conditions are fairly self-explanatory. However, the following information may be helpful.

Force Majeure

This is a French term that means "superior force." It refers to any event or effect that cannot be reasonably anticipated or controlled. If such an event occurs (for example, a war, a labor strike, extreme weather, or an earthquake) it may delay or terminate the project without putting the designer or client at fault.

Governing Law

This has to do with jurisdiction. You must identify the state whose laws will govern the signed agreement. Your client will usually request the state where its main office is located.

Dispute Resolution

There are three standard types of dispute resolution. Here is a brief description of each one:

- Mediation is a non-binding intervention between parties in an informal setting in order to promote resolution of a dispute. It involves the active participation of a third party (a mediator) who facilitates discussion in order to clarify issues, find points of agreement, and encourage cooperation. A commitment to mediation is often included in contracts. There are professional mediators and lawyers who offer mediation services.

- The next step beyond mediation is arbitration, in which an impartial third party (an arbitrator) hears both sides of the dispute in an out-of-court setting. The arbitrator is an attorney who acts much like a judge, listening to both sides of the story but not actively participating in discussion. You and your opponent will have the opportunity to present evidence and witnesses. After hearing the facts, the arbitrator will make a decision. In your contract, you will specify whether the decision of the arbitrator is binding or non-binding. Binding arbitration imposes a legal obligation on the parties to abide by the decision and accept it as final. Arbitration proceedings are held in an attempt to avoid a court trial. However, contract-required arbitration may later be converted into a legal judgment on petition to the court. The fees involved might be large (depending on the dispute, they could easily range from $3,000 to $20,000 or more), but usually they are less than those involved in pursuing a lawsuit. For the sake of convenience, many contracts identify a large, national arbitration service to be used in the event of a dispute. However, it may be preferable for you to replace this national name with a local name, particularly if you can find a service that is geared toward the arts.

- Litigation means that you are pursuing a lawsuit through the court system in order to resolve a dispute. The time and expense involved may be considerable.

Attorneys' Fees

When a decision has been reached concerning a dispute, either through arbitration or litigation, the losing side may be liable to pay the winning side's costs and attorneys' fees. Under copyright law, a winning plaintiff is entitled to recover his or her attorneys' fees if the copyright was registered before the infringement occurred. For other types of liability, the obligation to pay the prevailing party's legal expenses must be established in your contract.

NOTES ON SCHEDULE A: INTELLECTUAL PROPERTY PROVISIONS

Every designer produces original work that is covered by copyright protection, and additional work that could possibly be registered under trademark or patent laws. Because of this, every design contract needs to address the issues of ownership and usage of intellectual property. These can be negotiated in a variety of ways, based on the nature of the work and the specific needs of the client.

Preliminary Art Versus Final Art

There is an important distinction to be made between preliminary and final art. Early in each project, a designer may produce a lot of discussion materials (such as sketches, rough layouts, visualizations, or comps). These are prepared solely for the purpose of demonstrating an idea or a message to the client for acceptance. Normally the client does not receive legal title to or permanent possession of these items, so it's important for your contract to be clear on this point. Many preliminary concepts will later be modified or rejected entirely. Usually only one concept will be taken through to completion and it is only the approved and finished final art that will be delivered to the client.

Third-Party Materials

If intellectual property owned by a third party is to be used in a project (for example, an illustration or a photograph), the designer should state that the client is responsible for respecting any usage limitations placed on the property. You may even want the client to negotiate usage rights with the third party and make payments directly to it.

Trademarks

Issues related to trademarks are discussed in the warranties and infringement sections above.

Designer Tools

This deals with the issue of background technology. If any code that is proprietary to the designer is necessary to develop, run, display, or use the final deliverables, then the designer needs to retain ownership of it while granting a non-exclusive license for the client to copy and use it. This way you can use that same technology on any other clients' projects.

License

A license is a limited grant by a designer to a client of rights to use the intellectual property comprising the final art in a specified way.

Scope of License

The extent of the license that you grant will vary based on the type of work involved. The rights may be limited to use on certain products, in particular media, in a certain territory, and/or for a specified time period. Other basic limitations include whether or not you will allow the client to modify your work in any way, or to turn around and license the work to a third party without your permission. If the client later decides that it needs additional rights, it will have to come back to you, renegotiate, and pay additional fees.

Exclusive License

If a license is exclusive, it means that even though you have retained ownership of the work, you will not be giving permission to anyone else to use it. This means that you will not be able to generate additional licensing income from other sources. Because of this, designers need to negotiate higher prices for exclusive licenses.

Liquidation for Unlicensed Use

When licensing rights, you may want to consider agreeing in advance on the amount of damages that would be payable by the client upon a breach of contract. These are called liquidated damages. At some point in the future, the client may be tempted to exceed the original scope of the license that you have granted. Instead of coming back and renegotiating with you, as they should, it might just begin unlicensed usage. (It's a challenge that is faced all the time by stock photography businesses and illustrators.) Since you can't know in advance the extent of the actual damages that would be caused by the unlicensed usage, the amount of money to be paid is calculated as a multiple of the original contract price (300 percent is common). An agreement on liquidated damages can help to avoid potential lawsuits and serve as an incentive for the client not to exceed the scope of the license. However, you'll want to weigh your other options carefully. If you reserve the right to sue for breach of contract or infringement, it's conceivable that the amount of money awarded to you in a lawsuit could be higher.

Assignment of Rights

An assignment is a full transfer of intellectual property rights to your client. It might include copyright, patent, trademark, trade dress, or other types of intellectual property. For example, when a new corporate identity is developed and sold to a client, the sale typically includes an assignment of all rights. The client will go on to complete U.S. and international registration of copyright, trademark, patent, and other rights in its own name. Designers should charge a higher fee for any project that involves a full assignment of rights.

NOTES ON SUPPLEMENTS

Beyond the basic issues discussed above, additional language may be needed in the agreement to clarify issues that are specific to a particular design discipline. For example, Web developers have particular concerns that are different from those of packaging designers. Out of the many possible variations, we have focused in on three areas that we feel will be most relevant to the majority of AIGA members. Most of the items in the supplements are fairly self-explanatory. However, the following information may be helpful.

SUPPLEMENT 1: PRINT-SPECIFIC TERMS AND CONDITIONS
Samples

You will want to specify the number of printed samples to be provided to you.

Finished Work

In the printing industry, it's not unusual to encounter slight variations of specifications or materials (for example, substitution of a comparable paper stock due to limited availability) as well as a variance of plus or minus 10 percent on the final, delivered quantity. These should be considered normal and acceptable. Much more information is available about standard trade practices in the printing industry from organizations such as PIA/GATF (Printing Industries of America, Inc., and the Graphic Arts Technical Foundation).

SUPPLEMENT 2: INTERACTIVE-SPECIFIC TERMS AND CONDITIONS
Support Services

If you're bidding on a Web site and the scope of services described in your proposal includes testing, hosting, and/or maintenance, you are taking on additional legal responsibilities that need to be described in the agreement. Try to limit any additional liability as much as possible. On all interactive projects, you'll want to be very specific about how much support or maintenance you will provide after delivery, and whether or not those services will be billed in addition to the original contract price.

Compliance with Laws

Section 508 of the Workforce Investment Act of 1998 is of particular importance to user interface designers as well as software and hardware developers. This law requires electronic and information technology purchased by the U.S. government to be accessible for people with disabilities. It sets accessibility and usability requirements for any Web sites, video equipment, kiosks, computers, copiers, fax machines, and the like that may be procured by the government, thereby essentially affecting all such products in the American market. (The United Kingdom and Japan have also put accessibility guidelines into place.)

SUPPLEMENT 3: ENVIRONMENTAL-SPECIFIC TERMS AND CONDITIONS

Photographs of the Project

After completion of an environmental/3-D project (such as a signage system, a trade show booth, a retail interior, or an exhibit) you need the right to photograph the result. This involves being able to access it and take your photographs under optimal circumstances.

Additional Client Responsibilities

Environmental design projects often require various types of government approval, such as building permits or zoning reviews. Be sure to state that the client is responsible for these.

Engineering and Implementation

You will be providing specifications for materials and construction details that will be interpreted by other professionals, such as architects, engineers, and contractors. Typically the client will contract and pay for such implementation services directly. Your agreement should include a disclaimer that you are not licensed in those fields and that responsibility for the quality, safety, timeliness, and cost of such work is the responsibility of the client and the architect, engineer, or contractor involved. The client should indemnify you against any claims in this regard.

Compliance with Laws

Your project may be subject to the Americans with Disabilities Act (ADA), which is a civil rights act that affects private businesses as well as governmental organizations. ADA requirements are of particular importance to industrial designers, interior designers, and architects.

Client Insurance

Ask your client to provide you with proof that it has adequate insurance coverage in place for the duration of the project (one million dollars is a common minimum amount).

FINAL CHECKLIST

Before you send the draft agreement to the client, look through it one more time for quality control purposes. In the terms and conditions pages, there are several blanks that need to be filled in and some very important options need to be selected.

BASIC TERMS & CONDITIONS

2.   Number of days that the unsigned proposal will remain valid.

3.2 Standard markup percentage for expenses (and perhaps standard rate for mileage reimbursement).

3.4 Number of days allowed for payment of invoices.

4.1 Hourly billing rate to be used for general client changes.

4.2 Percentage of original project schedule or budget that will be used to determine whether or not changes are substantive instead of general.

12.5 Name of state identified for governing law.

12.8 Identify which supplements are attached, if any.

Last Add your name, signature, and date.

Schedule A: Intellectual Property Provisions

Choose only one of these three options:

IP 2.A (1) (a) and IP 2.1

- ❏ A license for limited usage; client may not modify the work.
- ❏ Indicate whether it is for print, interactive, or environmental.
- ❏ Describe the category, medium, duration, territory, and size of initial press run.
- ❏ Indicate whether the license is exclusive or nonexclusive.

IP 2.A (1) (b) and IP 2.2

- ❏ A license for unlimited usage; client may not modify the work.
- ❏ Indicate whether it is for print, interactive, or environmental/3-D.
- ❏ This license is exclusive.

IP 2.A (1) (c) and IP 2.3

- ❏ A license for unlimited usage; client may modify the work.
- ❏ Indicate whether it is for print, interactive, or environmental/3-D.
- ❏ This license is exclusive.

And, with any of the three options above, be sure to include the following liquidation clause just in case the client later exceeds the usage rights that you have granted:

IP 2.A (2) and IP 2.4
Fill in the percentage that will be used to calculate the amount of additional compensation.

Or skip all of the above and go directly to:

IP 2.B and 2.5
This assigns all rights to the client, with no limitations.

Supplement 1: Print-Specific Terms & Conditions

P 1. Enter the number of printed samples that you want to receive.

Supplement 2: Interactive-Specific Terms & Conditions

I 1.1 Enter the number of months in the warranty period and enter the number of support hours to be provided at no additional cost.

I 1.2 Enter the number of months in the maintenance period and enter the flat fee to be charged per month, or the hourly billing rate for maintenance.

Supplement 3: Environmental-Specific Terms & Conditions

3-D 3. Remove either the brackets or the text within them in order to indicate whether you are or are not a licensed engineer or architect.

3-D 6. Insurance requirement for the client: enter a dollar amount.

NEGOTIATING

Present the draft agreement to the client in person, if possible, so that you can explain the contents and answer any questions. Don't be surprised if the client asks for modifications or additional items to be included. Here are some of the issues that may come up:

Pricing

Often the initial client response will be to ask for a lower price. It's best for you to avoid getting into a discussion of standard hourly rates. Discuss the scope of work instead. Focus on the main objectives. Can portions of the project be scaled back? Are there components that can be broken out as later projects? Reducing the scope of work will reduce the overall price.

Deposits

Whenever possible, you should ask for a deposit at the beginning of a project. There are different approaches to this. Some designers apply the deposit to the first progress billing (making it essentially a pre-payment of phase one). Others state that the deposit will be held until the end of project and applied to the final billing. If that's the case, point out that no interest will be paid while it is being held. If the project is cancelled, the deposit will be refunded less any amounts due to the designer.

Product Liability

If you are working on the development of a product that will eventually be sold to the public, this will be an important issue. Your client may ask to have it included in the agreement. Product liability refers to the legal responsibility of product designers, manufacturers, distributors, and sellers to deliver products to the public that are free of any defects that could harm people. If a product is defective, the purchaser will probably sue the seller, who may then bring the distributor or manufacturer or product designer into the lawsuit. Any one of the parties may be liable for damages or may have to contribute toward a judgment.

Designer Insurance

Large clients often specify minimum insurance levels for the designer's business. Standard business requirements include general liability, workers' comp, and automobile coverage. In addition, you may need to carry professional liability insurance to cover such things as intellectual property infringement or errors and omissions. You'll need to analyze your own needs in this area and do some research with an independent insurance agent. Certain types of professional liability coverage may be limited in scope and rather expensive. If designer insurance requirements are added to the agreement, you must provide proof of coverage in the form of a certificate of insurance that is sent from your insurance agent directly to the client.

ADDENDUM TO THE AGREEMENT

There are two ways to record the changes that result from your negotiations with the client. The most direct is to go back into the body of the agreement and change the original language. This is, in fact, what you should do for all changes that relate to the scope and specifications in the proposal document at the front of the agreement. However, things can become quite confusing if you start to rewrite the attached terms and conditions. It is sometimes better to list negotiated changes to the terms and conditions on a separate sheet, called an addendum. The addendum must clearly describe exactly what is being changed and it must not create any contradictions or ambiguities. If you do go back into the original terms and conditions and make the changes directly, then you must be cautious when you are drafting your next client agreement. If you're in a hurry, it's all too easy to copy the modified terms by mistake. Be sure that you always go back to the standard language and not your most recent adaptation. The original text must always be your starting point—otherwise you can stray quite far from the original intent.

NEGOTIATING JUST ONCE FOR THE ENTIRE RELATIONSHIP

Terms and conditions can be negotiated separately for each and every project, or they can be negotiated just once for the entire relationship. If you start with a complete set and state that it will apply to all projects, then future proposals can just refer back to it. This can save on paperwork, time, and legal expenses for both you and your client.

FINDING AND WORKING WITH AN ATTORNEY

It can be a challenge to find the right attorney and to use his or her time in an efficient way. Most attorneys specialize in a single category of law, such as real estate or labor law. As a creative professional, you need to find an attorney who specializes in issues related to intellectual property (copyrights, trademarks, patents, trade secrets, and moral rights). Attorneys are licensed state by state, so you need to find one in your own area. Start your search by visiting these online directories:

- Volunteer Lawyers for the Arts
  http://www.vlany.org/
  (A nonprofit listing of legal resources for artists in twenty-five U.S. states plus Canada and Australia)

- Martindale-Hubbell
  http://www.lawyers.com/
  (A commercial directory of U.S. and Canadian attorneys that you can search by specialty and location)

- FindLaw
  http://www.findlaw.com/
  (A searchable commercial database of attorneys, along with articles on various legal topics)

It's a good idea to look for an attorney who has other designers as clients. Speak with established members of your own design community—one of them may be able to provide you with a local recommendation. Seek out an appropriate attorney when you are first establishing your business. Getting preventative advice on basic issues is much better than waiting until you're already in some sort of legal difficulty.

Initial discounts are sometimes available through groups such as Volunteer Lawyers for the Arts, but in general legal services are not inexpensive. Attorneys may charge a flat fee for assisting with certain basic transactions such as setting up an LLC, but for the most part services are billed on a time-and-materials basis. For this reason, you need to be efficient in the way that you interact. Make the best use of your attorney's time by being very well prepared. Bring copies of any correspondence that you have already received from or sent to the client. Gather sample documents from your industry and become familiar with the basic legal issues relevant to the creative services that you offer. You may be able to use one of these reference documents as a draft for further discussion with your attorney. Be completely honest and ask questions about anything that is not clear to you. Together you will then craft a final version to send to your client.

If your client is a small business, it may respond with some basic questions that you will have no trouble answering. With large clients, though, you may find that your document is routed to an in-house legal department. If questions come to you from an in-house attorney, consider having that person negotiate the fine points directly with your own lawyer. If the in-house counsel is a specialist in some other area of law, your intellectual property attorney can explain the context for the agreement language that you are requesting. Attorney-to-attorney negotiation creates additional expense, but if the resulting terms and conditions can be accepted as the basis of an ongoing relationship, then you won't have to go through the process a second time.

BASIC TERMS & CONDITIONS

1.   DEFINITIONS. As used herein and throughout this Agreement

1.1   *"Agreement"* means the entire content of this Basic Terms and Conditions document, the Proposal document(s), Schedule A, together with any other Supplements designated below, together with any exhibits, schedules or attachments hereto.

1.2   *"Client Content"* means all materials, information, photography, writings and other creative content provided by Client for use in the preparation of and/or incorporation in the Deliverables.

1.3   *"Copyrights"* means the property rights in original works of authorship, expressed in a tangible medium of expression, as defined and enforceable under U.S. Copyright Law.

1.4   *"Deliverables"* means the services and work product specified in the Proposal to be delivered by Designer to Client, in the form and media specified in the Proposal.

1.5   *"Designer Tools"* means all design tools developed and/or utilized by Designer in performing the Services, including without limitation pre-existing and newly developed software including source code, Web authoring tools, type fonts, and application tools, together with any other software, or other inventions whether or not patentable, and general non-copyrightable concepts such as Web site design, architecture, layout, navigational and functional elements.

1.6 *"Final Art"* means all creative content developed or created by Designer, or commissioned by Designer, exclusively for the Project and incorporated into and delivered as part of the Final Deliverables, including and by way of example, not limitation, any and all visual designs, visual elements, graphic design, illustration, photography, animation, sounds, typographic treatments and text, modifications to Client Content, and Designer's selection, arrangement and coordination of such elements together with Client Content and/or Third Party Materials.

1.7 *"Final Deliverables"* means the final versions of Deliverables provided by Designer and accepted by Client.

1.8 *"Preliminary Works"* means all artwork including, but not limited to, concepts, sketches, visual presentations, or other alternate or preliminary designs and documents developed by Designer and which may or may not be shown and or delivered to Client for consideration but do not form part of the Final Art.

1.9 *"Project"* means the scope and purpose of the Client's identified usage of the work product as described in the Proposal.

1.10 *"Services"* means all services and the work product to be provided to Client by Designer as described and otherwise further defined in the Proposal.

1.11 *"Third Party Materials"* means proprietary third party materials which are incorporated into the Final Deliverables, including without limitation stock photography or illustration.

1.12 *"Trademarks"* means trade names, words, symbols, designs, logos, or other devices or designs used in the Final Deliverables to designate the origin or source of the goods or services of Client.

2. Proposal.

The terms of the Proposal shall be effective for _____ days after presentation to Client. In the event this Agreement is not executed by Client within the time identified, the Proposal, together with any related terms and conditions and deliverables, may be subject to amendment, change or substitution.

3. Fees and Charges.

3.1 *Fees.* In consideration of the Services to be performed by Designer, Client shall pay to Designer fees in the amounts and according to the payment schedule set forth in the Proposal, and all applicable sales, use or value added taxes, even if calculated or assessed subsequent to the payment schedule.

3.2 *Expenses*. Client shall pay Designer's expenses incurred in connection with this Agreement as follows: (a) incidental and out-of-pocket expenses including but not limited to costs for telephone calls, postage, shipping, overnight courier, service bureaus, typesetting, blueprints, models, presentation materials, photocopies, computer expenses, parking fees and tolls, and taxis at cost plus Designer's standard markup of _____ percent (_____%), and, if applicable, a mileage reimbursement at _____ per mile; and (b) travel expenses including transportation, meals, and lodging incurred by Designer with Client's prior approval.

3.3 *Additional Costs*. The Project pricing includes Designer's fee only. Any and all outside costs including, but not limited to, equipment rental, photographer's costs and fees, photography and/or artwork licenses, prototype production costs, talent fees, music licenses, and online access or hosting fees, will be billed to Client unless specifically otherwise provided for in the Proposal.

3.4 *Invoices*. All invoices are payable within _____ (_____) days of receipt. A monthly service charge of 1.5% (or the greatest amount allowed by state law) is payable on all overdue balances. Payments will be credited first to late payment charges and next to the unpaid balance. Client shall be responsible for all collection or legal fees necessitated by lateness or default in payment. Designer reserves the right to withhold delivery and any transfer of ownership of any current work if accounts are not current or overdue invoices are not paid in full. All grants of any license to use or transfer of ownership of any intellectual property rights under this Agreement are conditioned upon receipt of payment in full which shall be inclusive of any and all outstanding Additional Costs, Taxes, Expenses, and Fees, Charges, or the costs of Changes.

4. Changes.

4.1 *General Changes*. Unless otherwise provided in the Proposal, and except as otherwise provided for herein, Client shall pay additional charges for changes requested by Client which are outside the scope of the Services on a time and materials basis, at Designer's standard hourly rate of _____ per hour. Such charges shall be in addition to all other amounts payable under the Proposal, despite any maximum budget, contract price, or final price identified therein. Designer may extend or modify any delivery schedule or deadlines in the Proposal and Deliverables as may be required by such Changes.

4.2 *Substantive Changes*. If Client requests or instructs Changes that amount to a revision in or near excess of _____ percent (_____%) of the time required to produce the Deliverables, and or the value or scope of the Services, Designer shall be entitled to submit a new and separate Proposal to Client for written approval. Work shall not begin on the revised services until a fully signed revised Proposal and, if required, any additional retainer fees are received by Designer.

4.3 *Timing.* Designer will prioritize performance of the Services as may be necessary or as identified in the Proposal, and will undertake commercially reasonable efforts to perform the Services within the time(s) identified in the Proposal. Client agrees to review Deliverables within the time identified for such reviews and to promptly either (i) approve the Deliverables in writing or (ii) provide written comments and/or corrections sufficient to identify the Client's concerns, objections, or corrections to Designer. The Designer shall be entitled to request written clarification of any concern, objection, or correction. Client acknowledges and agrees that Designer's ability to meet any and all schedules is entirely dependent upon Client's prompt performance of its obligations to provide materials and written approvals and/or instructions pursuant to the Proposal and that any delays in Client's performance or Changes in the Services or Deliverables requested by Client may delay delivery of the Deliverables. Any such delay caused by Client shall not constitute a breach of any term, condition or Designer's obligations under this Agreement.

4.4 *Testing and Acceptance.* Designer will exercise commercially reasonable efforts to test Deliverables requiring testing and to make all necessary corrections prior to providing Deliverables to Client. Client, within five (5) business days of receipt of each Deliverable, shall notify Designer, in writing, of any failure of such Deliverable to comply with the specifications set forth in the Proposal, or of any other objections, corrections, changes, or amendments Client wishes made to such Deliverable. Any such written notice shall be sufficient to identify with clarity any objection, correction, change or amendment, and Designer will undertake to make the same in a commercially timely manner. Any and all objections, corrections, changes, or amendments shall be subject to the terms and conditions of this Agreement. In the absence of such notice from Client, the Deliverable shall be deemed accepted.

5. CLIENT RESPONSIBILITIES.

Client acknowledges that it shall be responsible for performing the following in a reasonable and timely manner:

    (a) coordination of any decision-making with parties other than the Designer;

(b) provision of Client Content in a form suitable for reproduction or incorporation into the Deliverables without further preparation, unless otherwise expressly provided in the Proposal; and

(c) final proofreading and in the event that Client has approved Deliverables but errors, such as, by way of example, not limitation, typographic errors or misspellings, remain in the finished product, Client shall incur the cost of correcting such errors.

6. ACCREDITATION/PROMOTIONS.

All displays or publications of the Deliverables shall bear accreditation and/or copyright notice in Designer's name in the form, size, and location as incorporated by Designer in the Deliverables, or as otherwise directed by Designer. Designer retains the right to reproduce, publish, and display the Deliverables in Designer's portfolios and Web sites, and in galleries, design periodicals, and other media or exhibits for the purposes of recognition of creative excellence or professional advancement, and to be credited with authorship of the Deliverables in connection with such uses. Either party, subject to the other's reasonable approval, may describe its role in relation to the Project and, if applicable, the services provided to the other party on its Web site and in other promotional materials, and, if not expressly objected to, include a link to the other party's Web site.

7. CONFIDENTIAL INFORMATION.

Each party acknowledges that in connection with this Agreement it may receive certain confidential or proprietary technical and business information and materials of the other party, including without limitation Preliminary Works ("Confidential Information"). Each party, its agents and employees shall hold and maintain in strict confidence all Confidential Information, shall not disclose Confidential Information to any third party, and shall not use any Confidential Information except as may be necessary to perform its obligations under the Proposal except as may be required by a court or governmental authority. Notwithstanding the foregoing, Confidential Information shall not include any information that is in the public domain or becomes publicly known through no fault of the receiving party, or is otherwise properly received from a third party without an obligation of confidentiality.

8. RELATIONSHIP OF THE PARTIES.

8.1 *Independent Contractor.* Designer is an independent contractor, not an employee of Client or any company affiliated with Client. Designer shall provide the Services under the general direction of Client, but Designer shall determine, in Designer's sole discretion, the manner and means by which the Services are accomplished. This Agreement does not create a partnership or joint venture and neither party is authorized to act as agent or bind the other party except as expressly stated in this Agreement. Designer and the work product or Deliverables prepared by Designer shall not be deemed a work for hire as that term is defined under Copyright Law. All rights, if any, granted to Client are contractual in nature and are wholly defined by the express written agreement of the parties and the various terms and conditions of this Agreement.

8.2 *Designer Agents.* Designer shall be permitted to engage and/or use third party designers or other service providers as independent contractors in connection with the Services ("Design Agents"). Notwithstanding, Designer shall remain fully responsible for such Design Agents' compliance with the various terms and conditions of this Agreement.

8.3 *No Solicitation.* During the term of this Agreement, and for a period of six (6) months after expiration or termination of this Agreement, Client agrees not to solicit, recruit, engage, or otherwise employ or retain, on a full-time, part-time, consulting, work-for-hire, or any other kind of basis, any Designer, employee or Design Agent of Designer, whether or not said person has been assigned to perform tasks under this Agreement. In the event such employment, consultation or work-for-hire event occurs, Client agrees that Designer shall be entitled to an agency commission to be the greater of, either (a) 25% of said person's starting salary with Client, or (b) 25% of fees paid to said person if engaged by Client as an independent contractor. In the event of (a) above, payment of the commission will be due within 30 days of the employment starting date. In the event of (b) above, payment will be due at the end of any month during which the independent contractor performed services for Client. Designer, in the event of nonpayment and in connection with this section, shall be entitled to seek all remedies under law and equity.

8.4 *No Exclusivity.* The parties expressly acknowledge that this Agreement does not create an exclusive relationship between the parties. Client is free to engage others to perform services of the same or similar nature to those provided by Designer, and Designer shall be entitled to offer and provide design services to others, solicit other clients, and otherwise advertise the services offered by Designer.

9. WARRANTIES AND REPRESENTATIONS.

9.1 *By Client.* Client represents, warrants, and covenants to Designer that (a) Client owns all right, title, and interest in, or otherwise has full right and authority to permit the use of the Client Content; (b) to the best of Client's knowledge, the Client Content does not infringe the rights of any third party, and use of the Client Content as well as any Trademarks in connection with the Project does not and will not violate the rights of any third parties; (c) Client shall comply with the terms and conditions of any licensing agreements which govern the use of Third Party Materials; and (d) Client shall comply with all laws and regulations as they relate to the Services and Deliverables.

9.2   *By Designer.*

(a)   Designer hereby represents, warrants, and covenants to Client that Designer will provide the Services identified in the Agreement in a professional and workmanlike manner and in accordance with all reasonable professional standards for such services.

(b)   Designer further represents, warrants, and covenants to Client that (i) except for Third Party Materials and Client Content, the Final Deliverables shall be the original work of Designer and/or its independent contractors; (ii) in the event that the Final Deliverables include the work of independent contractors commissioned for the Project by Designer, Designer shall have secured agreements from such contractors granting all necessary rights, title, and interest in and to the Final Deliverables sufficient for Designer to grant the intellectual property rights provided in this Agreement; and (iii) to the best of Designer's knowledge, the Final Art provided by Designer and Designer's subcontractors does not infringe the rights of any party, and use of same in connection with the Project will not violate the rights of any third parties. In the event Client or third parties modify or otherwise use the Deliverables outside of the scope or for any purpose not identified in the Proposal or this Agreement or contrary to the terms and conditions noted herein, all representations and warranties of Designer shall be void.

(c)   EXCEPT FOR THE EXPRESS REPRESENTATIONS AND WARRANTIES STATED IN THIS AGREEMENT, DESIGNER MAKES NO WARRANTIES WHATSOEVER. DESIGNER EXPLICITLY DISCLAIMS ANY OTHER WARRANTIES OF ANY KIND, EITHER EXPRESS OR IMPLIED, INCLUDING BUT NOT LIMITED TO WARRANTIES OF MERCHANTABILITY OR FITNESS FOR A PARTICULAR PURPOSE OR COMPLIANCE WITH LAWS OR GOVERNMENT RULES OR REGULATIONS APPLICABLE TO THE PROJECT.

10.   INDEMNIFICATION/LIABILITY.

10.1   *By Client.* Client agrees to indemnify, save, and hold harmless Designer from any and all damages, liabilities, costs, losses, or expenses arising out of any claim, demand, or action by a third party arising out of any breach of Client's responsibilities or obligations, representations or warranties under this Agreement. Under such circumstances Designer shall promptly notify Client in writing of any claim or suit: (a) Client has sole control of the defense and all related settlement negotiations, and (b) Designer provides Client with commercially reasonable assistance, information and authority necessary to perform Client's obligations under this section. Client will reimburse the reasonable out-of-pocket expenses incurred by Designer in providing such assistance.

10.2 *By Designer.* Subject to the terms, conditions, express representations and warranties provided in this Agreement, Designer agrees to indemnify, save, and hold harmless Client from any and all damages, liabilities, costs, losses, or expenses arising out of any finding of fact which is inconsistent with Designer's representations and warranties made herein, except in the event any such claims, damages, liabilities, costs, losses, or expenses arise directly as a result of gross negligence or misconduct of Client provided that (a) Client promptly notifies Designer in writing of the claim; (b) Designer shall have sole control of the defense and all related settlement negotiations; and (c) Client shall provide Designer with the assistance, information, and authority necessary to perform Designer's obligations under this section. Notwithstanding the foregoing, Designer shall have no obligation to defend or otherwise indemnify Client for any claim or adverse finding of fact arising out of or due to Client Content, any unauthorized content, improper or illegal use, or the failure to update or maintain any Deliverables provided by Designer.

10.3 *Limitation of Liability.* THE SERVICES AND THE WORK PRODUCT OF DESIGNER ARE SOLD "AS IS." IN ALL CIRCUMSTANCES, THE MAXIMUM LIABILITY OF DESIGNER, ITS DIRECTORS, OFFI-CERS, EMPLOYEES, DESIGN AGENTS, AND AFFILIATES ("DESIGNER PARTIES"), TO CLIENT FOR DAMAGES FOR ANY AND ALL CAUSES WHATSOEVER, AND CLIENT'S MAXIMUM REMEDY, REGARDLESS OF THE FORM OF ACTION, WHETHER IN CONTRACT, TORT, OR OTHERWISE, SHALL BE LIMITED TO THE NET PROFIT OF DESIGNER. IN NO EVENT SHALL DESIGNER BE LIABLE FOR ANY LOST DATA OR CONTENT, LOST PROFITS, BUSINESS INTERRUPTION, OR FOR ANY INDI-RECT, INCIDENTAL, SPECIAL, CONSEQUENTIAL, EXEMPLARY, OR PUNITIVE DAMAGES ARISING OUT OF OR RELATING TO THE MATERIALS OR THE SERVICES PROVIDED BY DESIGNER, EVEN IF DESIGNER HAS BEEN ADVISED OF THE POSSIBILITY OF SUCH DAMAGES, AND NOTWITHSTANDING THE FAILURE OF ESSENTIAL PURPOSE OF ANY LIMITED REMEDY.

11. TERM AND TERMINATION.

11.1 This Agreement shall commence upon the Effective Date and shall remain effective until the Services are completed and delivered.

11.2 This Agreement may be terminated at any time by either party effective immediately upon notice, or the mutual agreement of the parties, or if any party:

(a) becomes insolvent, files a petition in bankruptcy, makes an assignment for the benefit of its creditors; or

(b) breaches any of its material responsibilities or obligations under this Agreement, which breach is not remedied within ten (10) days from receipt of written notice of such breach.

11.3 In the event of termination, Designer shall be compensated for the Services performed through the date of termination in the amount of (a) any advance payment, (b) a prorated portion of the fees due, or (c) hourly fees for work performed by Designer or Designer's agents as of the date of termination, whichever is greater; and Client shall pay all Expenses, fees, and out-of-pockets together with any Additional Costs incurred through and up to the date of cancellation.

11.4 In the event of termination by Client and upon full payment of compensation as provided herein, Designer grants to Client such right and title as provided for in Schedule A of this Agreement with respect to those Deliverables provided to, and accepted by Client as of the date of termination.

11.5 Upon expiration or termination of this Agreement: (a) each party shall return or, at the disclosing party's request, destroy the Confidential Information of the other party, and (b) other than as provided herein, all rights and obligations of each party under this Agreement, exclusive of the Services, shall survive.

12. GENERAL.

12.1 *Modification/Waiver.* This Agreement may be modified by the parties. Any modification of this Agreement must be in writing, except that Designer's invoices may include, and Client shall pay, expenses or costs that Client authorizes by electronic mail in cases of extreme time sensitivity. Failure by either party to enforce any right or seek to remedy any breach under this Agreement shall not be construed as a waiver of such rights nor shall a waiver by either party of default in one or more instances be construed as constituting a continuing waiver or as a waiver of any other breach.

12.2 *Notices.* All notices to be given hereunder shall be transmitted in writing either by facsimile or electronic mail with return confirmation of receipt or by certified or registered mail, return receipt requested, and shall be sent to the addresses identified below unless notification of change of address is given in writing. Notice shall be effective upon receipt or in the case of fax or e-mail, upon confirmation of receipt.

12.3 *No Assignment.* Neither party may assign, whether in writing or orally, or encumber its rights or obligations under this Agreement or permit the same to be transferred, assigned, or encumbered by operation of law or otherwise, without the prior written consent of the other party.

12.4 *Force Majeure.* Designer shall not be deemed in breach of this Agreement if Designer is unable to complete the Services or any portion thereof by reason of fire, earthquake, labor dispute, act of God or public enemy, death, illness, or incapacity of Designer or any local, state, federal, national or international law, governmental order or regulation, or any other event beyond Designer's control (collectively, "Force Majeure Event"). Upon occurrence of any Force Majeure Event, Designer shall give notice to Client of its inability to perform or of delay in completing the Services and shall propose revisions to the schedule for completion of the Services.

12.5 *Governing Law and Dispute Resolution.* The formation, construction, performance, and enforcement of this Agreement shall be in accordance with the laws of the United States and the state of _____ without regard to its conflict of law provisions or the conflict of law provisions of any other jurisdiction. In the event of a dispute arising out of this Agreement, the parties agree to attempt to resolve any dispute by negotiation between the parties. If they are unable to resolve the dispute, either party may commence mediation and/or binding arbitration through the American Arbitration Association, or other forum mutually agreed to by the parties. The prevailing party in any dispute resolved by binding arbitration or litigation shall be entitled to recover its attorneys' fees and costs. In all other circumstances, the parties specifically consent to the local, state, and federal courts located in the state of _____. The parties hereby waive any jurisdictional or venue defenses available to them and further consent to service of process by mail. Client acknowledges that Designer will have no adequate remedy at law in the event Client uses the deliverables in any way not permitted hereunder, and hereby agrees that Designer shall be entitled to equitable relief by way of temporary and permanent injunction, and such other and further relief at law or equity as any arbitrator or court of competent jurisdiction may deem just and proper, in addition to any and all other remedies provided for herein.

12.6 *Severability.* Whenever possible, each provision of this Agreement shall be interpreted in such manner as to be effective and valid under applicable law, but if any provision of this Agreement is held invalid or unenforceable, the remainder of this Agreement shall nevertheless remain in full force and effect and the invalid or unenforceable provision shall be replaced by a valid or enforceable provision.

12.7 *Headings.* The numbering and captions of the various sections are solely for convenience and reference only and shall not affect the scope, meaning, intent, or interpretation of the provisions of this Agreement nor shall such headings otherwise be given any legal effect.

12.8 *Integration.* This Agreement comprises the entire understanding of the parties hereto on the subject matter herein contained, and supersedes and merges all prior and contemporaneous agreements, understandings, and discussions between the parties relating to the subject matter of this Agreement. In the event of a conflict between the Proposal and any other Agreement documents, the terms of the Proposal shall control. This Agreement comprises this Basic Terms and Conditions document, the Proposal, Schedule A, and the following documents as indicated by the parties' initials:

_____ _____ Supplement 1: Print-Specific Terms & Conditions

_____ _____ Supplement 2: Interactive-Specific Terms & Conditions

_____ _____ Supplement 3: Environmental-Specific Terms & Conditions

By their execution below, the parties hereto have agreed to all of the terms and conditions of this Agreement effective as of the last date of signature below, and each signatory represents that it has the full authority to enter into this Agreement and to bind her/his respective party to all of the terms and conditions herein.

DESIGNER: CLIENT:

[Designer name]   [Client name]

[Address]   [Address]

Signed: _____   Signed: _____

Date: _____   By: [Client officer name]

                                           Title: _____

                                           Date: _____

SCHEDULE A: INTELLECTUAL PROPERTY PROVISIONS

IP 1. RIGHTS TO DELIVERABLES OTHER THAN FINAL ART.

IP 1.1 *Client Content.* Client Content, including all pre-existing Trademarks, shall remain the sole property of Client or its respective suppliers, and Client or its suppliers shall be the sole owner of all rights in connection therewith. Client hereby grants to Designer a nonexclusive, nontransferable license to use, reproduce, modify, display and publish the Client Content solely in connection with Designer's performance of the Services and limited promotional uses of the Deliverables as authorized in this Agreement.

IP 1.2 *Third Party Materials.* All Third Party Materials are the exclusive property of their respective owners. Designer shall inform Client of all Third Party Materials that may be required to perform the Services or otherwise integrated into the Final Art. Under such circumstances Designer shall inform Client of any need to license, at Client's expense, and unless otherwise provided for by Client, Client shall obtain the license(s) necessary to permit Client's use of the Third Party Materials consistent with the usage rights granted herein. In the event Client fails to properly secure or otherwise arrange for any necessary licenses or instructs the use of Third Party Materials, Client hereby indemnifies, saves, and holds harmless Designer from any and all damages, liabilities, costs, losses, or expenses arising out of any claim, demand, or action by a third party arising out of Client's failure to obtain copyright, trademark, publicity, privacy, defamation, or other releases or permissions with respect to materials included in the Final Art.

IP 1.3 *Preliminary Works.* Designer retains all rights in and to all Preliminary Works. Client shall return all Preliminary Works to Designer within thirty (30) days of completion of the Services and all rights in and to any Preliminary Works shall remain the exclusive property of Designer.

IP 1.4 *Original Artwork.* Designer retains all right and title in and to any original artwork comprising Final Art, including all rights to display or sell such artwork. Client shall return all original artwork to Designer within thirty (30) days of completion of the Services.

IP 1.5 *Trademarks.* Upon completion of the Services and expressly conditioned upon full payment of all fees, costs, and out-of-pocket expenses due, Designer assigns to Client all ownership rights, including any copyrights, in and to any artworks or designs comprising the works created by Designer for use by Client as a Trademark. Designer shall cooperate with Client and shall execute any additional documents reasonably requested by Client to evidence such assignment. Client shall have sole responsibility for ensuring that any proposed trademarks or Final Deliverables intended to be a Trademark are available for use in commerce and federal registration and do not otherwise infringe the rights of any third party. Client hereby indemnifies, saves, and holds harmless Designer from any and all damages, liabilities, costs, losses, or expenses arising out of any claim, demand, or action by any third party alleging any infringement arising out of Client's use and/or failure to obtain rights to use the Trademark.

IP 1.6   *Designer Tools*. All Designer Tools are and shall remain the exclusive property of Designer. Designer hereby grants to Client a nonexclusive, nontransferable (other than the right to sublicense such uses to Client's Web hosting or Internet service providers), perpetual, worldwide license to use the Designer Tools solely to the extent necessary with the Final Deliverables for the Project. Client may not directly or indirectly, in any form or manner, decompile, reverse engineer, create derivative works, or otherwise disassemble or modify any Designer Tools comprising any software or technology of Designer.

IP 2.   RIGHTS TO FINAL ART.

Final Art ownership options: choose A-License (either limited usage, exclusive license with no modification rights, or exclusive license with modification rights—all licenses include liquidation for unlicensed use) or B-Assignment. Be sure to delete or cross-out all alternates not chosen. Check appropriate media for each provision:

IP 2.A (1) (a) License for limited usage, no modification rights:

IP 2.1   For _____ *print,* _____ *online/interactive,* _____ *three-dimensional media*: Upon completion of the Services, and expressly subject to full payment of all fees, costs, and out-of-pocket expenses due, Designer grants to Client the rights in the Final Art as set forth below. Any additional uses not identified herein require an additional license and may require an additional fee. All other rights are expressly reserved by Designer. The rights granted to Client are for the usage of the Final Art in its original form only. Client may not crop, distort, manipulate, reconfigure, mimic, animate, create derivative works or extract portions, or in any other manner alter the Final Art.

Category of use: _____

Medium of use: _____

Duration of use: _____

Geographic territory: _____

Initial press run: _____

With respect to such usage, Client shall have (check one)

_____ Exclusive / _____ Nonexclusive rights

OR

IP 2.A (1)(b) *Exclusive license, no modification rights*:

IP 2.2 *For _____ print, _____ online/interactive, _____ three-dimensional media*: Designer hereby grants to Client the exclusive, perpetual, and worldwide right and license to use, reproduce, and display the Final Art solely in connection with the Project as defined in the Proposal and in accordance with the various terms and conditions of this Agreement. The rights granted to Client are for usage of the Final Art in its original form only. Client may not crop, distort, manipulate, reconfigure, mimic, animate, create derivative works or extract portions, or in any other manner alter the Final Art.

OR

IP 2.A (1) (c) *Exclusive license, with modification rights*:

IP 2.3 *For _____ print, _____ online/interactive, _____ three-dimensional media*: Designer hereby grants to Client the exclusive, perpetual, and worldwide right and license to use, reproduce, adapt, modify, and display the Final Art solely in connection with the Project as defined in the Proposal and in accordance with the terms and conditions of this Agreement.

AND

IP 2.A (2) *Liquidation for unlicensed use*:

IP 2.4 Client's use of the Final Art shall be limited to the usage rights granted herein for the Project only. Use of the Final Art, Deliverables, or any derivative works thereof by Client at any other time or location, or for another project or outside the scope of the rights granted herein require an additional fee and Designer shall be entitled to further compensation equal to _____ percent (_____%) of the original Project fee unless otherwise agreed in writing by both parties. In the event of nonpayment, Designer shall be entitled to pursue all remedies under law and equity.

OR

IP 2.B *Assignment*:

IP 2.5 Upon completion of the Services, and expressly subject to full payment of all fees, costs, and expenses due, Designer hereby assigns to Client all right, title, and interest, including without limitation copyright and other intellectual property rights, in and to the Final Art. Designer agrees to reasonably cooperate with Client and shall execute any additional documents reasonably necessary to evidence such assignment.

SUPPLEMENT 1: PRINT-SPECIFIC TERMS & CONDITIONS

P 1. *Samples.* Client shall provide Designer with _____ (number) of samples of each printed or published form of the Final Deliverables, for use in Designer's portfolio and other self-promotional uses. Such samples shall be representative of the highest quality of the work produced.

P 2. *Finished Work.* The printed work and the arrangement or brokering of the print services by Designer shall be deemed in compliance with this Agreement if the final printed product is within the acceptable variations as to kind, quantity, and price in accordance with current or standard trade practices identified by the supplier of the print and print-related services. Whenever commercially reasonable and if available, Designer shall provide copies of the current or standard trade practices to Client. Notwithstanding, Designer shall have no responsibility or obligation to negotiate changes or amendments to the current or standard trade practices.

SUPPLEMENT 2: INTERACTIVE-SPECIFIC TERMS & CONDITIONS

I 1. SUPPORT SERVICES.

I 1.1 *Warranty Period.* "Support Services" means commercially reasonable technical support and assistance to maintain and update the Deliverables, including correcting any errors or Deficiencies, but shall not include the development of enhancements to the Project or other services outside the scope of the Proposal. During the first _____ (insert number) months following expiration of this Agreement ("Warranty Period"), if any, Designer shall provide up to _____ (insert number) hours of Support Services at no additional cost to Client. Additional time shall be billed at Designer's regular hourly rate, then in effect upon the date of the request for additional support.

I 1.2 *Maintenance Period.* Upon expiration of the Warranty Period and at Client's option, Designer will provide Support Services for the following _____ (insert number) months (the "Maintenance Period") for a monthly fee of $_____ [or Designer's hourly fees of $_____ per hour]. The parties may extend the Maintenance Period beyond one year upon mutual written agreement.

I 2. ENHANCEMENTS.

During the Maintenance Period, Client may request that Designer develop enhancements to the Deliverables, and Designer shall exercise commercially reasonable efforts to prioritize Designer's resources to create such enhancements. The parties understand that preexisting obligations to third parties existing on the date of the request for enhancements may delay the immediate execution of any such requested enhancements. Such enhancements shall be provided on a time and materials basis at Designer's then in effect price for such services.

I 3. ADDITIONAL WARRANTIES AND REPRESENTATIONS.

I 3.1 *Deficiencies.* Subject to the representations and warranties of Client in connection with Client Content, Designer represents and warrants that the Final Deliverables will be free from Deficiencies. For the purposes of this Agreement, "Deficiency" shall mean a failure to comply with the specifications set forth in the Proposal in any material respect, but shall not include any problems caused by Client Content, modifications, alterations, or changes made to Final Deliverables by Client or any third party after delivery by Designer, or the interaction of Final Deliverables with third party applications such as Web browsers other than those specified in the Proposal. The parties acknowledge that Client's sole remedy and Designer's sole liability for a breach of this Section is the obligation of Designer to correct any Deficiency identified within the Warranty Period. In the event that a Deficiency is caused by Third Party Materials provided or specified by Designer, Designer's sole obligation shall be to substitute alternative Third Party Materials.

I 3.2 *Designer Tools.* Subject to the representations and warranties of the Client in connection with the materials supplied by Client, Designer represents and warrants that, to the best of Designer's knowledge, the Designer Tools do not knowingly infringe the rights of any third party, and use of same in connection with the Project will not knowingly violate the rights of any third parties except to the extent that such violations are caused by Client Content, or the modification of, or use of the Deliverables in combination with materials or equipment outside the scope of the applicable specifications, by Client or third parties.

I 4. COMPLIANCE WITH LAWS.

Designer shall use commercially reasonable efforts to ensure that all Final Deliverables shall be designed to comply with the known relevant rules and regulations. Client, upon acceptance of the Deliverables, shall be responsible for conformance with all laws relating to the transfer of software and technology.

SUPPLEMENT 3: ENVIRONMENTAL-SPECIFIC TERMS & CONDITIONS

3-D 1. PHOTOGRAPHS OF THE PROJECT.

Designer shall have the right to document, photograph, or otherwise record all completed designs or installations of the Project, and to reproduce, publish, and display such documentation, photographs, or records for Designer's promotional purposes in accordance with Section 6 of the Basic Terms and Conditions of this Agreement.

3-D 2. ADDITIONAL CLIENT RESPONSIBILITIES.

Client acknowledges that Client shall be responsible for performing the following in a reasonable and timely manner:

(a) Communication of administrative or operational decisions if they affect the design or production of Deliverables, and coordination of required public approvals and meetings;

(b) Provision of accurate and complete information and materials requested by Designer such as, by way of example, not limitation, site plans, building plans and elevations, utility locations, color/material samples, and all applicable codes, rules, and regulation information;

(c) Provision of approved naming and nomenclature, securing approvals and correct copy from third parties such as, by way of example, not limitation, end users or donors as may be necessary;

(d) Final proofreading and written approval of all project documents including, by way of example, not limitation, artwork, message schedules, sign location plans, and design drawings before their release for fabrication or installation. In the event that Client has approved work containing errors or omissions, such as, by way of example, not limitation, typographic errors or misspellings, Client shall incur the cost of correcting such errors;

(e) Arranging for the documentation, permissions, licensing, and implementation of all electrical, structural, or mechanical elements needed to support, house, or power signage; coordination of sign manufacture and installation with other trades; and

(f) Bid solicitation and contract negotiation, sourcing, establishment of final pricing, and contract terms directly with fabricators or vendors.

3-D 3. ENGINEERING.

The Services shall include the selection and specifications for materials and construction details as described in the Proposal. However, Client acknowledges and agrees [that Designer is not a licensed engineer or architect, and] that responsibility for the interpretation of design drawings and the design and engineering of all work performed under this Agreement ("Engineering") is the sole responsibility of Client and/or its architect, engineer, or fabricator.

3-D 4. IMPLEMENTATION.

Client expressly acknowledges and agrees that the estimates provided in the Proposal, at any time during the project for implementation charges such as, including, but not limited to, fabrication or installation are for planning purposes only. Such estimates represent the best judgment of Designer or its consultants at the time of the Proposal, but shall not be considered a representation or guarantee that project bids or costs will not vary. Client shall contract and pay those parties directly responsible for implementation services such as fabrication or installation ("Implementation"). Designer shall not be responsible for the quality or timeliness of the third-party Implementation services, irrespective of whether Designer assists or advises Client in evaluating, selecting, or monitoring the provider of such services.

3-D 5. COMPLIANCE WITH LAWS.

Designer shall use commercially reasonable efforts to ensure that all Final Deliverables shall be designed to comply with the applicable rules and regulations such as the Americans with Disabilities Act ("ADA"). However, Designer is not an expert and makes no representations or warranties in connection with compliance with such rules, codes, or regulations. The compliance of the Final Deliverables with any such rule, codes, or regulations shall be the responsibility of Client. Designer shall use commercially reasonable efforts to ensure the suitability and conformance of the Final Deliverables.

3-D 6. CLIENT INSURANCE.

Client shall maintain, during the term of this Agreement, at its sole expense, construction and maintenance liability, product liability, general business liability, and advertising injury insurance from a recognized insurance carrier in the amount of at least _____ million dollars ($_____,000,000.00) per occurrence. Such insurance shall name Designer individually as an additional named insured. Client shall provide a copy of said insurance policy to Designer at Designer's request.

8

Hidden Intellectual Property Hazards in Web Design

CARL BRUNSTEN

THE DESIGNER OF a Web site or Web application can sin against the intellectual property ("IP") rights of others in many, many ways. Some of the obvious legal blunders in Web work could occur just as easily in print work or in any other medium: unauthorized use of a celebrity's name or likeness, inaccurate or deceptive presentation of a third party's trademark, or exploitation of a stock or custom photograph in any way beyond the limit of its accompanying license. Web design, however, brings its practitioners into contact with much less publicized but still serious IP hazards unique to the medium and stemming from the surprisingly unsettled legal status of certain commonplace Web site technologies. Careless application of these technologies can potentially cost design firms lots of money and, even worse, force them to spend lots of quality time with lawyers. We'll look at some of these technologies and we'll also look at the uncomfortable implications for design firms in a recent U.S. Supreme Court decision expanding the range of people who can be held liable for Web-based copyright infringement.

DEEP LINKING

"Deep linking" is the creation of hyperlinks to the "underneath" pages of an unaffiliated party's Web site. As Web designers well understand, Web sites are often developed with a particular architecture allowing the visitor access to certain information only by passing through a home page and perhaps additional layers of information, security, screening, or advertising. While some subscription sites create walls to prevent the unwashed from directly linking into their deeper content, many Web site owners want to simultaneously preserve technological openness and respect for the Web site's architecture. Ticketmaster sued Microsoft over links created from Microsoft's Seattle Sidewalk Web site to deep locations in Ticketmaster's Web site. Ticketmaster complained that these deep links bypassed Ticketmaster's marketing and appropriated Ticketmaster's trademarks to help Microsoft, not Ticketmaster, sell advertising. The federal district court ruled against Ticketmaster on these specific claims, but also said there could be liability if the deep links create a confusion of source or if a license agreement posted on the target site gives reasonable and effective notice to the public against deep linking.

FRAMES

The Web site *chillingeffects.org* has posted some instructive examples of suspect but nevertheless worrisome cease and desist letters from holders of various Web patents. In one example, SBC (the telecom company) demands a patent royalty from a company called Museum Tour, whose Web site offers educational toys and museum-related products. SBC claims exclusive rights over a rather basic and unexceptional feature of Museum Tour's home page: a frame. The home page displays a row of buttons, one for each different product category. Clicking on any particular button presents below, within a frame, a detailed listing of the items for sale in that category, while the buttons for the other product categories remain persistently viewable above the frame. To that, most Web designers would say, paraphrasing Jimmy Durante, "I've seen a million of 'em." Yet SBC claims patents not only on this frame but on several basic Web site user interface elements. If SBC's patents are valid and as broad as it contends, then nearly all Web sites with a menu or navigation tool appear to have infringing features.

Some of the Web design firms my office represents have received similar demand letters from various patent holders. In several cases where redesigning around the patent claim was not a satisfactory option, we advised our client that the patent in question was doubtful—particularly in light of recent judicial decisions scaling back Web patents—and that the patent holder would be foolish to allow the patent's validity to actually be tested in court. Those conversations inevitably moved to the next topic: how much would it cost to fight? Frequently, before we could even pencil out an estimate, our client said, "Maybe the license is still the easy way out."

Frames present another unsettled legal question, arising from their common use in integrating content from two (or more) unaffiliated Web sites. This sort of framing has, of course, led to litigation. The *Washington Post* filed suit against an entity called TotalNEWS for creating a "parasitic" Web site featuring content from the *Post* framed by the TotalNEWS logo and advertising from which the *Post* derived no revenue. The *Post* won the early legal rounds in court, and then, as so often happens, the case settled, leaving behind no reliable legal precedent.

MASHUPS

The friction between evolving web technologies and IP laws is only going to increase with an emerging set of services being marketed under the umbrella term "Web 2.0." "Mashups," a key Web 2.0 technology, are new applications, services, or content created by melding together the pages, data, or services already available from disparate sources on the web. An early mashup was *housingmaps.com*, a combination of Google Maps and real estate listings from Craigslist. Mashups are also rapidly being developed for internal use within enterprises. The French bank Societe Generale, for example, maintains an in-house portal for its employees to share information and documents on pending deals. SG recently paid consultants to reinvent the portal with mashups blending into the database Yahoo News feeds, Google Maps, and Alta Vista's Babel Fish for automated English-French translation. Mashups come in several different flavors. Presentation-level mashups re-use the Web interface of an existing Web site. Logic-based mashups integrate functionality from an existing Web site into a new Web site or application. Content-based mashups simply scrape and serve data from an existing Web data source.

Corporate dollars for these customizations are increasingly flowing to the value added by the keen eye of the designer. Design firms have a wonderful opportunity to help their clients develop exciting new products and services. But if the legality of simpler techniques like deep linking or frames has not been fully resolved, then mashups are going to reside in an even thicker IP morass. While some companies flying under the Web 2.0 flag, like Google, have embraced mashups and readily publish APIs for independent developers, many other companies feel quite proprietary about their services and their data, even as they grant public access through the Web. Discovery Networks is now challenging an independent Web site's mashup that creates parodies of Discovery's marketing campaign by allowing users to embroider their own commentaries onto images from Discovery's Web sites.

WHO IS LIABLE FOR INFRINGEMENT?

In the absence of an effective client agreement to the contrary, a Web design firm has a duty to indemnify (that is, reimburse) its client with respect to any IP lawsuits against the client and connected, in some fashion, to the design firm's advice or deliverables. Even if the client agreement includes language limiting the design firm's duty to indemnify, the plaintiff copyright, trademark, or patent owner can in some circumstances directly hale the design firm into court, even though the design firm does not own or operate the Web site. For years the courts imposed significant constraints on this secondary form of exposure, but at least in copyright cases the constraints are beginning to come off.

In 2003 MGM, seeking to prevent unauthorized video downloads, brought an infringement action against the developers of Grokster, a peer-to-peer file-sharing network. Grokster's developers defended themselves with the U.S. Supreme Court's landmark decision in the *Betamax* case, holding that the maker of a product capable of substantial non-infringing uses cannot be held liable for customers' use of the product to commit copyright infringement. In 2005, to the surprise of many, the Supreme Court retrenched the *Betamax* rule and held that Grokster's developers could be monetarily liable for *offering a product or service that is likely to induce future infringement by others, or makes a material contribution to known infringement by others.* Web sites (as distinct from file-sharing networks) theoretically have an additional safe harbor in the "takedown" provision of the 1998 Digital Millennium Copyright Act, which immunizes a Web site owner from liability for infringements committed by the Web site's users, so long as the owner removes the offending content promptly after receiving notice from the copyright owner. On the heels of *Grokster,* this safe harbor has come under attack in an action by Viacom against the video-sharing Web site YouTube. Viacom argues that YouTube's features are inherently unlawful because those features support a volume of infringing content with which Viacom's "takedown" remedy can never keep pace.

Why should independent Web design firms worry about these cases? Because the holding in *Grokster* and potentially in *YouTube* point to the broad proposition that liability can attach to *anyone* involved, for his own profit, in designing, building, or implementing a Web feature that facilitates copyright infringement either by the Web site owner or by visitors using the Web site, and that the takedown remedy is not always a safe harbor. Web design firms working for "online community" or "user-supplied content" Web sites obviously must be concerned, but there is also risk in helping to build any kind of Web site with problematic features like mashups, deep links, or frames. Indeed, in *Grokster*, the entertainment industry argued that liability should be found against anyone who is in a position to "redesign a product to reduce infringing uses" but does not. In the new legal environment, independent Web design firms cannot feel safe relying on a boilerplate assertion that the client retains final control over the choice of Web site features and content. Cases involving significant dollars and tough plaintiffs are going to take this inquiry much deeper.

The major content industry players have turned up the pressure in Web-based copyright cases by litigating not only against deep pockets, but against everyone they can find in the infringement loop, including employees, investors, outside consultants or designers, and individual end users. On the patent side, as we saw in the discussion of frames, so-called "patent trolls" often prefer to go after small or medium sized targets, who are less likely to put up a fight.

Design firms are not utterly helpless against these hidden IP hazards. Intelligent steps still can be taken in client agreements and in the firm's internal practices to reduce exposure, and those steps will be outlined in an upcoming article. In the meantime, remember that designers sometimes comfort each other with talk that following various "rules of thumb" or "accepted industry practices" can inoculate them against IP disasters. That sort of talk is legal truthiness, at best. Remain skeptical at all times.

9

Payment Strategies

EMILY RUTH COHEN

IT'S THE NATURE of working in a creative industry; each job and client has unique characteristics, requirements, and needs. Although the professional flexibility can be rewarding, devising a consistent payment strategy can be another matter altogether. What may work for one client may not be quite right for another. Your best strategy is to approach your payment schedule as you would any design project, personalizing your methodology with forethought, research, and creativity.

Several proactive measures and precautions to define your payment schedule can help prevent future obstacles to a successful relationship with your client.

START WITH THE PAPERWORK

Before starting a project, provide your client with all necessary project documentation. This includes proposals, estimates, letters of agreement, contracts, schedules, and change orders. Where applicable, get your client's signed approval. Although oral agreements are legally binding, they are harder to prove. If all written documentation is clear and appropriately detailed, you will establish a professional relationship from the start, allowing for any potential disagreements and stumbling blocks to be ironed out beforehand.

UP-FRONT PAYMENT

Establish a standard policy that requires partial payment from clients prior to the start of the project and before any billable work is incurred. This strategy, termed up-front payment, is becoming a common procedure within our industry and is usually based on a percentage of the total project fee or estimate. For this up-front payment strategy to work effectively, it is crucial that you enforce it consistently, firmly, and without apology for all your clients.

Be cautioned. This simple request can often become a time consuming struggle. Clients may give you objections ranging from the reasonable, "Our corporate procedures preclude me from processing any up-front payment without either receipt of work or an approved, internal purchase order," to the plausible, "As a small business, our cash flow is tight and overhead payments, such as rent and utilities, may need to take priority," to the red-flag, "Why should I pay for work I haven't seen yet?" or "We don't have any money right now, but are expecting a large check in soon." Respond to these scenarios calmly and creatively.

First, emphasize that up-front payment is a reasonable request and a common procedure within the design industry. If you do not receive any up-front payment, then you are, in affect, incurring billable hours and extending the client credit. This reasoning can also apply to asking for a deposit or retainer against out-of-pocket expenses.

Also, without up-front money it may appear that you are working on spec with payment promised only upon acceptance. Like other professionals, such as architects and lawyers, you're hired based on experience. This means that you're entitled to be paid regardless of whether your work is accepted or approved— provided, of course, that your services follow the client's initial creative direction and are of the same quality and creativity you were initially hired for.

MANAGING INVOICES

Familiarize yourself with your client's payment policy and keep your invoices in manageable increments. Many corporations and businesses will not pay unless an approved purchase order (PO) has been processed; the absence of a PO at the time of invoicing will delay payment.

For large expenditures, your client may have to go through several rounds of time-consuming approvals, often involving upper management and accounts payable, before a PO will be issued or an invoice processed. As a rule of thumb, smaller invoices are often easier to process. Ask your client how much is too much before an invoice or PO gets delayed because of internal processing and approval procedures. Once you know the cutoff amount for a large expenditure, you can adjust your progress payments accordingly.

When you do receive a PO, read it carefully. Clients will often include conditions or descriptions that are standard for them but may or may not be applicable to your project and relationship.

Typically, a client will compensate you for only up to 10 percent beyond the fee indicated in the PO—this relates to protection for possible scope creep. Check with your client for the exact percentage he or she can pay. If the scope of the project changes and additional fees are incurred that exceed 10 percent of the PO, inform the client and request a revised or additional PO.

Many clients have an established policy for how soon they pay invoices and have timetables that range from thirty to ninety days. It is important to find this out in advance and invoice accordingly. For example, if a client pays all in "net 60," and the project can be completed within two or three weeks, you may want to issue all invoices at the start of the project. This will help shorten the approval and processing time, and ensure payments are made closer to the project's completion, rather than three months later. If this isn't possible, you can ask for a large percentage of your total costs to be paid up front, thereby reducing your financial liability later in the project.

GET IT IN WRITING

When establishing a job contract, negotiate a written and equitable payment schedule, including a due date for each payment and your specific responsibility or presentation to be delivered or completed by that date. Don't use vague terminology that can be misinterpreted such as "Payment due midway through the project." Another important strategy is to indicate that payment is due upon completion and delivery of the specified presentation or responsibility, *not* upon client approval. Such approvals can get delayed by several days or weeks for reasons beyond your control, or the project can get put on unlimited hiatus.

Don't rely on client-defined target dates that reflect client objectives since these may get delayed for reasons beyond your control. For example, one designer I know who was responsible for a comprehensive identity project for a store opening was asked to delay the last invoice until the store opened. Unfortunately, the opening was delayed several months after the target date. Luckily, the designer based the final payment on the date when her client first anticipated the store was to open, rather than agreeing to the general statement, "Payment to coincide with the opening of the store."

CHECK IT OUT

During the negotiation process, ask the client for credit references—three names are standard—and call the references to confirm credit history. The references should include, if available, a contact within a related industry like a photographer, copywriter, or illustrator. Then run a credit check on your client through a company like Dun and Bradstreet. Keep in mind that a credit report can't predict your client's dependability, reliability, or ethics. The report simply provides a useful credit history on the client.

Include a termination or cancellation clause in your agreement or estimate like, "In the event of cancellation of this assignment, at any time, the Designer will retain the first payment and the Client will be charged an additional cancellation fee that will include full payment for all work completed, expenses incurred, and hours expended. The cancellation fee will be based on the prices outlined in this agreement and subsequent change orders."

Trust your instincts. Gut reactions to a client or project can often guide you in the right direction in formulating a payment plan—or even working with the client in the first place.

ESTABLISHING YOUR SCHEDULE

Once you complete your research and fully evaluate the unique needs of each client and project, you can develop an effective payment schedule that includes several progress payments. Progress payments are based on a percentage or portion of your estimated costs. As mentioned earlier, each payment should be due at a specified, defined project phase and encompass defined deliverables and responsibilities.

An advantage to receiving incremental payments throughout a project versus one lump-sum payment at the end of a job is that your financial liability throughout the project will be greatly reduced, especially if the client delays payment later on. Of course this advantage is contingent upon you effectively managing and enforcing the payment schedule.

The following payment schedule is commonly followed: the first third of the estimated project total due prior to the start of the project, a second third due midway through the project, and the final third due upon delivery and completion of all responsibilities. Typically out-of-pocket expenses and unanticipated costs, like additional responsibilities and client revisions or AAs, are either billed upon completion or billed incrementally throughout the project.

Each project or client may require different solutions and options. For smaller projects with quick turnaround, two payments of one-half of the estimated project total may be more appropriate. However, a lengthy, multileveled project will require several payments due either on a monthly basis or at specified dates for each project phase. Progress payment can be the same amount (determined by a percentage of the project total) or can be different amounts (determined by the specific costs estimated for each project phase).

Depending on your business goals and cash flow, you may be able to negotiate less common, but sometimes viable, alternative arrangements. Although it's less popular, bartering can be an acceptable alternative for a cash-starved client offering an exciting creative opportunity. First check with your accountant; barter arrangements may be taxable. When bartering, make sure you negotiate, in writing, an equal value exchange. For pro bono and nonprofit work, or for projects you accept at a reduced rate, you can also ask for full creative control and compensation for all out-of-pocket expenses. If you decide to negotiate such nontraditional agreements, treat them like your other professional relationships and have them approved, in writing, by the client. Also, always emphasize that you're posing a nontraditional, one-time agreement that may or may not be applicable for the next project. The downside is that you risk establishing a reputation for these types of arrangements, possibly lessening the perceived value of your services.

Once you've negotiated a payment schedule, don't assume the client will follow through. After you mail an invoice, follow up with a friendly phone call to confirm its receipt and then, a few days before it is due, call the client to remind them of the upcoming payment deadline. This last call may be more effective if you can couch it within a project-related conversation. Most importantly, discuss payment and collections in a win-win scenario, maintaining a proactive position. For example, ask if there's something you can do to expedite payment. You can also offer a discount to clients for invoices that are paid early, although this option may not be advantageous for firms with tight cash flow and should be discussed with your accountant first. Once you have received payment, follow through with a note or phone call to show your appreciation.

IF ALL ELSE FAILS

Even if you follow every precaution, there will be clients who won't pay for various reasons. In those cases, you have several choices. You can accept the loss as part of doing business and learn from the experience, or you can seek help through arbitration, collection agencies, claims court, or, as a last resort, civil court. A clause in your project documentation clarifying how potential conflicts will be handled can help. For example, if you prefer arbitration, the American Arbitration Association recommends including the following clause in your contract: "Any controversy or claim arising out of or relating to this contract, or the breach thereof, shall be settled by binding arbitration in accordance with the rules of the American Arbitration Association and judgment upon the award may be entered in any court having jurisdiction thereof." In general, payment strategies, and the processes you go through to develop, negotiate, schedule, and collect payments should be flexible and adapt to the needs of you and your client. Just because you're in a creative business doesn't mean that your finances can't be straightforward.

10

Discount Requests and Retainer Agreements

CAMERON FOOTE

IT'S A COMMON business expectation that the more one buys, the cheaper the price. It should not be a surprise, then, for some clients to expect a price break, a discount, when providing steady work.

Discounts are a way that sellers reward loyalty by passing along some of the cost reductions generated through higher volume. They aren't arbitrary or altruistic; they're based on lower costs generated by increased sales. That is, they aren't provided as a favor; they are just smart business practice. As an example, when a manufacturer makes more items, manufacturing costs drop. Likewise, so do stocking costs when a retailer sells more. By passing along some of these savings, more sales are encouraged, which drives costs even lower, which encourages more sales, which drives costs still lower.

Everyone—seller and buyer—benefits.

THE REALITIES FOR SERVICE BUSINESSES

But the volume savings that are possible in manufacturing and retailing (scale economies) are seldom achievable by small service businesses. It takes about as long to do something the hundredth time as the first time. And because most functions are labor intensive, an action that takes as long, costs as much. So there are few cost savings to pass along, which invalidates the very rationale that justifies volume discounts.

The only consistent rationale for a creative firm giving a volume discount is that repeat business lowers marketing costs. It also is occasionally possible that a firm can work more productively because of prior client knowledge, but this is usually already reflected in lower time estimates.

Assuming that a firm is active in regularly pitching new business (marketing), the bottom line is that working with a large repeat client is probably 5 percent to as much as 15 percent less expensive than working with a new one. This difference provides a window of opportunity. It allows a firm to be more competitive in meeting the needs of larger, cost-conscious, and reward-worthy clients. More important, it also offers a way to change the dynamic of a relationship, to enhance client loyalty, and to score more work.

QUALIFYING CLIENTS

Whether for a client request to lower pricing or volunteered suggestion to strengthen an ongoing relationship, discounting is a strategy that should apply only to those who have provided significant business or have the potential to do so. It is not for small clients whose aspirations exceed their budgets. Work for small clients is seldom profitable enough for justification. With them, any discount comes directly from profit.

Turning down small clients

The rationale for denying a discount on future business to a small client who asks is explained above: there just isn't enough savings to warrant it. Also, because each new job is separately estimated, any efficiency from having previously worked together will already be reflected in lower time estimates. While it might be in a firm's interests to answer a small client's request for lower prices for other reasons, it cannot be justified on the basis of business volume alone.

Helping large clients

Today, as in the past, most continue to evaluate each proposal on its merits. An increasing number, however, look beyond this. They look for ways to build ongoing relationships while at the same time reducing costs through consolidating their purchasing. Creative firms approached by a client with these objectives in mind need to know how to respond. Even better, being proactive and approaching a client before being asked is not only a way to increase loyalty and build business, but it also does an end-run around competition. Either way, passing along some of the savings that would be generated through increased volume can be a marketing differentiator. Whenever discussing a price reduction, though, always keep in mind the need for a *quid pro quo*—that is, the need for each side to give up something to gain something.

The straight discount option

This is a price break generally offered to large clients based on a promise of more work. While the terms are negotiable, begin by offering a 10 percent reduction in return for a promised 25 percent increase in the next six months. Any agreement will usually be informal—a handshake basis—and thus carries some risk. But with a profitable client, it should pay for itself even when the promised work falls short. (See the profitability consideration in the sidebar on page 96.) Invoices should show both normal and discounted pricing as validation for the client. A variation of this arrangement would be to give a smaller rebate (typically 5 percent) at the end of a given period—say six months. This has the advantage of not being paid out until earned, and providing a financial "float." But the other side is that it requires the financial discipline of putting aside money to fund a potentially large future obligation.

Offer a retainer

This is the second option and the subject of the rest of this article. A retainer is nearly always better for the creative firm. Because it is more conventional, it is often preferred by clients as well. However, it relies on a more formal arrangement.

DEFINING A RETAINER

A retainer is an agreement whereby a firm sets aside a given amount of time every month for the client. The client agrees to pay a predetermined fee for this time in advance, whether or not it ends up being used. Retainer agreements are usually for a period of six months or one year. (In other professions, such as accounting and law, a one-time deposit against future billings is also called a retainer.)

A reduction in a firm's fees is usually offered in return for the client's commitment, but not necessarily. The client also receives other benefits, such as guaranteed availability, that might preclude its necessity. Although always negotiable, a fee discount of 10 percent is most common. Higher discounts are difficult to justify on a financial basis, but they might be a way to gain entry to a desirable client.

Each month can be started fresh, or any unused or excess work hours in a month can be "banked" and carried forward for future use. In the latter situation, time accounting is brought up to date every few months. Banking or rolling over retainer time provides more client flexibility, so is often preferred by them. On the other hand, banking time can lead to scheduling difficulties and requires increased record keeping for the creative firm. In a worst-case situation, a client might expect to use all its banked hours together, causing a workflow crunch. For this reason, it is unwise to roll over time for more than a month or two.

When the client provides more work than can be accomplished within the period allocated, it is billed separately. Pricing for this "excess" time can be at a firm's normal hourly rate, or a retainer's discounted rate, depending on the agreement. Most significantly, there is no refund if the client does not use all the time allocated by the retainer within the agreed period. This is the very essence of a retainer and should never be subject to negotiation. The logic is simple: the time was set aside and was, therefore, not available to sell to other clients. Once gone, time cannot be reclaimed.

WHERE RETAINERS ARE USED

Whatever a firm's specialty and clients, retainers are a way to satisfy the mutual needs of buyers and sellers, just as with any good business arrangement. They are appropriate for use by creative firms of all sizes with any client having enough volume to make the arrangement attractive for both parties.

In PR firms. Retainers originated and are most common among public relations firms and their clients. The reason is that public relations often requires constant involvement in a client's business. In addition, when there is a crisis, PR services are required immediately. No client wants to run the risk that its needs can't be addressed because of unfortunate timing or a heavy workload at its PR firm. Paying a retainer is a type of insurance, analogous to paying firefighters to sit in a firehouse for the occasional disaster.

In ad agencies. Retainers are also common among advertising agencies. They are used to cover some or all the fee-for-service activities associated with an account. Media and other expenses, not being billable time, are not included. Whether an agency has an exclusive (agency of record) arrangement or shares the client with others is of no consequence.

In design and interactive firms. Although less prevalent, retainers continue to gain in popularity. (In the latter primarily for site maintenance contracts.) For all the reasons that follow, they can benefit both a firm and its clients. They are, therefore, worth suggesting whenever there is a substantial volume of work over an extended period, frequent client contact, or a premium put on immediate response by the client.

RETAINER PROS AND CONS FOR YOU

As indicated below, the advantages of a retainer for a creative firm are few but very substantial. The disadvantages, while there are more of them, are much less significant.

Advantages

The greatest retainer benefit for most firms is reliable revenue. There's a client check that can be counted on to arrive at the same time every month. A reliable revenue stream allows better planning and reduced operating expenses, not to mention the psychic benefit of fewer financial concerns.

The other major attraction is the possibility for more and better work. Retainer clients are not only motivated to use the time they have contracted for, but doing so often results in even more work than they might otherwise have planned. They are also more likely to assign new projects to a firm on retainer. It is more convenient, the firm's capabilities have been proven, and there is less paperwork. Work begets more work. Even more important, working with a client on a more regular basis encourages them to think of a firm in terms of partnering.

Disadvantages

For firms whose retainers provide discount pricing, the most significant downside is the potential loss of revenue. The anticipated additional work never materializes, or it isn't enough to compensate for the discount. In other cases, an increase in discounted work cuts into time available to work for other clients at the firm's full rate.

Otherwise, the most significant downside of a retainer is that it allocates a percentage of billable hours to a single client, for better or worse. Even in the best scenario, this means responding more or less immediately when the client calls, despite current workload. In the worst case, a sudden client need or a spike in workload could mean tying up a firm's capacity and jeopardizing the schedules of other client work.

Then, too, without taking care, a retainer can result in a firm being treated as a client's "in-house" supplier. When this happens and there is too much familiarity, client expectations and demands tend to rise. It is easy for a firm to be taken advantage of unintentionally. Tying up a large block of time with work for any one client, month-in and month-out, can also affect a firm's ability to be competitive. It is easy to become too closely identified with certain types of clients and work. Also, clients that compete with the retainer client might pass the firm by, fearing a conflict of interest. In either case, domination by one client could limit a firm's ability to compete for larger, more exciting assignments. And, not incidentally, too much routine work—more of the same old, same old—can have a negative impact on creative innovation and employee morale.

Finally, there's the danger of being seduced by easy money. Marketing efforts tend to slide while retainers provide a steady income. When this happens, a business becomes unnecessarily vulnerable after the retainer ends.

RETAINER PROS AND CONS FOR THE CLIENT

Requests to consider working on a retainer occasionally come from knowledgeable clients. More often, though, it makes sense for a firm to propose the arrangement, either to address a client's pricing concerns, or to get an inside track on more work. Whichever the case, it helps to understand what is, and isn't, appealing to clients.

Advantages

The major benefit of a retainer for many clients is savings. As previously indicated (see "Defining a Retainer" above), fees are typically discounted by 10 percent. In other words, if a firm's normal labor rate is $150 per hour, work done under a retainer would be billed at $135. Any work in addition to that covered could be provided at the same reduced rate, or at a firm's normal rate, depending on the retainer negotiation.

For other clients, particularly those with fast turnaround needs, a major attraction is preferential treatment. This is often a factor among clients who are already providing a significant volume of ongoing work. With a retainer they get special recognition. In essence, the perception is that they become Client Numero Uno.

Another consideration, especially for large clients, is that guaranteeing a certain steady volume of work will allow them to justify making investments in training a creative firm. This can be particularly important to clients in complex organizations, or those dealing with sophisticated products and markets.

Disadvantages

The primary concern for many clients is paying for time that might never be used, especially if one of the reasons for the retainer was budget concerns. As covered earlier, this can be resolved, in part, by allowing time to be banked (rolled over) for a designated period. But remember that the other side of providing flexibility—carrying time forward—poses a risk to the workflow of the firm should the client decide to use it all at once.

There's also a feeling that because retainers are time-focused they encourage make-work or working slower. That is, that the costs of projects when a firm is "working by the clock" will be greater than when it works on project fees. And some clients fear that they will become vulnerable to padding the time sheet. It is difficult for a client to verify how much time was expended on which tasks and setting up a procedure to do so can be time-consuming, negating some of the retainer benefits. Finally, it may also be difficult or accounting-intensive for them to apportion the monthly payment among various projects, departments, and budget accounts.

SETTING UP A RETAINER

As a legal, contractual agreement that will obligate both parties, a retainer can be set up in any way that both agree to. There are, however, certain elements that should always be included:

❑ The period covered—e.g., January 1st to July 1st.

❑ The types of services to be provided—e.g., design.

- The number of hours reserved during a specific period—e.g., forty hours per month.

- When and where the hours will be made available—e.g., normal business hours where specified by the client.

- Payment amount and terms—e.g., $4,000 payable on the first of each month.

- Payment for excess and credit for unused time—e.g., excess billed at $125 per hour; unused carried forward one month.

- Ownership of materials—e.g., copyrights owned by client.

- Terminations—e.g., thirty days written notice.

The form reproduced below shows a format that incorporates these and additional elements. It is suitable to use as a draft for your own retainer agreement. Before asking a client to sign, however, be sure to check your form with a lawyer.

IS A RETAINER RIGHT FOR YOUR CLIENTS?

As a final step before considering whether to enter into a retainer agreement, ask yourself the following questions:

1. **How much pressure is there to reduce prices or be instantly available?** These are the two primary motivators for most clients. Without a strong desire for one or both, most clients will be suspicious of a retainer proposal.

2. **How important is cash flow to you?** The more volatile your income, the smaller your cash reserve or line of credit, and the higher your fixed expenses, the more a retainer will make sense.

3. **How enjoyable is the client and their work?** Retainers encourage closer relationships and spawn more work. If you enjoy the client and their assignments, whatever money is given up will seem like a bargain. If you're neutral, it could seem costly. If you dislike the client, it will be a devil's bargain.

4. **What percentage of your income will it be?** It is financially risky to have too much business tied up with one client. One or two small retainers can provide much desired financial stability. But too much of a good thing can be a financial disaster just waiting to happen. (For guidelines, see the sidebar on the following page.)

Considerations Before the Fact

Whether responding to a client request for lower prices or to offer greater accessibility, be sure to consider the following beforehand.

How profitable will the additional work be? It is easy to fall into the "any business is good" trap. In the absence of other benefits, such as providing more desired experience, any additional work has to be profitable enough to more than support a discount. *A firm that does not track the profitability of its jobs and accounts should not provide discounts or retainers.*

Will more work from one client increase vulnerability? Too much business from too few clients is a major risk for firms of all sizes. When more than a quarter of its income comes from one client, or half from two, it is courting disaster. The only exception is when a firm has enough money in the bank to cover a prolonged financial drought after the sudden loss of a client.*

Is this a short-term consideration? If so, forget it. Providing discounts or retainers changes the way a firm works, and has long-term repercussions. Some are good, some not so.

Might it mean foregoing more profitable business? Creative firms mostly sell time, and only so much is available. If it is sold to one client at a cheaper rate, it isn't available to sell to others at a higher rate. In addition, when a firm is kept busy handling lower paying work it is less likely to have the incentive to do the prospecting that will lead to more profitable work.

What will be the effect on morale? Employees and firms are stimulated and grow stronger from variety and exposure to new challenges. Yet, most clients want more of the same old. Don't be quick to sacrifice future creative growth for a little temporary cash.

This article was originally published in the Creative Business *newsletter, a publication devoted exclusively to helping freelancers and creative firm principals address business issues. Newsletter information and downloadable forms and articles are available at* www.creativebusiness.com.

---

* If 25 percent of income comes from just one client, *Creative Business* recommends funds should be available to cover two months of future expenses; if 50 percent, enough for three months; if 75 percent, enough for four months; if 100 percent, enough for five months, the maximum time it should take to get replacement business.

RETAINER AGREEMENT

This will constitute an agreement between (client) and (creative firm) for (graphic design/writing/public relations consulting/advertising/Internet-based) services for the period (date) to (date).

During this period, (creative firm) agrees to devote up to (number) hours per month on work to be determined by (client). It will normally be performed at the offices of (creative firm), but occasionally may take place at other locations as required. Priority and scheduling will be at the discretion of (client), but acknowledge the need to work within previously established schedules and processes of (creative firm). Work will normally occur between the hours of 9 and 5 on weekdays.

Payment for these services will be to (creative firm) at the rate of (amount in dollars) per month and will be made no later than the 30th day of each month that this agreement is in force. No invoice will be submitted by (creative firm).

In the event fewer hours are used during a one month period, unused hours may be carried forward to the following month. Any hours unused at the end of the second month will be forfeited without compensation.

Work in excess of (hours) per month will be at the rate of (amount in dollars) per hour and will be billed separately. Any expenses exclusive of normal overhead are not included in this agreement and will be invoiced separately at cost. Examples of such expenses include but are not limited to: delivery services, travel beyond 25 miles from (creative firm) or (client) facilities, and meals when traveling. All invoices will be payable within 30 days (net 30). Invoices paid after 30 days will be subject to interest at 1.5% per month.

All materials furnished by (client) will remain the property of (client) and will be returned upon request, or not more than 10 days from the termination of this agreement.

The results of any and all work performed under this agreement, including original creative work (with the exception of _____), will become the property of the (client). (Client) may use this material in any way deemed appropriate.

All materials developed by (creative firm) for production purposes, including but not limited to computer formats, files and code, will remain the property of (creative firm).

This agreement may be terminated on 30 days written notice by either (creative firm) or (client). In event of termination, (creative firm) shall make a reasonable attempt to finish work in progress.

(Insert more paragraphs here with other terms and conditions as may be appropriate.)

(Signed) _____   (Signed) _____

(Name) _____   (Name) _____

(Title) _____   (Title) _____

(Creative Firm) _____   (Client Company) _____

(Date) _____   (Date) _____

11

Finding the Perfect Job

MICHAEL JEFFERSON

THE DEFINITION OF the perfect job is different for everyone. Whether you are seeking your first job, or thinking about changing jobs or careers, you need to be able to consider what you want, and evaluate your situation. If the mere thought of going to your job makes you angry, you should find a different one. If you want to find a job that is right for you, you need to know what you want from an employment opportunity. Once you know what you want you can go about finding it.

As a member of the full time work force, I work for eight hours, five days a week. There is no way I would spend forty hours a week working a job I hate. People that work jobs they hate become miserable. It took me a few years to find a job that is perfect for me, but I finally did in 2006 and I am a lot happier as a result. I encourage everyone reading this to keep looking until you find your perfect job. Whether you are a recent graduate or you have been working for many years, keep looking.

The first and most important step to take when looking for your perfect job is often the most difficult. That step is deciding on a career path. If you know the career you want to pursue, you will be able to prepare yourself to find employment in that field. A large part of that preparation is education.

Whether you have never held a job, or you are looking to make a career change, you will need a degree in graphic design or a closely related discipline to become a graphic designer. There is a slim possibility that you can find a design job without a degree, but your employment search will be very long and very difficult. In the design field, a Master's degree will not hurt your chances of finding a job, but obtaining one is not necessary. A degree of any kind along with a strong portfolio is enough to get a career started.

Discovering a career path that you are passionate about can only come from learning more about yourself and what you find interesting. After you know the career path you want to take, you need to get some experience. If you have never done any professional design work in a professional environment how could you possibly know what kind of setting is appropriate for you? Internships are a great place to start. If you are in school and you want an internship, visit your school's career services office. They should have a list of companies that offer internships. If you are not in school, finding an internship will be very similar to searching for a full time position. You should search the internet for opportunities, contact companies you want to work for and ask if they have an internship program, and network. Ask everyone you know if they are aware of any available design internships. After working an internship you will have relevant experience to put on your resume. You will also have a better understanding of the kind of environment you want to work in.

If you have already worked in a professional environment, you should have an idea of the kind of environment that will allow you to be comfortable. There are several factors you should analyze when deciding if an employment opportunity is right for you.

TYPE OF WORK

For designers who are starting their careers, the type of work that will be done is extremely important to consider. Beginning designers should aspire to build their portfolios. Making photocopies and answering phones will not help you build a stronger library of work. Working for a company that solely designs toilet paper may not be the best skill building position either. An ideal internship will allow you to work on challenging, skill enhancing projects. Any experience working in the design field is better than none, but you should make efforts to find a position that will allow you to develop your skills and grow as a designer. If you are a more experienced designer, you should already have a strong portfolio. Instead of portfolio building, you should seek a position that will be more closely aligned with your interests. If you work on brochures and you develop the desire to work on identity projects, don't allow yourself to be complacent. Look for companies that specialize in creating identities until you find one that wants to hire you. No matter how many years you have been working, it is never too late to start something new.

WORK ENVIRONMENT

Every workplace is different. They are often similar, but every work environment is unique. Would you be comfortable working in a room with ten other people? Would you be comfortable working with people who feel the need to talk all day instead of working? Can you deal with a boss who micromanages and constantly asks for project updates? Can you work in a fast paced, chaotic environment? Those are the kinds of questions you should ask yourself when considering your ideal working situation. Your job should be a place where you can be comfortable. The thought of going to your job may not make you happy enough to do cartwheels but it shouldn't infuriate you either. Through on the job experience you will be able to discern the type of work environment that will allow you to be a happy employee.

SALARY

This aspect of job searching can be a humbling experience, especially for recent graduates. First time job seekers do not have much room for negotiation. With a little research you will be able to discover the salary for entry level design positions. *AIGA/Aquent Survey of Design Salaries (http://www.designsalaries.com/)* is a useful design salary resource. Salary is determined by location, experience, and ability among other factors. On average, entry level design positions in New York pay more than similar jobs in Idaho. The cost of living in New York is higher and salaries reflect that.

If you are in the beginning stages of your career and you are looking for a job that will pay you more than $45,000 per year, you will be looking for a long time. If you are offered a design position that will allow you to work on interesting and challenging projects, turning that job down because you are looking for an unrealistic amount of money is not wise. Don't let the offered salary keep you from accepting what might otherwise be a great job.

Designers who have been working for a few years have more room to negotiate. If possible, you should avoid taking a salary that is lower than your current or previous salary. The large majority of people that change jobs receive a raise in pay. Do some research and find out what people with your level of experience are making. Your research should present you with a range of figures. Keeping your current or previous salary in mind, you can use those numbers to present a range to potential employers.

LOCATION

I know people that commute for two or more hours everyday to get to work. I will never be one of those people. The location of your job is important to consider. How far are you willing to travel every morning and every evening? Before you accept a job make sure you will be able to get there on time everyday.

LEARN MORE ABOUT THE JOB AND THE COMPANY

Once you know what you want from a job, you have to locate job listings and apply for them. By researching the companies that post job listings, you will be able to determine if those companies are able to give you the employment experience you are seeking.

If a company has a design department, it probably has a Web site. Visit that Web site. Read up on the company's history. Visit its "About" section. If it has press releases posted, skim through those. Visit the portfolio section. Ask yourself if you respect the product and if the company does the kind of work you want to do. After you have visited the Web site, do a few Internet searches and see what comes up. Is that company discussed by others in the design community? If so, what is being said? Independent research will give you a better understanding of its work and reputation in the design industry. After researching, you will know more about the company and you will be prepared if you are called in for an interview.

Job interviews are a great place to gather more information. At a job interview you answer a lot of questions. When that portion of the interview is over you get the valuable opportunity to ask questions of the employees that work for the company you are considering working for. If you ask good questions during the interviewing process, you get an insider perspective on the company's corporate culture. When those questions are answered make sure you are listening intently. Take notes if your memory is unreliable.

The questions below will give you a better understanding of the job and company you are interviewing for.

- What is this company's design philosophy? (The answer to this question may be on the company's Web site so check that first. It's not a good idea to seek answers that are readily available on the Web.)

- How did the position become available?

- Are there opportunities for career advancement?

- What qualities would you say are necessary for someone to be successful in this position?

- Could you describe the typical day for the person that will fill this position?

- What do you like most about working here?

IF YOU WANT A BETTER JOB, FIND ONE

Finding a new job is easier if you have a job. Being part of the work force demonstrates that you are employable. Most people change jobs at least seven times before retirement. If you have a job you love or a job you hate, you have every right to look for other opportunities. People that have a job they love probably don't spend much time seeking new opportunities but it never hurts to see what's available.

Try to be discreet about your search. Don't walk around your office saying, "I can't wait to quit!" Don't search monster.com while your boss is standing behind you. When you send out resumes, be sure to make a note or check the box next to your current supervisor's name that reads, "Do not contact." If you have a job that you enjoy, but you still want to seek better opportunities, make sure that you are obsessive in your efforts to learn the details about any other positions that are available to you. Effective fact-finding will ensure that you don't give up a job that makes you happy for a job that will depress you.

I have held three different positions since I graduated in 2004. Every job was an improvement on the last because I kept looking until I found my ideal position. I will be with the company I work for now for many years to come. The job I have has all the features I need. The pay is good, I like the people I work with, I like the work I do, my commute is less than an hour, there are many places to choose from for lunch (I love to eat), and my job doesn't add stress to my life. I searched until I found a job that is perfect for me. With research and determination you can do the same.

12

The Design Firm and Its Employees

ROZ AND JESSICA GOLDFARB

SUCCESSFUL BUSINESS ADMINISTRATION includes overcoming the challenges of a plethora of employment matters. From determining staffing needs, to interviewing, hiring, maintaining constructive relationships, and firing, this whole process presents a constant struggle for all companies. For design firms, those problems are increased by the need for balance between creative and business goals and personalities. In this creatively driven business, the essential fact is that the firm's people are its greatest assets and they walk out the door every night. The key ingredients to a successful employment relationship, therefore, are communication and respect between employer and employee.

First, the design firm, large or small, just like any business, must put into place fair business practices and develop standardized employment policies. The problem is that few design firms review or track how employment decisions are made, although many have been given these tools by their parent companies. Nor are individuals with these responsibilities trained as to how to interview or evaluate candidates, review or manage employees, or address problems properly. Even in small firms, one person should be identified to function as a "Human Resource Administrator" and given the appropriate training. It is recommended that all employment decisions should include or be channeled through this person, as should all documentation concerning resumes received, dated, and action taken (i.e., interviewed, considered, rejected, etc.) and all personnel files and other employment information (i.e., policies, health benefits, employee handbooks, etc.). This way, the firm will always have at its disposal some record of people who could be possible employees for the future, as well as documentation to protect against any possible legal actions. If the firm uses a recruitment firm, these records also can be essential to tracking referrals and pin-pointing possible conflicts from multiple referrals.

Second, firms must recognize that inter-personal dynamics are involved in these matters. The employment *relationship* is just that: an affiliation between an individual and a company, personified by individuals given the authority to make certain decisions. Given the extent to which we in American society identify ourselves by our job, this is one of the most important relationships in life. In creative firms, the value of the product is, obviously, its creativity, which is personality-driven. This means that the identification between the individual and the product, and, thus, the individual and the firm can be particularly strong. Managing creativity, therefore, poses unique challenges, requiring a sensitivity to the individual and the team.

Each of us has personal wants and needs in relation to the workplace. Those running firms often have a distinct vision of the type of environment they aim to create, which, not incidentally, has a direct effect on their ability to attract the quality of individual necessary to ensure success in the marketplace. Clear communication sets the right tone for a trusting, nurturing relationship in the workplace and provides a substantial foundation upon which to build the long-lasting relationship and promise of growth that both parties seek.

JOB DESCRIPTIONS, INTERVIEWING, AND HIRING

A respect for these priorities must be established at the very beginning of the relationship. Key hiring requirements need to be identified, prioritized, and described. It is the rare design firm that goes through the effort of writing a job description. But this is an essential part of the process, for it both forces the clarification of the qualifications needed and establishes expectations for the future of the relationship, thereby avoiding many problems down the road. It can also force the firm to question the realism of these requirements and expectations.

An important step toward creating a successful relationship is ensuring that the candidate understands the employer's needs and the employer recognizes the candidate's goals. Too often employers forget their own work history and the anxiety of looking for work. It may seem that the balance of power has shifted to the employer, but a savvy individual recognizes the underlying mutual dependence of the relationship.

The time to sort all this out is during the interview process, but unfortunately, few people are ever trained on how to conduct an interview. Common, tricky "interview questions" rarely tell anything truly useful about a candidate, unless the interviewer is very cunning. And, of course, this is also a time for romancing, when some employers may gloss over important points about the firm. Others, trying to be very honest, paint an unrealistically bleak picture of the working conditions. Either way, the candidate is left with an unclear perception and, in the end, both sides often come away knowing very little about each other.

Again, clarity is required. Job descriptions help the interviewer hone in on what information is crucial. Checklists of these skills or characteristics can help the interviewer, especially when comparing candidates. Moreover, employers should instruct interviewers not to ask questions that solicit excess information that could be a discriminatory basis for making the hiring decision, or that may simply imply such information was the reason for that decision.

If care is not taken during the hiring process, even after a job is accepted, there may be differing views of what the job entails (that is, its requirements, role, and duties) or the terms of employment (such as salary, bonus, review schedules, length of employment, and grounds for discharge). Either the employer or the employee, under these circumstances, will sooner or later become dissatisfied and the relationship is bound to deteriorate. To avoid such difficulties, everyone involved in the hiring process should take care that all aspects of the position are clearly defined and understood. For this reason a job description is often given with an offer letter, stating that the terms laid out are intended as guidelines and subject to change.

In practice, significant guideposts in making the decision to hire or accept a position are inevitably a combination of objective criteria (such as issues of skills, title, money, and the quality of the work), less tangible elements (office environment, work ownership, and access to clients, for example) and personal characteristics (such as personality, ambition, or cultural match)—not to mention office politics. Some reactions are harder to identify and are of an intuitive nature, often chalked up to "chemistry."

Candidates should always receive some "feedback," even if the standard response is: "it's just not right" or perhaps "it's not a fit." Understandably, designers find it hard to face these ambiguous responses. However, the word "fit" does tell a significant story. Fit means everything. But, in the last analysis, it is vital both to base the decision and, whenever possible, to articulate it on the basis of objective criteria as well as fit. For this purpose, a proper job description is indispensable. It will prove handy as a reference down the road during periodic evaluations and in case problems arise. If a person ultimately is to be let go, this history of information is invaluable to that decision-making process.

Where the reason for refusing to hire someone is not clear, an employer runs the risk of facing a lawsuit with the applicant claiming the reason was some type of illegal discrimination. If that is successful, it can be very costly to an employer: The applicant may obtain an order to be hired, may recover compensation for foregone pay, and, where proven, for mental suffering. In instances where the discrimination was considered especially flagrant, large punitive damages may be collected. A simple statement or notation to a file can fully eliminate this hazard.

AT-WILL VERSUS CONTRACTUAL EMPLOYMENT

Many people assume that an employer is bound by law to treat them "fairly," to have "just cause" for letting them go, or to give a specific amount of notice when doing so. However, without any particular contractual commitment, employers are not obligated to do any of these things. A largely unrecognized fact is that without a written contract stating a specific period of employment, employees are generally considered by law to be "at-will." That is, the law presumes that the employer reserves the right to change the conditions of employment or to discharge the employee at any time without notice for any nondiscriminatory reason—just as it assumes that an employee may quit at any time without providing advance notice.

In some instances, an applicant or employee can enforce oral or written promises (in a job application, job description, written offer, employee handbook, and so on) made during the interviewing and hiring process or period of employment. The key is whether it can be shown conclusively that those representations were reasonably relied on to a detriment (for instance, in hiring, that another offer was rejected or that a prior job was left on the basis of those statements), that the employer is guilty of intentional or negligent misrepresentation, or that the statements were part of an express or implied contract of employment. So, again, clarity becomes a key player in determining the rights involved.

FREELANCING AND CONSULTING VERSUS STAFF EMPLOYMENT

When a firm is in a hiring mode, issues of workload and the anticipated flow of projects dominate and create a sense of urgency. Often the solution is to hire a flexible workforce: freelancers, project-based employees, or "virtual" resources. The increasing unpredictability of clients or projects also creates pressures to hire in this way. The advantages may be obvious. To the firm there are lower costs, the capacity to bring in a talent base greater than might otherwise fit within a budget, and the ability to adjust easily and quickly to current work needs.

To the employee, the benefits include a variety of work, flexibility in the location or timing of work, the ability to deduct from income all business expenses, and the access to different retirement savings options. These advantages are so compelling, in fact, that more often it is the prospective employee that suggests alternative work arrangements in order to remain independent. The disadvantages, however, are too often overlooked. To the firm, these employees can be undedicated or unreliable, and legal and tax penalties are also involved. To the employee, it similarly means no loyalty from the employer, and benefits, such as health care and retirement accounts, are unavailable and more and more difficult to maintain on one's own.

While an employer and an individual may agree upon virtually any work arrangement they please, for tax purposes, the laws and regulations of the Internal Revenue Service, with increasing likelihood, may define workers as employees and require that they pay Social Security and Medicare taxes and withhold income taxes. Independent contractor status is allowed if the firm has a reasonable basis to treat the individual as an independent contractor and the IRS will consider industry practice on such a basis. The deciding factor is generally how dependent that individual is on one firm during a particular period of time, even if that period is relatively short. The firm must also take care to *treat all freelancers similarly; any* inconsistency can result in an IRS determination that that person is an employee. Part of this similar treatment requires that the firm file reporting forms (Form 1099 or 1099-MISC) for all independent contractors. The IRS also looks to issues of control, such as who has decision-making authority over the work (whether approval by the firm is required, for instance, or who, if anyone, determines details like where that individual performs the work) or over financial matters (whether the person is on salary or if payment is made by the hour or day, and whether expenses are reimbursed).

Benefits (such as medical insurance, pensions, profit sharing, and 401k plans) are also affected by this status, and employers cannot extend its benefits to non-employees. Where formal benefits plans are in effect, the Employee Retirement Income Security Act (ERISA) and other laws govern, and these matters become much more complex.

A word of warning is due because in recent years, as companies have sought to reduce labor costs by using more freelancers, federal and state authorities have become more aggressive in investigating and enforcing these issues. A failure to pay proper payroll taxes can result in an order for payment with interest and a substantial penalty. So it is safest to assume that anyone working at the design firm on more than just a temporary project is probably considered an employee. Firms should consult with an accountant or attorney if there is any doubt and always err on the side of caution.

Moreover, designers can face different levels of protection for their work dependent upon their employment status. Work completed by staff designers is normally considered "work made for hire" and property of the firm. Designs created by freelancers, however, are property of the designer. Because projects are often the product of collaboration by more than one designer, there can be confusion as to who owns these rights. Whatever the circumstance, firms must take care to acquire the specific rights necessary to meet the needs. For example, firms can negotiate with designers to buy all the rights to the work or to license it for a particular use.

PERSONNEL POLICIES AND EMPLOYEE HANDBOOKS

The clearest method to establish employment policies is to set them out in written personnel guidelines, policy statements, or manuals that have been reviewed by an attorney. These should be given to employees and/or kept in a place where they can be viewed. New employees should be given copies but should also ask whether these policies exist.

Most employers claim their right to determine responses on a case-by-case basis or make changes at any time simply by including a clear disclaimer on all documents that the statements are *guidelines only*. Employees are sometimes required to sign an acknowledgment to ensure that the policy statements or manual have been received.

In rare instances, oral or written promises are enforced against an employer and are usually limited to statements which appear to be definitive terms of employment (such as, "guaranteed bonus," "discharges only for cause," or "our company will ... "). Some reasonable and harmful reliance on these promises is required before any recovery can be had.

Enforcement of these policies against an employee (such as where an employee is disciplined or discharged as a result of failing to follow work conduct or performance policies or procedures), is usually done within the firm. These cases may be challenged if the employer has not applied the policies consistently. Whether by reason of discrimination or favoritism, all "special cases" for which rules are set aside create confusion, animosities, and dilute the force—and enforceability—of the rule.

DISCRIMINATION

Federal, state, and local discrimination laws do not create a general guarantee of fairness, but rather carve out particular categories for which any bias is made illegal. Under these laws, all *employment decisions*—including hiring, distributing benefits, promotions, or firing—must be based on objective criteria that are justified by business necessity and related to the position.

It is generally illegal for an employer to discriminate against an applicant for employment or an employee on the grounds of race, color, national origin (or that of his parents or spouse), religion, age, gender, sexual preference, marital status, citizenship, or disability (now including mental or physical disabilities, drug or alcohol dependency and AIDS or HIV+status). Additional laws protect against discrimination on the basis of union affiliation, "whistleblowing" on an employer's illegal practice, or having a criminal record.

As a result, throughout the hiring process and employment relationship, employers should not seek information, comment, or keep records concerning these issues. Only objective criteria such as skills, work experience, education, and work performance should be considered or included on all application forms, in interviews or screening processes, in performance evaluations, and in personnel files. While this may seem obvious, it is not always so clear which topics are permissible and which are forbidden. Therefore, employers must prevent the existence—or even the hint—of preference based on any of the proscribed characteristics.

The most common trouble arises when seemingly innocent statements imply unlawful discrimination by indirectly conveying an employer's intent to base the decision to hire on a particular illegal ground. For example, questions or casual comments concerning certain physical characteristics may be taken as evidence of an employer's intent to discriminate on the basis of some physical disability. Jokes or off-color remarks on these issues may also lead to these misperceptions.

PROMOTIONS, TITLES, SALARY, AND PROFIT SHARING

Of all the possible incentives toward employee retention, the award of increased earnings and position with the company is the most powerful. How this is done and the relationship between staff in an organization is complex and dependent upon the variables within each organization. The following is a partial listing of issues that must be addressed by the firm in structuring these policies:

❑ *Existing organizational structure: Is there a system of grade levels and titles?* The premise is that a system is necessary and has to be defined. In larger organizations, titles, job descriptions, and salary ranges are often tied to a point gradation system. For example, under this type of system, entry-level administrative positions might be classified as a grade 1 position; grade 8 might be an assistant manager, whose salary would be in the $47 to $58,000 range; grade 10 might be a manager, earning $55 to $65,000; and grade 12 might be a director, earning $62 to $75,000. While smaller design firms may be able to utilize a simpler plan, they should still connect titles to a salary range.

❑ *Has any time frame or length of service been deemed necessary to attain a promotion? Have accomplishments been defined to justify a promotion such as excellence in performance or advanced education? Who should be moved up through this system and when?* These three questions relate to a difficult judgment, evaluating objective standards that have been established (some that should be outlined in personnel guidelines or manuals) and personal, highly subjective factors. They also depend on the quality of communication established between the employer and employee, especially during scheduled and ad-hoc employee review sessions. While experience is given primary weight in most businesses, creatively-driven businesses often value performance or talent over proven longevity. The inherent danger in promoting a junior over a senior person is the possibility of friction and the implied message to the senior members that it may be time to seek another position.

❑ *Maintaining parity with other staff members and with the marketplace: basic equality of salary, title, and relationship to the length of term of employment.* A rule of thumb is that there are few secrets inside or between organizations, so the importance of parity cannot be over-emphasized. Another management strategy pegged to a successful and established structure is to link titles to salary ranges. Each new hire by a firm offers the opportunity to review the existing salary structure to see if it is current with the marketplace. While keeping up may put additional pressures on budgets and profit margins, falling behind can mean losing staff to other higher-paying companies or losing prospective employees to counter-offers.

❏ *Establishing a financial cap to a defined position.* It is recommended that a cap on a salary range for a specific title be established. If the employee is with the firm long enough to "outlive" the normal increases allowed for the position and cannot be promoted, the employer should consider the other alternative compensations outlined under Employee Retention.

❏ *Should a title change necessarily mean increased salary?* In a word, yes.

❏ *Considering profit sharing/stock/equity alternatives to annual salary increases.* Many companies utilize an annual system of bonuses and/or profit sharing as a way of sharing the benefits of business growth as well as increasing employee incentives to motivate the perception that they are a part of the process. Most employees recognize that these moneys are not guaranteed, but that the benefits of shared involvement and loyalty to the firm are substantial. Pension plans that are tied to years of tenure and vestment are very successful in bonding the employee to the company. For some firms, the bonus/profit sharing plans supersede the emphasis on raises allowing for lower annual increases. The inherent value in this case is to lower fixed overhead in favor of sharing concepts for "good years." Generally, issues of equity only come into play when the individual has become a key member of the firm. There are two key hallmarks of this form of reward: (1) Does the individual participate in the administration of key decision-making processes of the firm? (2) Would the individual's contribution (creative or business side) mean a significant loss of business if that person were to leave? If that person is responsible for controlling a substantial portion of revenues and is part of the firm's management, then some portion of equity should be a just consideration. A recent trend has been to offer equity at earlier stages as an enticement to join new ventures.

EMPLOYEE RETENTION AND RECRUITING

Finding and keeping quality employees are significant and costly problems for many design firms. Attracting and retaining valuable employees and avoiding turnover, therefore, become priorities. Techniques can include offering increased financial rewards and incentives, as well as finding new creative challenges for employees to stay "fresh" and interested.

From the financial point of view, the standard incentives (such as salary increases, promotions, and change of titles) work best in the early years of the relationship. However, the employer's capacity to increase these benefits decreases in direct proportion to the length of tenure. Profit margins do not expand in proportion to the prospect of increased overhead and, in fact, the margins may decrease as the design field experiences a shakedown from the influences of technology. For those who wish to avoid the problems and costs of turnover, re-staffing (whether or not through recruiters), advertising, re-training, and continuity issues with clients and disruption within the firm, there are solutions to consider.

Recent years—particularly in the post-dot com bust and post-9/11 world—have seen a real shift in emphasis on Quality-of-Life issues and time has been as valuable a benefit as money. Employers do well to consider offering increased vacation, holidays, or other paid time-off allotments, as well as sabbaticals or even other unpaid time-off options. Permitting shorter workweeks, flex-time, or telecommuting has given many employers a real advantage.

The following list represents various options for additional incentives or "perks." Some of these are often negotiated at the time of hiring—and at a time when the focus is on the short-term needs of attraction and not the long-term issues of retention—but perhaps are better left for a later stage in the relationship when expanded incentives are advantageous. Some to be considered are:

- Increased insurance benefits: expanded health, dental, optical, life, and disability
- Health club memberships
- Defined expense accounts
- Transportation and/or commutation to and from work
- Increased participation in pension plans, if company-wide
- Education and professional improvement reimbursement
- Seminars and conferences
- Bonuses, company stock-options, equity and/or profit sharing
- Child or elder care
- Flex-time or job-sharing

Some employees are content with maintaining a singular role within an organization. The employer must be creative in managing these people by finding ways to sustain the creative momentum to stimulate them and avoid staleness. Keeping up-to-date on esthetics, design trends, and technological advances is both the employer's and the employees' responsibility.

Others who desire professional growth can face a glass ceiling where internal organizational structures and overhead restrictions tie the employer's hands. The reality is that certain people will leave for these reasons and some people will need to leave because the organization may have outgrown them as well.

While employee retention can be an important goal, there are advantages to turnover that offer creative growth and financial stability to a design firm. This includes the option to replace individuals with less-experienced talent that is perhaps also newer and fresher, and offer savings to the firm. The over-riding challenge to the firm is to know when to pursue which of these directions.

TERMINATION, RESIGNATION, AND FIRING

In the best of circumstances, an employment relationship will end relatively amicably, quietly, and with a mutual sense that it "just didn't work out" or "it's time." In many of these cases, the employee simply outgrows the position and no longer finds it challenging. In others, the employer's needs were either not evident or changed over time making it impossible to give the employee the type of role or responsibility commensurate with his or her background and experience.

Sometimes employment is terminated by the employer because of matters unrelated to the specific employee, based on a business or economic reason. These are generally called "layoffs" rather than "firings" and can be precipitated by the general business climate, a downsizing, a company re-organization, or the closing of a division or business. Layoffs are governed by specific legally required procedures.

Under more unfortunate circumstances, the relationship ends by one party only and is a disappointment, if not complete surprise, to the other. Unwelcome resignations, stemming from employee discontent, often occur when there is lingering confusion over job duties, differing expectations concerning the growth of the position, or simply poor work conditions. Firings are caused by employer discontent when there is unsatisfactory performance, unacceptable behavior, or insubordination.

All too often, the pertinent complaints have rarely, if ever, been communicated before the surprise announcement to end the relationship. These regrettable situations should be addressed quickly and in open discussions so that the problem can be corrected. The firm is, of course, in the best position to establish policies and procedures to address each situation. For the employee, this may be trickier so battles must be chosen carefully and handled diplomatically.

Whatever the reason, the best manner to deal with these matters is by taking the time for quality communication. Most situations can be solved through a straightforward discussion; usually it seems that the practical route for all involved is to move on. But without an adequate resolution, the end of an employment relationship is often marked by blame, denial, anger, and insecurity, which may lead to an unnecessary, on-going dispute or simply the public bad-mouthing of the employer.

The best practice is to establish voluntary (via initial acceptance of the position), clear, written rules of conduct for the workplace and expectations for work performance in statements and personnel manuals. These should include specific penalties for non-compliance and internal procedures, if any, to review any problems as they arise. Employees should routinely be given copies or notices of these policies so that they are aware that they will be bound to them. Employers can reserve their right to change these policies and to determine their responses on a case-by-case basis by simply stating this right on the document.

Employers should also avoid treating any one employee differently than others by excepting them from policies covering work conduct or performance. These so-called "special cases" only create confusion as to what is required and resentments among the staff based on perceptions of favoritism. Ultimately, they dilute the force—and enforceability—of the rule.

Regular, periodic performance evaluations will ensure clarity in the employment relationship by giving all involved the opportunity to communicate. Written evaluations provide the best documentation and should be discussed at the reviews and included in personnel files. These efforts put the employee on notice of problems, provide the chance to respond or defend himself against any charges, as well as raise his own questions or problems. It is preferable for everyone involved to provide an opportunity to correct a problem and to follow-up with periodic employee performance evaluations These steps also set the groundwork in case there is a need to discipline or fire the employee.

An employee may behave in a manner that is simply unacceptable and requires a response. Common misconduct is lateness, absenteeism, on-the-job drug use, foul or abusive language, open discriminatory treatment of others, or disruptive behavior. Nonperformance or insubordination can also be a failure to follow rules, whether from more obvious or objective concerns, like the refusal to follow an employer's instructions in fulfilling the duties of a job, to nuanced or subjective issues, such as appearance or dress. These matters should always be investigated and addressed quickly.

Firms should, whenever possible, use "progressive discipline" or disciplinary measures that become increasingly more severe as the employee continues to engage in misconduct or fails to improve. Generally, employees are first given a verbal warning (with a written memo added to the personnel file). If the behavior continues, a written warning is given, followed by suspension from work without pay, and, ultimately, the employee should be fired. It is wise to set up meetings with the employee to discuss discipline and methods for correction, and to provide notice of steps that the employer will take if the problem continues. This way, the employee has been treated fairly by having several chances to correct the behavior.

Some misconduct or performance delinquencies are sufficiently severe to warrant an immediate suspension or discharge. These may include gross insubordination (such as disobeying work rules by coming to work intoxicated), violations of codes on conduct (such as yelling at a client or fighting with a colleague), or engaging in illegal activities (such as theft, falsification of records, or sale of drugs) on the employer's premises. But typically, the employee will be sent home while the employer investigates the matter and determines the appropriate penalty.

Of course, once circumstances have reached a certain level, the employee must be fired. Many employers require approval from a neutral manager or a human resources specialist before the action is taken. Firing, while never pleasant, can be eased by a few simple procedures. Advance notice allows an employee time to tie up loose ends and find alternative work. Notice may be given at home, the end of a working day, or the end of a pay period to give the employee time to deal with the situation before spending time in the office(s). In some cases, however, it is necessary to move quickly, sometimes even requiring immediate departure, to ensure that the employer's property (including business files or documents related to trade secrets) is not taken.

A final meeting or exit interview should be held in all cases to give notice of the termination and/or to discuss separation issues (such as the effect on benefits), as well as reviewing any previous disciplinary actions or poor performance appraisals. At this time, the firm may offer letters of reference or confirmation of employment (or one can be requested by the employee) and a copy should be included in the employee's personnel file.

It is always helpful to be very clear with the employee about the reason for the termination without being insulting or inflammatory. Here, as always, glossing over the truth leads only to confusion over the actual cause and resentment at the decision. If this information is not forthcoming, the employee may want to request it at a meeting or in a follow-up letter. It is best, however, to avoid extended, overly emotional conversations about the situation. Written notice of the reason can be given where possible; this documentation should be kept in a personnel file and can be helpful in case of a challenge or to counter claims for unemployment insurance if the termination was for cause.

In extreme instances, employers have tried to dodge actually firing someone by forcing someone to quit. However, if an employer establishes work conditions which are so unbearable that a reasonable employee would quit (such as extremely abusive treatment by a supervisor or sexual harassment), that termination is deemed under the law as a constructive discharge caused by the employer, rather than a voluntary action of the employee. The employer is then liable just as if the employee had been fired. So no one wins.

Most employees will choose not to protest a termination because it requires a significant investment of time, money, and emotional energy to deal with complex litigation. The employer's vulnerability here may be prevented or limited by the employee's "at-will" status or the lack of any other specific legal right. To be binding, employment commitments must be contractual, established in a personnel manual, or by law, such as in the case of discharges related to discrimination. These rigorous requirements can be overwhelming to the individual who may decide that it is just not worth it. Of course, if there is significant cause to believe that there was wrong-doing by the employer or if the person fired is angry or hurt enough even if wrong, a legal action may be filed. Whenever action is taken, it is costly and time-consuming for all involved. That is why firms should always remember the ancient adage that "an ounce of prevention is worth a pound of cure."

TERMINATION, SEVERANCE, NON-DISCLOSURE, AND NON-COMPETE AGREEMENTS

Sometimes an employer and employee may enter into a contract to set the terms for the termination of the employment. These may be negotiated in advance, at the initial hiring, or after the decision to end the relationship. These contracts may cover grounds for dismissal, a means for disputing the termination (such as alternative dispute resolution), and severance payments or other benefits.

Severance payment agreements usually depend upon the salary of the position and/or the length of service with that employer. Severance pay is given for a specified period and may end when the employee is hired elsewhere. In most cases, the amount of severance pay is conditioned upon the signing of a waiver and release of all claims against the employer. Termination and severance agreements often contain a provision requiring that the terms of agreement be kept confidential and be revealed only to those with an established need-to-know. Special issues concerning severance and termination agreements arise for reductions-in-force (RIFS) and older workers (defined as anyone over forty).

These agreements vary widely and can also govern the behavior of the parties after termination. They may include a so-called "non-disclosure agreement," which restricts a former employee against divulging trade secrets—that is, things not generally known by the public or discovered through other means. They may also contain so-called "non-compete agreements"—which prohibit a former employee from soliciting the clients or staff of the employer or from otherwise competing against the employer. To be enforceable, these must be limited in scope, geographical boundaries, and duration so as not to unduly limit one's ability to earn a living. Additional limitations include prohibitions against publicly disparaging the employer or cataloguing specific grounds upon which the termination may be contested or the employer may be sued and/or the methods for these disputes. Non-disclosure or non-compete agreements also can be entered into at any stage of the employee's tenure with the company. If these are included in separation agreements, however, they should be accompanied by some additional benefit to the employee in order to be enforceable, such as requiring that a specific person at the firm answer all reference requests concerning the employee or by giving additional severance pay.

ASSIGNING WORK CREDIT, AND USE OF COMPANY'S PORTFOLIO

Industry practice dictates that a designer should be credited for his or her creative role on a project, especially if the work is published. In recognition of the designer's contribution, access should always be given to samples of the work, including team-based projects, to use for a portfolio. The only exception to this rule should be for projects with confidentiality restrictions, such as products that have not yet been released to the public. While some employers can make it difficult, and while there are no legal regulations per se (with the exception of proprietary or confidential projects), common past business practice indicates this system of accreditation for creative roles.

It is the designer's responsibility to present the work accurately, indicating the level of her responsibility and giving the proper credit to the design firm and other team members. If a person leaves a firm and starts a new company, prior work may be displayed in a portfolio as a demonstration of her past experience. The ethical issue is always how the credit is assigned.

CLOSING

Design firms have grown in sophistication over the decades. Today, in an ever more competitive marketplace, and with an educated pool of designers and marketers, design firms of all sizes must function as structured businesses. Remaining sensitive to their creative cultures, firms need to develop systems allowing them to function as an organizational unit. Smoothing out these processes will eliminate many problems, ease morale, and cultivate an environment with the freedom to create.

As we have noted, businesses with a creative product have distinctive requirements. The quality of employee relationships is the nucleus around which all else revolves. Communication, equality in the workplace, identifiable structure, planned decision-making, and, finally, the balance between the objective and the subjective are the day-to-day concerns facing these firms. Although too frequently left to the bottom of the pile in the face of client demands, taking the time to handle these matters thoughtfully can save everyone time, money, and the emotional hardships that can adversely affect workplace morale. Most importantly, an emphasis on these priorities and decisions will create the positive synergy needed between employer and employee for successful, long-term relationships.

13 Managing Creatives

STEVE LISKA

I APPROACH MY responsibilities as a design manager from the following perspective: Design firms are first a business and second a producer of applied art. Knowing that I'm primarily responsible for keeping the lights on, paying salaries, and building a company with long-term viability grounds my approach to managing the creative staff. I layer onto that foundation the realization that graphic design is an *applied* art. It is not art for art's sake, nor primarily an act of self-expression. Graphic design uses art to communicate something about a company, product, or service. This may arguably make the actual business of design more of a problem-solving enterprise than a creative endeavor. Minimally, it suggests that we apply our knowledge of art in order to develop business communication solutions.

We use creativity to help companies communicate. We make choices about color, shape, texture, sound, and language to convey information in a way that words on a page can rarely achieve on their own. The "products" of design are artifacts that engage audiences aesthetically on many levels and through multiple senses.

At the end of the proverbial day, we are artists, but always applied artists. Managing creatives, then, involves finding a balance among the many and often competing interests related to objective business demands and subjective aesthetic principles. Here are some ways I've done that over the past twenty-five-plus years.

ENVIRONMENTAL DESIGN

Intentional planning and investment in the working environment are an integral part of both the business side of design and design management. In many ways, the studio environment sets the tone for the way business is conducted and how work is created. In the same way that design professionals talk about the need for holistic branding for our clients, I've made a concerted effort to create a studio environment that reflects the level of professionalism and design quality that I expect as a business owner and design manager.

Everything from architectural design and in-house resources to operational policies and design methodologies communicates to our associates the type of professionalism that defines our company. As a management tool, the environment communicates to associates that while we work with creative tools, we are first and foremost a professional business. We have protocols for answering the phone, greeting clients, and we adhere to a standard business workday.

We invest in the best technology and resource library and work in an office designed by leading international architects. Our commitment to environment communicates to associates that (a) we're a highly professional company and (b) we respect the craft and the designer enough to provide every possible tool that will help them produce their best work.

That said, we balance the buttoned up office environment with a relaxed dress code and with a flexibility that accounts for the things in life that sometimes disrupt the workday. We're professional, but not rigid; disciplined but not intransigent.

OPEN BOOKS

As a design manager, if I need to be accountable for achieving objective business goals, it is in my best interest to share those goals with my associates. We regularly invite designers into the business details of projects, discussing budget, anticipated hours, client management tactics, etc., as well as keeping the office informed of client billing and new business development activity. Making designers aware of the day-to-day aspects of running the business reinforces the primary message that our firm is a business that happens to create "products" through the use of applied art. It also helps align internal project goals, and for designers looking to move into more project management, it provides a solid foundation in business basics that will prepare them to become design managers. They learn quickly and accurately that providing an artifact or deliverable that satisfies the client is only one part of the larger business process.

OUT OF OFFICE EXPERIENCE

Sharing information about the primary function of the company as a business enterprise is critical. Equally important is reinforcing our position and vocation as artists. We've not chosen to be financial analysts or accountants; we're designers (or managers of designers) who do, indeed, create artful communication solutions across multiple mediums. As a design manager, it is important to encourage our associates to experience art and design in its many forms within the graphic design world and beyond.

Design managers can be role models by taking time to experience multiple art forms outside the office and sharing those experiences with the office. As a company, the studio can actively invest in providing corporate benefits that include access to cultural events. Broad exposure to wide variety of art and culture, from fashion to opera or architecture to dance, will add a type of crosspollination that will always benefit the designer and, ultimately, the work she or he produces for the company.

FRAMEWORK AND PARAMETERS

I've long been an advocate of providing a basic framework coupled with clear parameters for each project. While individual projects certainly have unique elements, there are steps common to most projects. At Liska, we created basic methodologies, processes, and structures for approaching a variety of projects, from naming to Web site and advertising to identity. These frameworks aid the efficiency of the design process and provide clear checkpoints for the project on the table. They're a critical tool for not only getting the project done on time and within budget but also for creating clear expectations and milestones for the designer.

It's a framework, not a house.

The framework puts in place the basic guidelines, but the individual designers need to be supported consistently in their efforts to explore and experiment with a wide variety of design. Navigating this space between structure and free exploration is the perennial and prominent challenge of managing creatives.

Each designer will have a different comfort level with exploration and also bring an individual aesthetic to the project. As much as it is a constant goal to design in ways that express the client's brand attributes and not our own preferences, designers do bring individual style and tendencies. The challenge grows with the designer's daily reality that whatever she or he creates must be approved by the design manager, who, in turn, also has a particular aesthetic preference and responsibility to the client's vision. It is the responsibility of a design manager to allow designers creative exploration while also encouraging them to consider the rest of the team, including the client. In order for a design solution to be successful, it needs the approval of the design manager and the client.

Perhaps the most important factor in managing a creative staff is an awareness that there are always multiple layers influencing the designer's choices. It's been my approach as a design manager to recognize the many factors in play; to know my associates' communication preferences, individual styles, limitations, and potential; and to adapt my communication technique and professional expectations accordingly.

My role is to be cognizant of my employees' perspectives, to appreciate and acknowledge their efforts, and to provide consistent encouragement and clear direction toward project goals. Some of that involves assigning designers to projects in which I think they will be successful as well as knowing when a staff member is ready to take on a project that is outside his or her comfort zone.

But it has to be a house by the end of the day.

Encouraging designers to explore beyond their comfort level is critical. Finding effective ways to do that is a large part of daily project management. It requires a balancing act that is primarily practical, consistently encouraging, and eternally optimistic.

On the practical side, the design manager must know the capabilities and sensitivities of the individual designer. Exploration takes time, courage, and a full awareness that the exploration process is a valid and worthwhile exercise, whether or not it yields a fruitful result every time. This requires patience from the design manager and consistent encouragement for a process that may or may not produce a result that will pass either the design manager's filter or meet the client's need.

Experimentation is challenging for the designer, and design managers can help make that process more comfortable by providing an environment that supports and encourages the designer's efforts. One of the lines spoken by an associate years ago still holds true today, especially when designers are pushed beyond their comfort zone or continually directed to refine their work. After exploring and refining for several hours, she sighed and said with full dramatic emphasis, "Design is hard." It's true. Design is hard. It's a lot of trial and error, of putting one's well-intended efforts on the wall for a design manager to step up and say, "no, no, thanks, but no" to most of the work. Encouragement and positive feedback is a critical tool for mitigating some of the painstaking processes required of creatives.

It is critical to encourage designers continually to press their work and to explore and experiment on their own rather than by looking at the piles of design magazines for inspiration. It's hard to translate ideas into tangible items every single day for every single project. The design manager can enable or support the continued efforts of designers by consistently encouraging and appreciating the efforts of designers to push their boundaries, especially while they have multiple people to please, deadlines to meet, and projects to complete.

Equally important for the design manager is the ability to be eternally optimistic. There's something that does drive us day in and day out. Surely some of that is the challenge of solving problems and growing our business. In our core, as designers and especially as design managers, the element of optimism is critical, because exploration and experimentation does pay off, eventually and often serendipitously. It's that elusive spark of creativity that, through a framework and with aggressive exploration, produces the "perfect" design solution. It happens. It happens more often, I believe, through a studio environment that provides structure, balance, and continual commitment to design processes that build in room for exploration, that provide consistent feedback and encouragement, and that continue the pursuit even when and maybe partly because, "design is hard."

14

The Design Firm and Its Suppliers

DON SPARKMAN

IN THIS AGE of ever-changing design, what applies to one kind of company may not fit another. If you are involved in print, you'll have an entirely different group of suppliers than those supporting a design firm specializing in Web pages or multi-media. Some design firms are part advertising agency and part direct marketing. Some are corporate or government in-house design groups using outside design consultants.

There is only one common denominator: good and ethical standards that apply to all businesses. Business ethics aren't taught like selling techniques. Ethical questions are often complex and vary from one situation to another. With selling, there are tried and proven approaches that work for any business, whether it's graphic arts or insurance. Ethics, on the other hand, is often a gray area and needs to be approached on a case-by-case basis. Because there are never two cases that are alike, each needs to be analyzed carefully. If you feel you don't know the correct answer to an ethical question, call a respected peer. Usually this will provide you with the right solution.

SUPPLIERS ARE A COMPANY'S LIFE BLOOD

A company without suppliers is like a person without food who will starve. Like nourishment, the businesses that support you are needed on a regular basis. You must realize that because they support you, they are no less important than you are to your clients. There is an old saying, "You are only as strong as your weakest link." If your suppliers let you down, you will let your clients down and, ultimately, you are the real loser.

123

It is important to forge a strong relationship with every one of your support businesses. The most successful companies include their suppliers in their successes. Many companies use holidays to send gifts of appreciation to their suppliers. They feel that this is as important as sending gifts to clients. After all, clients come and go—but suppliers are always there.

THE FOOD CHAIN OF DESIGN

When you think of suppliers, you often take a lofty position in the food chain of design. After all, the designers are the important folks. You make it all happen. The buck stops with you; or does it? Aren't you a supplier to your clients? The United States Government labels designers as vendors. Your clients often see the service as a necessary evil, like suppliers with an attitude.

There is disdain for any client that stalls in paying for services rendered. Designers want to lynch anyone reselling or reusing work without due compensation. In essence, designers want to be treated fairly for work produced in good faith and with due diligence. Unfortunately, sometimes suppliers are not seen in the same light. Designers often think, "They're there to make me look good or they won't get any more of my valuable business." It's human nature to view things from one perspective.

Successful designers realize they must be respected as good business people. If you are anything less, you will lose the respect of your clients. After all, how can your clients feel that you can affect their bottom line if you appear not to control your own? In this day of "partnering," clients don't want vendors. They want a much more interactive relationship with design and their designers.

If you are a part of your client's team, then your vendors must be part of your team. Know the rules of doing business the right way. If you don't, you may end up with a bad reputation amongst your suppliers that will be irreversible. To think they don't communicate with each other is to forget how much we communicate with each other as designers.

RULES FOR WORKING WITH SUPPLIERS

1. **Never falsely represent yourself or your needs.** Asking for a low price because of all the "potential" work is a prime example. Over and over again, even if made in earnest, this promise is a jinx. Besides, you hate it when this carrot is dangled in front of you by a potential client.

2. **Don't ask for speculative work.** Asking freelancers to do what you would never do—speculative design—plays on their need for work. Some design firms will only pay a freelancer if the work done by the freelancer is accepted by their client. No other industry would think of asking a worker to do this for services rendered.

   Asking a printer for free work for future projects is an example of "work for ransom." For example, you ask a printer to print your company brochure because of a big project in the offing or the promise of an account you really don't have control over. This is just another form of asking for spec work.

3.   **Never ask for under-the-table remuneration.** An example of this is a "finder's fee." This is a one-time commission paid to you for work you've brought to a supplier. Let's say you are purchasing printing for a client, or referring a client directly to a printer. You tell the printer that you expect a commission for finding this project. This should be something that has been agreed on in advance. Don't bring it up after you've referred the printer to this account. Don't expect a finder's fee to be a continuing royalty for future work. Just like it sounds, it is a fee for finding, not keeping your client happy.

     Kickbacks or hidden commissions are done under the table. Suppliers don't have margins of profit large enough to make sure there is always something in the job to pay a commission to you. They will need to add your commission to the top. There is a good rule of thumb: "If you can't explain your commission to your client, it's wrong."

4.   **Don't take unfair advantage of a supplier in a captive situation.** An example of this is a design firm coercing an inexpensive printer into a team situation on a design and printing project. For instance, a magazine is sent out for bids to three designers and three printers. The design firms are all competitive in pricing and caliber of work. Two of the printers are known to be expensive and the third will most certainly be low. One of the design firms controls a substantial amount of work done by the inexpensive printer. The design firm forces the printer to agree not to offer a quote to the magazine publisher without including a quote for design by them. Other design firms and printers bidding separately stand less of a chance of staying competitive. The "combined only" bid makes the design firm look good, but severely limits the printer.

5.   **Don't prepare vague Requests for Quotations (RFQs).** This is deliberately asking a vendor for a price knowing you have wiggle room to get more than they'd normally give. An example of this is confusing a photographer or illustrator by minimizing the actual assignment, which, for them, will mean more time than they've included in their estimate.

     If you are sincere in your RFQ, you will do your homework so there are no loose ends. Designers are often given vague specifications by clients out of ignorance. Creativity is hard enough to price, but specs that are open ended can be disastrous. A good example is an RFQ for the design and production of a publication with no mention of the number of pages. The firms bidding aren't mind-readers and, unless the scope of work is defined by the client, a bid is useless.

6. **Don't ask suppliers for materials that you know won't lead to a sale.**
   Stock photography is often a victim of cavalier designers. For years,
   advertising agencies would use stock transparencies as images for major
   campaign pitches and not pay for them. They would order the images
   for consideration, use them for layouts, and then return them. Now the
   stock houses offer low-resolution images for the designer to use in layouts. These images won't offer the unscrupulous designer enough definition for print. When it comes to the Internet, and the creation of Web
   sites, the low-resolution image is good enough and the stock photo
   agencies depend on honest designers.

   Paper merchants are often victims of misuse. Typically a designer
   will request paper samples/dummies and make up a layout for the client.
   The finished work is turned over to the printer. Here is where the problem lies. Paper mills typically let more than one merchant carry their
   products and this allows printers to shop price. The friendly merchant,
   who helped the designer, may never get the final sale. Designers can do
   several things to alleviate this situation. One is to let the printer know
   that a certain merchant has been a great help and that you would like
   him to be considered. Another is to let the paper merchant know who
   the printer is. This at least gives him a chance to approach the printer.
   The optimum is to make the paper merchant part of the bid process.
   This can be done by simply including the merchant within the printing
   specifications. In your RFQ, the bidders are told that your paper merchant will be the only supplier used on this specific job. You may get
   some disgruntled printers, but at least they all have the same restriction.
   You'll be in the minority of design firms doing this, but you'll have the
   undying gratitude of the paper merchant.

7. **Don't mislead suppliers in billing procedures.** Telling the supplier to
   bill your client at the end of a project when it's always been assumed that
   you'd be invoiced, is taking unfair advantage of a situation. The better
   your relationship is with the vendor, the worse the sin. If you know your
   client is "slow-paying," this is unforgivable.

8. **Don't provide false schedules.** This is the opposite of building in time
   so that there will be a cushion for both you and the supplier. Don't go
   into a project planning to compress the schedule once work has begun.
   If the supplier knew the real schedule, overtime would have to be a factor within the quote. Clients sometimes do this to designers; they get a
   quote for a normal turnaround, then compress the schedule. Doing this
   to your suppliers is not fair play.

9. **Never establish new credit terms after a job's completion.** If you
   know you can't live with thirty-day terms, be up front about it. Your
   suppliers are not there to finance your business. Never agree to credit

terms you know you can't adhere to. This is false representation and will come back to haunt you when you need this supplier. Your word is your credit and vice versa.

10. **Don't reject work to elicit corrections of your own mistakes.** Printing is often a vehicle for this type of abuse. The scenario is this: a printing job is commercially acceptable but the designer or client has made a mistake. Because of a minor printer's error the designer then demands a reprint and asks for additional changes or corrections. Making any changes other than correcting their own mistake is not a practice followed by most printers and should not be asked for by the designer. Normally they will offer to make the original correction, but nothing else. This is detailed in the Printing Trade Customs because it is often a way for a customer to correct its own mistake or mistakes for free. Unfortunately some printers may be hungry enough to break this rule. Fortunately most won't.

11. **Protect yourself, know your liabilities.** Take proper precautions when the property of suppliers is in your possession. Some materials won't need to be returned, while others may be originals and require insurance coverage on your part. Original paintings, original photography in film versions, and other valuable property may exceed your normal business insurance. You are responsible for the replacement value and you should obtain a rider when these items are in your possession.

   The best way to cope with an unforeseen loss of client's valuables is to list every scenario and every type of valuable paper in your possession or that could possibly be in your possession. Then sit down with your insurance agent and find out what you need.

12. **Treat your suppliers as you would like to be treated.** We will get far more positive response when we offer our suppliers the professional respect and consideration we expect from our clients. If we don't, we will get more than just bad service, we will have a bad reputation and that can be irreversible. Think about the suppliers you've been warned about and remember: word travels quickly.

   Like us, our suppliers have their own suppliers. Because they are so conscious of their own vulnerability, they treat their suppliers well, knowing they need all the support they can get.

   To better understand business ethics and liabilities, ask questions first. Every facet of design has experts available to answer your questions. These are some, but hardly all of the ethical abuses that may tempt designers as well as their clients. While you can't go to jail for abusing ethics, you can ruin your reputation with your suppliers and impede your ability to compete successfully.

15

Print Design and Environmental Responsibility

DON CARLI

Reprinted from AIGA Design Business and Ethics,
"Chapter 7: Print Design and Environmental Responsibility."

LETTER FROM THE DIRECTOR

AIGA IS OFTEN associated solely with its role in celebrating examples of design that are unforgettable for their creativity, finesse, effect, and beauty. Yet AIGA also is committed to advancing professional and ethical standards for the design profession, and to encouraging greater understanding of the fundamental value and relevance of design to business and society.

This chapter (reprinted from the brochure created for the *AIGA Design Business and Ethics* series) provides designers and other graphic communications professionals with an introduction to design and print production practices that demonstrate respect for the challenges of one of the truly critical issues of our age: the balance between economic gain and environmental degradation. For design to be responsive to a client's needs, it should be responsible and appropriate. Appropriateness, in the twenty-first century, will entail respect for resource constraints.

This primer includes best-practices tips and links to resources that will enhance your ability to design, produce, and purchase print responsibly. Social responsibility has economic and environmental dimensions. This broad perspective is often described as a commitment to "sustainability," which has become a term-of-art for advancing economic activity while ensuring that we can sustain our activities in a sometimes fragile world without harming the future's potential. Showing respect for these consequences is no longer a fringe issue. Businesses are driving this agenda, and designers must learn to be trusted advisors on responsible communication techniques to serve clients effectively.

Business is beginning to understand how important a commitment to sustainability is in its strategic positioning and long-term economic well-being. This awareness of the issue—if not demonstrable performance—is becoming mainstream in business thinking. It is critical to the designer, as a trusted advisor to business on communication and positioning issues and as a crafter of design artifacts, that the profession also make these issues mainstream in its thinking.

We hope that this primer will address myths and misconceptions that reduce the impact of design, help designers understand the criteria they should use in taking a project to print, and address practical questions that will help designers in their quest.

—Richard Grefé, Executive Director, AIGA

PRINT DESIGN AND ENVIRONMENTAL RESPONSIBILITY

> Design decisions are among the most critical issues in determining the external impacts of a product, service, or communication over its entire life cycle. Designers, in pursuit of appropriate responses to client needs, have ethical responsibilities to provide work that minimizes adverse (i.e., unreasonable or inappropriate) consequences, creates value, and engenders positive results.[1]

The highest and best use of a designer's special talents is creativity and skill in addressing a client's communication needs while balancing the economic, social, and environmental consequences of his or her design recommendations. Designers, along with those in many other professions, have an obligation to "do no harm." Designers serving clients, stakeholders, and the public in pursuit of this goal can create special value and play a crucial role in supporting the requirements of business to be environmentally and socially responsible.

While there are comparatively few negative environmental effects *directly* associated with the design and procurement of print, design decisions made in the initial stages of a product life cycle, even when the product is a communication strategy, predetermine many of the waste streams and environmental damages associated with printed matter.

Whether your design decisions are governed by the inspiration of a muse, the rational arguments of business logic, or some combination of the two, this guide should help you see more clearly a path toward responsible design for print.

There are many interpretations of the term "sustainability," and its definition continues to evolve as global debate on the topic widens. For some it means maintaining the status quo. For others it is equated with notions of responsibility, conservation, and stewardship. However, for a growing number of people, sustainability is a concept associated with "sustainable development," the first definition of which was articulated in the United Nations World Conservation Strategy of 1980. "Development" in this context includes economic growth, human rights, and the satisfaction of basic human needs:

> For development to be sustainable, it must take account of social and ecological factors, as well as economic ones; of the living and non-living resource base; and of the long-term as well as the short-term advantages and disadvantages of alternative action.

Regardless of which definition of sustainability resonates with your views, there are several myths and misconceptions about it that this guide will help you confront.

Myth 1

Print design is not an environmental issue.

The production of paper and printing have never been more sensitive to environmental concerns than they are today. Yet there has never been a greater need for continuing to improve upon the *status quo.*

Despite predictions that digital media will result in less printing, the use of print has been on the rise since the invention of movable type by Bi Sheng in the year A.D. 1045. Americans in particular are prodigious consumers of printed products and paper. Although the United States represents less than 5 percent of the world's population, it consumes more than 25 percent of the world's paper and printed products.

Americans receive over 65 billion pieces of unsolicited mail each year, equal to 230 appeals, catalogs, and advertisements for every person in the country. According to the not-for-profit organization Environmental Defense, seventeen billion catalogs were produced in 2001 using mostly 100 percent virgin fiber paper. That is sixty-four catalogs for every person in America.

According to the American Forest and Paper Association, the average American uses more than 748 pounds of paper per year, and waste paper is America's single largest export by weight. It takes about sixty-eight million trees per year to produce the catalogs and appeals we receive annually, yet nearly half of this mail is thrown out unopened. For companies like Anheuser Busch and Coca-Cola, primary packaging is their single largest expenditure, and discarded packaging represents over 30 percent of the solid waste buried in U.S. landfills each year.

A common perception is that the adverse environmental impact of paper use is the consumption of trees. In fact, since trees are a renewable resource, their use in paper is not as detrimental to ecological balance as the damage incurred in the process of converting wood to paper. Paper manufacturing alone is the third largest use of fossil fuels worldwide and the single largest industrial use of water per pound of finished product. Printing inks and toner are the second largest uses of carbon black, which is primarily manufactured by the incomplete combustion of oil. Even the manufacture of soy-based inks typically involves the extensive use of diesel fuel, petroleum-based pesticides, and herbicides. In addition, some question the use of ink made from genetically modified soy due to genetic pollution risks to organic farming.

If all of the world's more than six billion people were to design, produce, consume, and dispose of paper and print as North Americans do, we would require four times the resources available on our planet and would still not be able to achieve sustainable economic growth.

Design choices play a major role in determining the financial, environmental, and social consequences associated with the selection of raw materials and processes employed in the production of printed products. This places the design profession in a pivotal role in determining the character of the environmental impacts from printing, including the emission of greenhouse gases and persistent organic pollutants.

To those concerned with the fragile balance of our ecology, the dangers have been clear. From the perspective of designers, however, it is also important to observe an increasing influence on clients' behavior: growing pressure from investors, employees, and other stakeholders to change the manner of their consumption of forest products, paper, and packaging.

Myth 2

There is a limited market demand for environmentally responsible design and print production.

Green printing and environmentally responsible design have operated on the fringes of commerce since the publication of Rachel Carson's *Silent Spring* in 1962, but a "perfect storm" of corporate scandals and rising concern about global warming, water shortages, and other threats to life as we know it are changing the governance and purchasing priorities of business.

Both business and governmental leaders are now struggling to restore investor and consumer confidence in financial markets. This struggle has increased the number of major corporations that are embracing the concept of corporate social responsibility (CSR) and making it an organizing principle for public corporate governance reform and business management. One international business initiative to codify the reporting of corporate social responsibility is the Global Reporting Initiative (GRI), a coalition of businesses that are defining the measures for reporting corporate activity according to a "triple bottom line" of economic, social and environmental impacts.

Increasingly, it is likely that corporations will be asking designers to create CSR and GRI reports along with their traditional annual reports. A time may come when performance reports will combine the attributes of all of these into a single statement expected by the public and investing community. According to the annual report of the UN Global Compact, more than 1,000 companies from fifty-three countries are now participating in voluntary Global Compact initiatives for the management and reporting of corporate social responsibility (CSR) in their annual reports. This represents an increase of 100 percent in 2002/2003 alone.

Business leaders at companies such as DuPont, Johnson & Johnson, Procter & Gamble, and Toyota are moving from seeing environmental stewardship as a necessary evil to viewing sustainability as a driver of top-line growth and opportunity. For many of the world's largest transnational corporations, sustainability has become the central focus of efforts to secure their future economic growth and create new markets for their products. Yet few have managed to integrate it successfully into their current, ongoing operational decision-making and business practices. The need for print solutions with improved financial, social, and environmental performance is becoming a high priority for companies that rely heavily on print in industries like consumer goods, publishing, retail, and banking.

Designers have an opportunity to create measurable "triple bottom line" value for their clients by viewing their design and production decisions—a highly visible public expenditure of clients' funds, if not a major portion of their total expenditures—through a lens of sustainable business principles and ethical priorities. This challenge to designers involves both content and form: designers can counsel their clients on the form of the message, while also balancing their aesthetic decisions from economic, social, and environmental perspectives. The significance of print media to business has spawned a number of sustainable design initiatives that address core concepts and issues from which designers and other graphic communications professionals can derive valuable insights. Examples include the U.S. Environmental Protection Agency's (EPA's) Cradle-to-Cradle Design Award and the recently announced Resource Conservation Challenge.[2]

The economic, social, and environmental impacts of print are substantial, although they are hidden in plain sight. According to an analysis of 1999 U.S. Department of Commerce figures, paper and commercial printing expenditures represent 10 to 15 percent of all corporate expenditures exclusive of labor. For publishers, the figure is 35 percent. However, despite its magnitude, print is typically not the first area of concern subjected to scrutiny when companies make sustainability a priority. This is the case for at least five reasons:

- ❏ Printing is seen as a necessary evil rather than as a mission-critical activity.

- ❏ Print-related activities are not managed centrally.

- ❏ The total costs of print—direct and indirect, long-term lifecycle costs—to the enterprise are seldom measured.

❑ Print is so pervasive that it is taken for granted.

❑ Design and printing processes are seen more as art than science.

However, there is growing evidence that the environmental and social aspects of publishing, printing, and packaging cannot be ignored indefinitely. For example, there is a work group of the Global Environmental Management Initiative that is investigating ways in which companies can identify environmental issues along their supply chains, including environmentally preferable enterprise publishing, printing, and packaging.[3]

This increased attention to environmental responsibility can be an opportunity for designers to be seen as critical advisors to corporations on how to reduce their negative impacts without compromising the imperative for product differentiation and promotion through design and printing.

Prescient designers will neither be discouraged by lack of interest on the part of traditional print buyers, nor will they wait for environmentally preferable purchasing criteria to be established. Rather, they will seek out corporate sustainability officers, marketing and strategy executives, and other corporate executives for whom management of corporate social responsibility is a key priority. There is no need for environmentally preferable print to require aesthetic compromise or unreasonable premiums, and the brand image value of responsible print has measurable importance. For example, a partnership between CitiGroup and Environmental Defense[4] is expected to generate annual savings of 1,000 tons of solid waste, nineteen million gallons of wastewater pollution, and 2,000 tons of greenhouse gas emissions with no increase in direct costs. At Citibank's current rate of annual paper use, this change alone will result in potential savings of 6,700 tons of wood each year, enough to build 500 average single-family homes in the United States.

Myth 3

Business leaders are concerned only with reducing costs and generating profits.

The evidence is clear that there is abundant need for the restoration of trust in business. According to a recent survey of more than 160 senior executives conducted by Nima Hunter Inc. in conjunction with Ethical Corporation magazine, the management of corporate social responsibility in accordance with the principle of sustainability is seen as the key to regaining that trust.[5] In the words of Dow Chemical chairman William S. Stavropoulos:

Companies that don't meet their responsibilities to all their constituencies will have a difficult time. Responsible customers won't want to buy their products. Talented people won't want to work for them. Enlightened communities won't want them as neighbors. And wise investors won't entrust them with their economic futures.

One of the first steps taken by corporate leaders upon having a CSR epiphany is to commission the publication of a corporate social responsibility report to signal their conversion. With the erosion of trust in business brought about by the rash of recent scandals and a sagging economy, there has been a bull market in the number of corporate sustainability and environmental reports being published by Fortune 500 companies. Graphic designers with a sensitivity toward and knowledge of these issues are crafting the messages as well as the form of these reports.

According to a recent CSR Network and Cameron Cole survey of the environmental, social, and sustainability reporting practices of the one hundred largest companies in the world, almost half are producing global, environmental, or social reports. These reports typically exemplify the state of the art in sustainable design and printing. However, designers and printers should look beyond CSR reports and seek opportunities to apply sustainable design principles to advertising, direct mail, packaging, and other uses of print. Corporations are facing increasing criticism that CSR reports alone are not enough.

Investors, employees, and nongovernmental organizations (or NGOs, the large number of nonprofit organizations that are concerned with corporate responsibility and environmental issues) are looking for evidence that the concept of sustainability is being adopted root and branch at every level of the organization and throughout corporate supply chains. It is the need to put the principles of sustainability into practice at a grassroots level that presents graphic communication professionals with their most significant challenges and opportunities.

The challenge is to work as a partner with clients to design solutions that create less waste, less negative impact on the environment, and more value to stakeholders. Sustainable design strategies are the key to print's future. To quote designer/architect William McDonough: "You don't filter smokestacks or water. Instead, you put the filter in your head and design the problem out of existence."

Myth 4

Using paper with recycled content and soy-based inks will eliminate the negative impacts of print.

One way of dealing with complexity is avoidance. Another is oversimplification. The specification of postconsumer recycled paper and the use of ink based on renewable resources are important steps in the right direction. However, designers need to avoid simplistic approaches. They need to know more, do more, and demand more if design, printing, and printers are to contribute to sustainable processes of production. It is important to specify recycled paper, but it is not enough.

There are four essential aspects of recycling:

□ The design of products that use less virgin material and that themselves can be recycled;

□ The manufacture of these materials into new recyclable products;

□ The collection and processing of recyclable materials;

□ The specification, purchase, and use of recycled-content products.

Whether the issue is paper, ink, or the selection of a printer, designers and specifiers make environmentally preferable choices only when the environmental "lifecycle" aspects and impacts of their raw material and production process choices are evaluated against alternatives. A lifecycle analysis (LCA) involves measurement and/or estimation of how much energy and raw materials are used and how much solid, liquid, and gaseous waste is generated at each stage of the product's life, from the extraction of the raw materials used in its production and distribution, through to its use, possible reuse or recycling, and its eventual disposal.

The sustainability of a product or process requires an analysis of more than recycled paper content or soy ink content. How a product is printed, distributed, used, and recovered is as important as the raw materials it is made of. When developing designs or advising clients, designers should learn to consider the entire production process, from paper choices to printing methods to distribution, use, and recovery of resources.

Ask suppliers whether they can provide independently verified information about the lifecycle environmental impacts of materials and processes. Manufacturers can apply for the International Standards Organization (ISO) 14000 series of standards, an international benchmark for commitment to continuous improvement in environmentally responsible performance; as a consumer or specifier, the designer can ask whether a manufacturer is ISO 14000-qualified. Favor vendors and suppliers that measure, manage, and report on the total environmental performance of their products and services based on a standard such as the ISO 14042 Lifecycle Assessment model.[6] Companies such as HP offer best-practice examples, along with efforts of organizations participating in international Environmental Product Declaration initiatives.[7]

Manufacturers of printing equipment, paper, ink, toner, and other chemicals employed in printing and packaging like Heidelberg, HP, MeadWestvaco, Domtar, NewLeaf, Stora Enso, DuPont, 3M, and Dow Chemical recognize the value of sustainable development, yet much of what they have accomplished is not visible to customers. Ironically, some companies see little evidence of demand for sustainable solutions among printers and other buyers of their products. In part, this may be due to the complex specification and purchasing relationships that exist among designers, printers, and corporate clients. In part, it may be due to lack of information, lack of awareness, lack of knowledge, or apathy on the part of buyers.

One indication of this lack of attention is apparent in exploring the issue on the Web. At the time this guide was written, using the popular search engine Google yielded over 1.5 million citations for the term "sustainable development" and more than 178,000 citations for the term "corporate social responsibility." In contrast, searching the term "sustainable design" resulted in only 73,500 citations, most of which had to do with industrial or architectural design. Searching the term "sustainable print" yielded thirty-eight citations, while searching "sustainable print design" yielded none.

Designers have an opportunity to make their interest in environmentally preferable products and services known. To be credible, designers and graphic communication professionals will need to learn to speak the language of sustainability and to engage vendors, suppliers, customers and other stakeholders in this issue. Designers also have an obligation to themselves and to their profession to seek the knowledge and skill required to move sustainable design from the margins to the mainstream of design practice and business communications in print.

Myth 5

There are no sources of information, training programs, or services available to support efforts to design and produce print in a sustainable manner.

An abundance of information about sustainability exists, as does a vast array of training, education, and support services available from colleges, universities, community centers, federal and state government, consulting firms, and not-for-profit organizations. In addition to the footnotes in this guide, a list of Web links to useful resources is provided in the appendix.

Designers can seek assistance and support from not-for-profit organizations like Conservatree,[8] Environmental Defense,[9] or The Institute for Sustainable Communication.[10] Designers can also make use of certification systems and guides for the evaluation of lifecycle environmental impacts from organizations like the Forest Stewardship Council[11] and The Nordic Swan.[12] Efforts such as the United Nations Environmental Program's Lifecycle Thinking Initiative also provides tools, training, and support for lifecycle environmental management.[13]

The EPA's Design for the Environment program[14] is but one of many that promotes the integration of cleaner, cheaper, and smarter solutions into a wide variety of everyday products and business practices. Also, a coalition of fifty-six environmental groups recently crafted a common vision for environmentally preferable paper that is being adopted by a growing number of companies.[15]

Conservation of resources associated with paper use is among the high-priority challenges identified by the EPA's Resource Conservation Challenge (RCC).[16] The RCC program is a major national effort to find flexible yet more protective ways to conserve our valuable resources through waste reduction and energy recovery activities. These activities will improve public health and the environment and are also supported by the American Forest and Paper Association.

Recommendations and Information Resources

1. *Environmental issues to consider when designing or specifying raw materials or printing processes*:

   Design-for-environment and lifecycle-management principles are the most significant issues to consider when designing or specifying printing. Organizations like Nordic Swan[17] have proven that lifecycle concepts can be successfully employed in the design, specification, production, and procurement of a wide array of products and processes, including printing and packaging.

   It is important for designers to identify and partner with capable and responsible suppliers who share a commitment to "beyond compliance" environmental management in order to fully evaluate and minimize the adverse environmental impacts of design choices and production process alternatives.

2. *Principles of environmentally responsible print design.*

   ❏ Rethink features and functions to use less material and less energy.

   ❏ Consider closed-loop lifecycles from design through production, use, and recovery.

   ❏ Design for recyclability, reusability, and recoverability of energy and materials.

   ❏ Seek independently verified data about environmental aspects and lifecycle impacts.

   ❏ Select materials with less impact and toxicity (via air, water, and solid waste streams).

   ❏ Increase use of recycled and renewable materials.

   ❏ Optimize production techniques to eliminate scrap, error, and waste.

   ❏ Select lower-impact packaging and distribution systems.

   ❏ Design for reduced energy use, water use, and waste impacts during use.

   ❏ Maximize the length of the product's useful life.

   ❏ Recover, reuse, and recycle materials at end of the product's life.

3. *Criteria to consider in selecting a printer*:

   ❏ Management commitment to environmental stewardship that extends beyond legal compliance;

- All major suppliers and subcontractors are informed of the environmental policy and encouraged to adopt similar standards;

- A dedicated manager for environmental health and safety;

- Standards-based environmental and quality management systems;

- Evidence of lifecycle thinking and continuous improvement applied to key products, services offerings, and business practices.

In addition to the criteria listed above, designers and specifiers should evaluate printers based on a number of other factors. This checklist is not a set of threshold attributes for a responsible printer, although it does detail aspects of a printer's approach toward sustainable practices that a designer should know if he or she is to use a printer consistently while also advising clients on the choice of printers. Increasingly, clients may need to report information like this pertinent to their procurement and supply chain activities in their CSR reports and/or in their annual reports:

- Facilities location, orderliness, cleanliness, and environmental conditions;

- Published environmental performance improvement goals and objectives;

- Quality management processes;

- Stakeholder relationship management processes;

- Raw materials lifecycle analysis data;

- Worker health and safety data;

- Fuel and energy use data;

- Water use data;

- Air emissions data;

- Solid waste recycling and disposal data;

- Toxic emissions reporting data;

- Transportation and storage of raw materials and finished goods;

- Environmental violations, fines, and lawsuits;

- Community involvement and corporate philanthropic activities;

- Public disclosure and verification of performance and improvement goals;

- ☐ Innovative use of clean technologies and sustainable business practices;

- ☐ Environmental stewardship certifications, citations, and awards.

In addition, designers and specifiers should evaluate the degree to which printing companies support environmental and sustainability education, training, and awareness-building initiatives with supplier, community, governmental, and non-governmental organizations.

Finally, designers should assess the degree to which individual employees are encouraged to assume leadership and supporting roles as volunteers in community and industry efforts to promote sustainable development and corporate social responsibility.

It is important to note that due to more stringent regulatory environments, printers in Europe and Canada have adopted formal environmental management systems and certifications to a far greater extent than is the case in the U.S., but global transnational corporations are finding that there are advantages to adhering to a single set of strict standards.

The most prevalent standard for environmental management systems in existence is the International Standards Organization (ISO) 14001 standard. It is important to note that ISO 14001 does not mandate any specific level of environmental performance or reporting. Rather, it provides a continuous improvement framework, which can be adapted on a firm-by-firm basis. Therefore, one should not assume that ISO 14001 alone is a reliable indicator of sustainable business practices.

Some may believe that the list of issues and performance factors described above is an impossible, impractical, or economically infeasible threshold. Yet there are numerous examples of large, small, and medium-sized printers in Europe and Canada and the U.S. that score well on all of these factors.

One example of particular note is the British printing company Beacon Press Ltd.,[18] a sixty-person company founded in 1976 that is located in Uckfield, East Sussex. Beacon Press has won more than twenty-one awards for its environmental management system. Among its many achievements, Beacon Press has reduced its gas consumption by 46 percent and its water use by 57 percent since 1995. It has totally eliminated all alcohol used in the printing process. It uses vegetable-based inks, recycles 95 percent of all dry waste, uses green electricity generated from renewable sources, and 95 percent of its press-cleaning solvents are recycled for further use. Beacon Press has made a corporate commitment to participate in the British government's voluntary initiative to reduce CO_2 emissions, waste, and water consumption by 2005 and to report on the effectiveness of its efforts through a series of twenty-one performance indicators that are objectively measured each month. Beacon also donates 1 percent of its profit to community investment and is a member of the

Campaign to Protect Rural England (CPRE), Earthwatch, the World Wildlife Fund, the 95+ Group and the United Nations Pioneers in Responsible Enterprise Project.

Designers should note that there are many printing companies in Europe that have profiles similar to Beacon's, but there are comparatively few in the United States. At present, of the more than 40,000 printing companies in the U.S., only six currently have ISO 14001-certified environmental management systems. While printing companies that have taken a proactive stance are the exception rather than the rule in the U.S., several have made substantial investments and public commitments that are worthy of recognition. Such companies are forerunners in a "greening" of the American printing industry that will play a critical role in preserving the vitality of our economy, ensuring our international competitiveness, conserving essential natural resources, protecting the environment, and restoring trust in business.

Anderson Lithograph in Los Angeles, a division of Mail-Well Inc., has developed a comprehensive ISO 14001 based approach to the management of "everything that it takes, makes, and wastes." Anderson Lithograph was selected by AIGA as its partner in this brochure in the *AIGA Business and Ethics* series, since it offers a clear and noteworthy example of what can be expected from a printer with a commitment toward a responsible goal (although it is not alone in that role). In addition, Anderson Lithograph actively supports and participates in voluntary programs and pioneers in the application of innovative clean technologies. For example, all electricity is generated through an onsite natural gas-fueled cogeneration facility, which was customized to capture nearly all volatile organic compound (VOC) emissions of both Web and sheet-fed presses. This qualifies Anderson's facility for permanent total enclosure (PTE), as certified by the local Los Angeles County air quality regulatory body. Anderson Lithograph is a member of the Coalition for Environmentally Responsible Economies (CERES), is Forest Stewardship Council Chain of Custody certified, is a member of the California Climate Action Registry and is in the process of becoming ISO 14001 certified.[19]

While Anderson Lithograph is a large operation, another printer worthy of special note is Ideal Jacobs,[20] a small, fourteen-person printing company in northern New Jersey. Not only is it ISO 9000 and ISO 14001 certified, but it has been selected for inclusion in the EPA Performance Track program for companies that consistently meet their legal responsibilities and have implemented high-quality environmental management systems. Ideal Jacobs has also been selected for recognition by the OSHA Safety and Health Achievement Recognition Program (SHARP) for companies with exceptional health and safety systems.

It is through the emulation and encouragement of leaders like Anderson Lithograph and Ideal Jacobs that the environmentally preferable printing alternatives available to designers, print buyers, graphic communications professionals and the organizations they serve will grow. Similarly, it is through the active engagement of marketing communicators, corporate sustainability executives, supply chain executives, and procurement managers at companies that are publicly committed to environmental stewardship and corporate social responsibility management that designers will find new opportunities to put the principles of sustainable design into practice.

Successful engagement requires patience, persistence, and an open mind, as well as willingness to overcome challenges such as listening to critics; identifying champions; securing buy-in from stakeholders; coordinating the activities of internal functions and suppliers; ensuring clear communication between internal functions and suppliers; addressing technical difficulties that can arise and hinder implementation; or confronting difficulties encountered in correctly specifying new materials and production processes.

An excellent place to start your search for prospects is among the 296 companies with CSR reports listed on CSRwire.[21] Other places to connect with business leaders and managers that value environmentally preferable procurement are meetings and conferences associated with organizations such as the National Association for Environmental Management,[22] The Global Environmental Management Initiative (GEMI) Value Chain Workgroup, or the Institute for Supply Management's Commission on Social Responsibility.[23]

Where can I turn for information, training, education, and support for responsible design in print?

Sustainability is a journey rather than a destination. In turn, the following links and resources are offered to start you on the path toward greater awareness of the need for change. The knowledge that you acquire and share with others in the fields of business and print technology will expand the transformative power of design and increase the value of print. The responsibilities of designers and the power of design are aptly described by Stefano Marzano, CEO and chief creative director of Philips Design:

> Design plays a key role in the shift towards a sustainable future. Due to its very nature of bridging socio-cultural developments and technology, design is a powerful engine for sustainable development. And in their privileged role as interpreters and communicators between people and technology, designers can stimulate new ways to satisfy people's needs. In short, they can generate valuable solutions that are economically, socially, and environmentally sustainable. Taking responsibility for tomorrow, today.[24]

For many designers the exploration of sustainable development concepts like lifecycle analysis and triple bottom line analysis may be unfamiliar or challenging. Much of the literature pertaining to sustainable graphic design and environmentally preferable printing has yet to be written. However, there are many not-for-profit organizations, trade associations, educational institutions, and community groups that are converging on the concept of sustainability, and designers should monitor their progress in the interest of always staying ahead of their clients in understanding such critical issues.

Whether your motivation is a moral imperative, a business case, or some combination of the two, we invite you to explore the sources of information currently available (see Resource Links) and join AIGA in raising awareness and capacity for sustainable human communication through the power of design and print.

RESOURCES

AIGA Center for Sustainable Design
sustainability.aiga.org/

Alliance for Climate Protection
www.allianceforclimateprotection.org/

The Alliance for Environmental Innovation
www.environmentaidedefense.org/

American Forest & Paper Association Environmental & Recycling Info
www.afandpa.org/

Beyond Grey Pinstripes
www.beyondgreypinstripes.org/

Bioneers
www.bioneers.org/

Business for Social Responsibility
www.bsr.org/

Center for Design
www.cfd.rmit.edu.au/

The Center for Paper Business and Industry Studies
www.paperstudies.org/

Center for Responsible Business, UC Berkeley
www.haas.berkeley.edu/responsiblebusiness/

The Centre for Sustainable Design
www.cfsd.org/

Ceres
www.ceres.org/

College of the Atlantic: Human Ecology Program
www.coa.edu/

Conservatree
www.conservatree.com/

Cranfield University: Sustainability and Design
www.cranfield.ac.uk/students/prospectus/

Design With Memory
www.designresource.org/

The ECO Design Center
www.ecodesigncenter.com/pages/designer.html/

EcoMarket
www.ecomarket.net/

Eco-Procurement Good Practice Guide
www.iclei-europe.org/

Ecospecifier
www.ecospecifier.org/

The EnviroLink Network
www.envirolink.org/

Environmental Defense
www.environmentaldefense.org/home.cfm/

Environmental Product Declarations
www.environdec.com/

Ethical Corporation Magazine
www.ethicalcorp.com/

Forest Ethics
www.forestethics.org/

Forest Stewardship Council
www.fscus.org/

Global Citizen Center
www.globalcitizencenter.org/

Global Reporting Initiative
www.globalreporting.org/Home/

Global Spine
www.globalspine.com/

GreenBiz
www.grocnbiz.com/

Green Options
www.greenoptions.com/

Guiding Principles of Sustainable Design
www.nps.gov/dsc/dsgncnstr/gpsd/

IDSA Ecodesign Section
www.idsa.org/whatsnew/sections/ecosection/

Institute for Sustainable Communication
www.sustaincom.org/

Live Earth
liveearth.org/

Natural Capitalism
www.natcap.org/

The Natural Step
www.naturalstep.org/com/Start/

Pollution Prevention Pays (P2Pays)
www.p2pays.org/

Print Planet
www.printplanet.com/

Printers' National Environmental Assistance Center
www.pneac.org/

Rainforest Alliance
www.rainforestalliance.org/

Renourish
www.re-nourish.com/

Rocky Mountain Institute
www.rmi.org/

SustainAbility
www.sustainability.com/

United Nations Environment Programme
www.unep.org/

United National Global Compact
www.unglobalcompact.org/

The World Business Council for Sustainable Development
www.wbcsd.ch/

Viridian Design
www.viridiandesign.org/

World Changing
www.worldchanging.com/

World Resources Institute
www.wri.org/

World Watch
www.worldwatch.org/

END NOTES

1. *www.mbdc.com/challenge/*
2. *www.epa.gov/epaoswer/osw/conserve/*
3. *www.gemi.org/docs/work/workgroups.htm*
4. *www.environmentaldefense.org/pressrelease.cfm?ContentID=2861*
5. *www.nimahunter.com/reports.asp*
6. *www.epa.gov/nrmrl/lcaccess/lca101.html*
7. *www.environdec.com/*
8. *www.conservatree.com*
9. *www.edf.org/page.cfm?tagID=1439*
10. *www.sustaincom.org*
11. *www.fscus.org/*
12. *www.svanen.nu/Eng/*
13. *www.uneptie.org/pc/sustain/lcinitiative/background.htm*
14. *www.epa.gov/opptintr/dfe/*
15. *www.conservatree.com/paper/Choose/commonvision.shtml*
16. *www.epa.gov/epaoswer/osw/conserve/*
17. *www.svanen.nu/*

18. *www.beaconpress.co.uk*

19. *www.climateregistry.org/*

20. *www.idealjacobs.com/*

21. *www.csrwire.com/csr/home.mpl*

22. *www.naem.org/*

23. *www.napm.org/AboutISM/ComSocResp.cfm*

24. *www.design.philips.com/*

Part 2

Management

16

Legal Structures for the Design Firm

LEONARD D. DUBOFF

EVERY GRAPHIC DESIGN business has an optimal structure that will provide it with the maximum possible benefits. These may include tax benefits, protection from liability, continuity of existence, and the like. It is important for owners of small businesses to determine which business form will best serve their needs and whether their business objectives can be legally achieved.

SOLE PROPRIETORSHIPS

The simplest form of business is a sole proprietorship. This is the name given to a business that is owned and controlled by a single individual. Little need be done to create a sole proprietorship. All you have to do is obtain a business license if it is required in your jurisdiction and, if you are using a name for your business other than your own, register that as an assumed business name or fictitious name. This simple business form has a major downside though. Sole proprietors have full personal liability for all debts of the business. This means that your house, car, personal bank accounts, and the like will be exposed to the risks of your business. Certainly you can obtain insurance, but insurance policies have limits and some risks are not insurable.

If a sole proprietor hires an employee and the employee commits a wrongful act within the scope of the business, then the sole proprietor will have full personal liability for the employee's wrongful conduct. In addition, if the employee contracts on behalf of the sole proprietorship and the contract is within the scope of that business, the sole proprietor will be liable on the contract, even if it was not authorized or approved.

Sole proprietors pay income tax on their earnings at their individual rates. While most sole proprietors segregate their business bank accounts from their individual bank accounts for a number of practical reasons, the IRS lumps all of the sole proprietor's earnings together for tax purposes. That is, the sole proprietor's personal tax return will reflect business earnings as well as investment or bank interest.

PARTNERSHIPS

When two or more individuals join together for purposes of engaging in a business, then the relationship between them is known as a partnership. No formal acts are necessary to form a partnership, although it is always a good idea to put all of the parties' agreements regarding the business into writing so misunderstandings can be avoided.

A partnership is defined as an arrangement whereby two or more persons act as co-owners and engage in a business for profit. Note that the individuals need not be equal partners, although, if they have not specified a particular relationship, the law presumes that they are equal. Because there are numerous presumptions that attach to the relationship under state laws, it is important for individuals who become partners to specify in writing the terms of the partnership with some particularity in order to avoid confusion.

Each partner has full personal liability for the debts and wrongful acts of any other partner when they occur within the scope of the partnership business. In addition, partners have full personal liability for the acts and the contracts of all partnership employees. For example, if one partner engages in acts of copyright infringement, all partners will be liable for the wrongful conduct, even though only one of the partners was the wrongdoer.

Each partner pays tax on his or her distributable share of partnership profit and may deduct his or her share of partnership losses. Note that tax liability is imposed on the partner even if there is no actual distribution of profit. If, for example, two graphic designers have an equal partnership that earns $50,000 per year and decide to retain those earnings for purposes of expansion, then each partner has a tax liability for $25,000, even though the money was not distributed.

LIMITED PARTNERSHIPS

A type of partnership that can afford some partners' limited liability is known as a limited partnership. This business form is a partnership comprised of one or more general partners who have full personal liability and one or more limited partners who may enjoy limited liability so long as they are not actively involved in running the business. A limited partner may receive financial information and, in some states, retain the right to elect or remove general partners, but the limited partner may not, under any circumstances, conduct the day-to-day operations of the business.

If a limited partner becomes actively involved in determining policy and running the partnership's business, then the active limited partner will have full personal liability as if he or she were a general partner.

Partners in a limited partnership, whether they are general or limited partners, are taxed on distributable profits and may deduct distributable losses. The limited partnership is not taxed as such, though an information return must be filed; individual tax returns of the partners reflect partnership profits and losses. The partnership does file an annual return, but it is for informational purposes only.

One method by which business owners may be shielded from liability for business obligations is to have the business structured as a corporation or some other business form with limited liability.

CORPORATIONS

One of the most popular business forms is the corporation. It is a separate legal entity apart from its owner(s), even if it is owned by one individual. The corporation is responsible for all of its business activities and the owner generally is not. If an employee engages in wrongful conduct within the scope of the business or if the employee involves the corporation in an unfavorable contractual arrangement, the corporation, not the owner, will be liable. With few exceptions, the owners' only exposure when engaging in business in the corporate form is for the assets placed in the corporation.

A corporation is a taxable entity, and it must, therefore, file its own corporate tax return. There is, however, a special type of corporation which may elect, for tax purposes, to be treated as if it were not incorporated. This is the so-called S corporation. Unfortunately, S corporations do not truly pass through profits and losses as if the business were unincorporated, and there are a number of restrictions imposed on businesses with an S corporation status. This form of business is unavailable if any of the shareholders are not American citizens or resident aliens. Certain forms of trusts, nonprofit corporations, and S corporations may own stock in an S corporation. Other business entities such as C corporations may not. There must also be only one class of voting stock in an S corporation. An S corporation may have no more than one hundred owners.

Those who conduct business in the corporate form and desire to provide medical, dental, or prepaid legal insurance for employees may do so by adopting a plan permitting them to fund these benefits with pre-tax dollars. In addition, the benefits are not taxable to the employee recipients. This is available only for corporations that are considered taxable entities, not S corporations. A properly structured contract between the corporation and its shareholders could provide for a tax-deductible life insurance program. This type of arrangement is also available only for regular or C corporations, which are taxable entities.

A C corporation must retain its losses and carry them forward until it has earned profits that can be netted against those losses. The individual owners may not personally net those losses against their individual earnings. In addition, if money is paid to shareholders on account of their stock interest as dividends, then that money will be taxed to the recipient and may not be deducted by the corporation. Essentially, then, this money is taxed twice, though only at a flat 10 percent to the shareholder.

There are a number of methods by which a business attorney can structure a graphic arts business in order to maximize liability protection while minimizing tax. If, for example, the parties have conducted their business under a particular name or logo, then they can protect that trademark and continue to use it when they set up their business form. The trademark could be owned by the business, or a more sophisticated plan could be implemented. For instance, if the owners personally retain ownership of that mark and register it in their own names, they can license the mark to their graphic design business and obtain some benefits, including royalty payments. Royalty income is known as passive income and is exempt from certain employment related taxes. There are, thus, some tax benefits in having a licensing arrangement between the business owners who are also owners of the trademark.

It is common for owners of small businesses, including graphic design businesses, to be employees of their businesses. The money paid to employees as wages is known as earned income, and that income is subject to all employment taxes. Earned income is also deductible by a corporation, which is a taxable entity. This means that even though the corporation earned a considerable amount of money, it may pay that money out in salaries and payroll withholding expenses so long as the salary is reasonable, and, thus, have no taxable income at year-end.

LIMITED LIABILITY COMPANIES

One of the newest business forms is known as a limited liability company (LLC). This business form allows the individual owners to achieve the same kind of liability shield they would have in a corporation with greater flexibility. The LLC was initially created for the purpose of providing individuals and businesses who could not qualify for S corporation status and who wanted to create a business entity as a liability shield, while also enjoying the ability to pass through earnings as if the business were conducted as a sole proprietorship or partnership. In addition, the LLC provides a more informal business structure.

Today, creators of an LLC can elect tax treatment as if the LLC is a taxable entity like a C corporation or they can choose to be treated as if they are conducting business as a sole proprietorship or partners similar to an S corporation. All they need do is "check the box" and this can be accomplished either when the LLC is created or, if appropriate steps are taken, when the first tax return is filed.

LLCs can be run by a single manager or by the owners as a group. Here, too, the parties need only specify their choice in the LLC's documents. Unlike corporations, which are required to have annual meetings for the purpose of electing directors and appointing officers, LLCs can function informally. Once the articles of organization are filed with the state, the internal working document known as the operating agreement can specify whatever the parties wish for an organizational structure and any other formalities they deem appropriate.

S corporations and LLCs electing pass through treatment are not taxable entities. The owners must pay tax on their distributable profits and may deduct their pro rata share of business losses. It would, therefore, be important for you to determine whether your graphic design business is likely to lose money during the formative years. If so, it may be in your best interest to create an S corporation or an LLC. In this way, your business losses may be netted against your personal earnings from other sources.

Owners of small businesses frequently retain earnings in their business entities rather than drawing them out for purposes of growth and expansion. Accumulated earnings beyond certain maximums must be justified as reasonable for the needs of the business. Otherwise, they will be subject to a tax of 15 percent in addition to the regular corporate tax. A maximum accumulation of $250,000 is allowed for most businesses, though for businesses whose principal work is in the fields of health, law, engineering, architecture, accounting, actuarial science, performing arts, or consulting, the maximum is $150,000.

There are numerous other considerations that affect the determination of what business form will best serve your interests and maximize your business security. A skilled business lawyer can assist you in making that determination and helping you realize your objectives.

17

Principles of Design
Firm Management

SHEL PERKINS

PROFESSIONAL DESIGN FIRMS present unusual organizational and management challenges. How do we support something as intangible as creativity? How do we stabilize something in constant motion? What sort of valid comparisons can be made between things that are unique? How can personal needs and business needs overlap to a great extent yet not be identical? What happens when we have to make a decision that's good for the business but perhaps not for us personally? Each creative organization must meet these challenges in its own way. Organizing and nurturing a design studio means not only challenging, motivating, and rewarding the individual staff members but also perceiving and meeting the needs of the firm itself while maintaining a strong and consistent client orientation.

I'd like to share some thoughts about appropriate organizational structures and management approaches. These ideas are presented in fairly broad terms, and some important topics, such as marketing, will only be mentioned in passing. My emphasis here is on the vision of the firm, and how that is expressed in the business structure and supported by daily operations.

In order to successfully launch a new firm, the founders must be prepared. They must have experience in producing quality design. A vision of what they want to accomplish and what the focus of the new firm is is also necessary. This vision must be supported by a detailed business plan that includes an analysis of the market demand for the kind of services the firm will offer, an accurate evaluation of the competition, and a realistic budget of the revenues and expenses that can be expected during the first year of operations. Preparation of a business plan is essential because it is a declaration of mission—a narrative of who the firm is and what it cares about—and it establishes the standards for success.

It is important that the new firm be adequately capitalized. Exactly how much capital is required is a matter for discussion. A conservative advisor would say that it's not unusual for a new business to take two years to break even, so it should have enough cash and financing available to cover overhead for twenty-four months. My approach is less conservative because it is based on the assumption that a studio should not be opened until it already has client work lined up. Each new firm must have at least one major client account, plus a step-by-step plan for winning additional accounts in very short order. Having a major account from day one means that we are doing billable work that will be invoiced in the first thirty to forty-five days and payment from the client will be received thirty to forty-five days after the invoice has gone out. If we are certain that our billings will be enough to cover our overhead, and if we are certain that it will take no longer than ninety days for us to turn labor into cash, then the firm could start with enough money on hand to pay for start-up costs and at least the first ninety days of expenses.

I want to emphasize that founders need good advice from professionals outside of design: an attorney who can help with legal requirements and contractual issues in dealings with both clients and employees; an accountant to advise on general financial management and tax issues; a banker for assistance with financing and cash management for the growing firm; and a business insurance agent who can offer guidance on risk management. These advisors should be consulted well in advance of opening the doors. In particular, the accountant and the banker can be of great service in evaluating plans and advising on capital needs.

In observing the growth of new firms, I would suggest that there is a pattern. The first three or four years are the start-up phase, and those years are often quite turbulent. It takes that long for a firm to establish its client base and reputation, and to evolve its own internal organizational structure and culture to the point where projects can consistently be completed in a profitable way.

In the graphic design profession, firms that have successfully graduated from that start-up stage often find themselves to be mid-sized, with a staff of somewhere between eleven and twenty-five people. Continued success will create continued opportunities for growth. However, growth is not something that happens automatically. It is a conscious decision that is made in response to each opportunity that presents itself.

Decisions about growth must be tied into the overall business plan. There are positive aspects as well as risks. If a large new project or client account is accepted, how many new employees will be needed to service it properly? If and when that account ends, how many other accounts will be required to keep the expanded staff busy? On the other hand, a small studio that is largely dependent on one main account is vulnerable. What happens if that client goes out of business or its industry goes into a slump? A larger studio can consciously develop new business relationships that allow it to diversify with multiple clients in multiple industries, so that all of their eggs are not in one basket. Related to that, the firm must choose whether to expand its offer to include a more complete range of services or to concentrate in one special area where it can be perceived as a clear leader.

If the firm decides to grow, that continued expansion will lead to a second period of turbulence as the organization learns to manage larger projects, larger teams, and higher stakes.

OBJECTIVE

The overall objective is to evolve a structure that meets client needs and supports the creative process. There is no cookie-cutter solution to the challenges of establishing and growing a creative firm. There is no off-the-shelf solution from one firm that is going to be a custom fit for another. Each firm provides different services to clients in different markets. Each firm has a different mix of people. The work situation is very fluid and constantly evolving. Over time, each successful firm must evolve a flexible structure that is appropriate for its own activities and that supports coordination of its many commitments.

If the basic objective is to evolve a structure that meets client needs, we need to start by thinking about what those external needs are. Essentially they have to do with quality, efficiency, and service.

EXTERNAL NEEDS

Clients want design firms to bring a new perspective to their business challenges and add value to client enterprises through innovative thinking. They come to design firms for a competitive advantage. So adding value is at the top of the list of external needs. Clients need creative firms that can understand the context of a particular problem as well as provide a depth of understanding on larger issues. Clients want to hire firms that know them, their business, their market, their competitors, and can help them create and profit from opportunities.

Design studios need to provide fast responses for clients. I know we've all been there. We need to produce proposals quickly, and then more often than not the projects themselves need to move along as fast as humanly possible. Fast response is definitely an issue for creative firms.

Clients want to have no confusion about the work that is being done for them. There needs to be clear communication, clearly stated objectives, a shared road map, and frequent updates on progress. For a given project, one senior contact within the studio should be the decision-maker who receives the clients' information and answers their questions.

Clients need to be included in the process so that there are no surprises. They will have different comfort levels of how much they want to be included, but my personal feeling is, the more they are included, the better. An inclusive process features work sessions with the client, discussion documents, and signed client approvals at the end of each interim phase.

It is important to note that, from the client standpoint, the studio structure is not an issue. Clients rarely care how the creative firm is organized internally as long as the work is good and client needs are being met.

INTERNAL NEEDS

Obviously, the studio needs to be doing great design. Quality of design must be a given right from the start and design excellence must be an ongoing priority.

Within the studio, there needs to be a sense of continuity, a sense of history. Information about what the firm has done in the past needs to be available. Project types, professional tasks performed, resources needed, successful schedules, patterns of client activity—these are the design-specific measurements that are important to build into studio management systems.

New proposals need to be informed by past history. What we've done for the client before, how long the project really took, what the materials really cost. The studio needs to have a memory. By drawing on cumulative history, new projects have a better chance of being priced correctly and structured to succeed. The firm may be traveling fast, but it needs to remember where it has been. Reinventing the wheel and repeating past mistakes is wasteful and demoralizing.

In order for a studio to consistently provide fast response to clients, it must have sufficient internal resources. It's important to recognize that this is always going to be a moving target. We need to have the right kind of resources to do the sort of work that we have committed to do, but the work changes constantly. We must continually reevaluate the services that we are marketing and the core competencies of our staff, and get feedback from clients about how well they are being taken care of.

In order to work as effectively as possible, there needs to be excellent ongoing communication within the studio, and a clear understanding of individual responsibilities. Especially in small firms where each team member wears a number of different hats, it's important to know who's wearing which hat at any given time. Sorting the hats and doing some honest self-assessment will identify gaps in skill sets that can be addressed through future hires.

Each firm has a range of needs, and must hire staff members with core competencies in each area. Together, they comprise a spectrum of complementary skills. Small firms will outsource more of those skills, and larger firms will bring more of them in-house. I believe that every firm needs to hire the best across the board and create an all-star team. Let each of the players succeed in their particular area and make sure that there is excellent communication between them all. Distributing responsibilities to the most appropriate staff members will allow the founders of the firm to focus their own energies and prevent their attention from becoming scattered, as well as keep their personal workload manageable.

Active projects should be led by senior people who are good collaborators. Within design firms, these project leaders are often the primary contact for the client, as well as being a manager and mentor to their coworkers. A senior person is experienced in coordinating the activities of a multidisciplinary team. He or she must be well organized, able to prioritize, and achieve results in a sometimes-stressful environment.

A successful studio will establish and maintain a culture of cooperation and concern—a culture that supports negotiation and management of the network of commitments necessary to satisfy both internal and external needs. In addition, the internal structure and business practices need to support the creative process without getting in the way of it. From the point of view of the client and the larger business community, it is primarily the creative work itself that should be visible.

Project after project, year after year, it's important to build these values and concerns into the structure of the firm in such a way that success is sustainable.

MAKE IT SUSTAINABLE

Despite the fact that client services will evolve and there will inevitably be staff turnover, high standards have to be set and maintained in all areas. Design firms need to bring the same commitment and quality to all activities within the studio, both business-related and design-related. This includes selecting and developing good relationships that are mutually beneficial and making sure that all staff members are learning and growing—that a learning organization has been created. To remain in business, there is an obvious need to be consistently profitable. Another need is to have fun. Enjoyment of the work motivates designers and contributes to the freshness of creative solutions. If the fun ever drains away from the practice of design, it will be time to close the doors.

At the risk of stating the obvious, be very careful about managing the workload to make sure that too much isn't taken on at any given time. A good amount of time should be left for work and the appropriate resources should be available to successfully deliver what was promised. This requires effective coordination between all of the activities within the firm. The right hand needs to know what the left hand is doing.

Making the firm sustainable over time means that each individual project has to be structured for success. There are many aspects to a successful project.

STRUCTURING PROJECTS

It's important that the projects be well defined—that the scope of the work is understood and that the base situation is addressed, and not just the symptoms. Key information may come from the client in a request for proposal, but that needs to be fleshed out by the studio into a comprehensive project definition that states the business objective, the market positioning, the competitive environment, the expected business results, and all relevant specifications. It is necessary to establish common goals with the client right at the start and clearly define the deliverables. Management of the client's expectations as the project unfolds, particularly if the definition of the project shifts, is crucial. It is vital to identify those shifts and communicate them in an effective way.

Occasionally a project will be downsized. If the scope of the work is reduced, adjusting the billings downward is an easy matter. However, it is more typical for project changes to expand the scope of work. The studio needs to be diligent about letting clients know the implications of expanded requests by sending change orders that spell out the additional effort that will be involved. There should be no surprises. A change order not only documents who requested what and when, but it gives the client an immediate opportunity to reconsider and renegotiate. The process clarifies the studio's commitments and how those commitments will meet specific client needs.

Project schedules and budgets are obviously tied to detailed specifications. Appropriate pricing cannot be determined until realistic specifications have been agreed upon. Not only do budgets need to account for all costs, but they must also contain an expected profit margin for the studio. Beginning a project without sorting out all of these issues is a recipe for failure. The process of clarifying these issues strengthens the design brief and actually leads to better work.

At the end of each project, the client's satisfaction should be assessed, the services offered refined, and the studio positioned for additional work. It is an important practice to close the loop in this way. An ongoing series of well-managed projects with great design solutions spells success for the firm. Reliable fulfillment builds strong relationships with clients who value professionalism and the competitive advantage provided.

DESIGN-CENTERED ORGANIZATION

From an organizational standpoint, the design of client projects is at the center of the firm, supported by various kinds of support and feedback: marketing activities, traffic, financial management, network administration/IT support, and other administrative tasks. The design process is supported by these areas of expertise.

Within the design function, different studios have different job titles and sometimes describe the process in different ways. There tends to be senior level design and creative direction. There is the design staff, production, and project coordination/project management. This is the majority of what is taking place in the studio, and often represents 70 to 75 percent of the total number of employees.

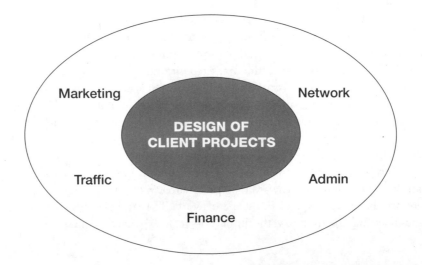

To support these activities, the combination of administration, finance, network management/IT, and marketing is usually no more than 25 to 30 percent of the staff. If we look at that with X-ray vision, what we are seeing is the differentiation between billable and nonbillable labor.

Since the work for clients is primarily tracked and measured in hours, time management is critical to the profitability of any design firm. An appropriate range of billable time needs to be established for each staff position. All hours need to be recorded, both billable and non-billable, and staff members need periodic feedback on where they stand in relation to targets. Realistic goals must have some relation to past levels of performance, which must have been measured in a comparable way. For these and other indicators, it's important to capture complete information, and the system for tracking activity must be current and consistent. Over time, each firm will develop a sense of norms, like temperature or blood pressure. Real activity will never be an average, but once we have defined acceptable ranges for each indicator—high and low, best case and worst case—we can watch actual performance move around within those parameters without becoming too alarmed.

BILLABLE TIME

For the studio to be profitable over the long haul, we need to maximize the billable time. If we look at that a little more closely, the time that people actually spend in the office is not going to be 100 percent billable. There is a certain amount of built-in downtime: vacation time, sick time, staff meetings, and various studio activities that will not be billable to clients. When these have been subtracted from the total, something in the neighborhood of 80 percent may be the maximum billable percentage for a creative firm with a standard forty-hour workweek.

Enough staff members need to be near that maximum billable percentage to support the few people who are primarily nonbillable. Marketing is probably going to be largely nonbillable, and financial management and administrative support will definitely be primarily nonbillable. As we structure the staff, we are creating a weighted average of the various billable percentages. Company wide, at least 60 percent of all regularly scheduled hours should be billable to clients. Here's an example:

	Project time	Studio time
Creative direction	80%	20%
Design	80%	20%
Production	80%	20%
Project coordination	80%	20%
Marketing	30%	70%
Admin, finance, network/IT	10%	90%
Overall	60%	40%

The Association of Professional Design Firms (APDF) provides some relevant information. Sixty percent as a benchmark for billable time is supported by survey information that the APDF has compiled over the years. The APDF collects, in confidence, and analyzes complete financial statements from a large number of independent design consultancies in the United States and Canada. Typically, the median billable percentage has ranged from 59 to 63 percent.

In past APDF surveys, firms have reported two different methods for determining the billable percentage. Most studios calculate billable time based on actual hours reported by each staff member. In contrast, a few firms look at job titles only; for example, a creative director is assumed to be 100 percent billable while an administrator is assumed to be 100 percent nonbillable. Job titles are not reliable indicators. Actual hours should be the basis of this calculation.

On a similar note, it's important to remember that recording time as billable on a timesheet is not the same as actually invoicing a client for it.

STAFFING

Over time, more people will be added, and new positions will be created in the various categories of the organization. Though the overall size will be increasing, the proportions should stay roughly the same. Each time the workload dictates that someone be added, be aware of how he or she will fit into the mix. If administrative staffing outweighs project staffing, then the firm will not be able to pay for its increasing overhead. Here's an example of how small and large staffs might compare:

	Total number of employees	
	Small firm	**Large firm**
70 to 75%:		
Creative direction	1	3
Design	4	12
Production	2	6
Project coordination	1	3
25 to 30%:		
Marketing	1	3
Admin, finance, network	2	6
Total	11	33

Questions about structure will arise in every firm that experiences growth. Various types of internal organizational structures are common for both midsized and larger creative firms. One is a corporate-style pyramid—a hierarchy of responsibility with a single authority at the top. This is often seen in firms where one person's name is on the door. Another structure has multiple segments that meet at the center, like a flower or star, allowing several principals to manage a separate staff without too much overlap. Regardless of the geometry, the point is to create an appropriate system based on the combined personalities involved and the range of services provided to clients. An appropriate system will facilitate the daily work being done, respond well to change, and support future growth.

TEAMS

As a studio grows and more people become involved in the creative process, the communication loops become quite large. If there are fifteen or twenty people involved in the creative process, it's appropriate to begin to think of them as teams. This is an intrinsic organizational issue that all growing firms face. Decisions about organization can either stimulate growth or prevent it.

There are many ways of organizing creative resources. Everyone in the studio is involved in different projects, so each person is probably on multiple project teams. But if designers pull back a little bit, it will leave space to think about client teams. Perhaps there are certain teams that service certain client accounts. Perhaps that is how designers are hired—to join the Client E team or the Client R team, and most of the work done is for that particular client.

It's also possible to organize resources around certain industries; some product design studios and some consulting firms are organized in this way. If there is a depth of understanding in particular areas such as software development, hardware manufacturing, biotechnology, or financial services, it might indicate a way of organizing internal resources.

There are also creative firms that are organized by design discipline—the creative service that is being offered. These firms might form as a corporate identity team that does its own hiring and manages its own activities. Another possibility is a brand identity and packaging team. Maybe there's a team that does three-dimensional work and creates retail environments. It's possible to organize resources based on various disciplines.

A related consideration is the fact that different disciplines sometimes have different pricing and contractual conventions. Fixed-fee agreements are typical for small graphic design projects, whereas time-and-materials contracts and royalties are more common for industrial design projects. For work in some disciplines, it may be appropriate to negotiate amounts per page or per square foot. For some deliverables, the frequency and scope of usage will determine the creative fees. Clients purchasing identity work need to receive full rights and ownership, but with some interactive projects, perhaps only a licensing arrangement is appropriate. Teams organized by discipline may have different norms in these important respects.

Finally, we might also consider sorting design and production staff based on personalities. That is to say, selecting complementary personalities with an appropriate range of skill sets for a team led by a strong senior person that they respect. Team building based on personal chemistry as well as professional competencies can reinforce good communication and facilitate cooperation when pressure builds on projects. The downside might be that ego could get in the way of effective coordination, and that clients could develop a loyalty to an individual rather than to the firm.

The choice of team structure will have an impact on marketing strategies and the way that the firm describes itself to clients. There will be a need to keep the different teams equally busy with appropriate assignments. It's necessary to think about whether an optimum mix of disciplines or categories exists for the firm, and whether future growth needs to be proportional in that respect.

Once a growing firm has sorted a large pool of creative resources into teams, the hard part is to make sure that everyone stays challenged—that everyone has new work and no one feels that they've been pigeonholed into a narrow area. What is the best way of coaching, challenging, evaluating, rewarding, and encouraging personal growth? How do we make sure that this structure remains open and flexible? Addressing these issues involves a lot of trust and effective communication between the various team members.

How is a shared vision maintained across the teams, the unifying purpose for the group reaffirmed and clarified, and individual activities put into a context that explains their relevance? In a busy studio, with resources being used in shifting configurations and individuals playing multiple roles, competing priorities can cause confusion and stress. To prevent burnout, there is an operational challenge to maintain a feeling of overall cohesion and direction, rather like a flexible background grid fitting for more than one design to play across.

FINANCIAL TARGETS

In reviewing monthly financial statements with an accountant, it becomes clear that some standard financial information is not industry-specific. Certain comparisons and ratios can reveal the general financial health of any type of business. Also, the best indicators, like percentages and multipliers, are scalable and are not affected by the size of the company.

Beyond standard measurements, though, creative firms have a strong need for indicators that are more specific to our activities. External benchmarks that are design-specific are not always easy to come by. Many firms develop their own internal measurements over time with the help of their accountants. When looking at a profit and loss statement, one important way to gauge revenue is to divide the billings for a period by the total number of employees during that period. There are two ways of doing this. One way is to look at fee billings (labor billings) only. The other way is to look at total billings, which includes labor and all other revenue (such as materials, other third-party costs passed through the studio, and mark-ups). Revenue per employee can be used as a way of setting personal targets for employees. It can be used to estimate future sales based on staff size or, conversely, to estimate staffing needs based on expected sales. If the studio is organized into teams, personal targets can be used as a modular way of constructing team targets.

Revenue is measured in currency, so it changes over time due to factors like inflation. In recent years, annual fee billings per employee have been roughly $91,000 according to APDF surveys. When billings are added in for project materials, total billings per employee reach $124,000 (with materials comprising about 27 percent of that total). Using these indicators, total income for a firm of ten people might be about $1.24 million per year, whereas a firm of thirty might expect to have a total income of $3.72 million per year, assuming that the right client relationships are in place. Here's a sample calculation:

Example	Small firm	Large firm
Number of employees	10	30
Total billings per employee	$124,000	$124,000
Total annual billings for firm	$1,240,000	$3,720,000
Less annual materials billings at approximately 27% of total	$330,000	$990,000
Fee billings for firm	$910,000	$2,730,000
Fee billings per employee	$91,000	$91,000

Another way to analyze a profit and loss statement is to look at individual cost categories as a percentage of total sales. For example, rent expense might be equal to 3 or 4 percent of total sales. Total salaries might equal 34 to 38 percent of total sales. Thus total income for any given period might be approximately three times our salary expense. This multiplier is affected by the number of billable hours being reported and the billing rates charged to clients for those hours.

One reason for tracking billable and non-billable hours is to split salary costs into direct labor and indirect labor categories on the profit and loss statement. Direct labor is added to the cost of goods sold, along with other project-related expenses such as materials and freelancers. Indirect labor goes into overhead along with items like rent, utilities, and employer taxes. In each accounting period, the cost of goods sold is subtracted from total revenue to calculate the gross margin. The gross margin must be large enough to cover all overhead and still leave a profit. A gross margin equal to 45 or 50 percent of total revenue is typical for graphic design firms. For many design firms, pre-tax profits might be 4 to 10 percent or higher, depending on how much money is disbursed through retirement plans and discretionary incentive programs.

These are just a few of many possible measurements. Percentage indicators, ratios, and multipliers can be expected to stay within certain parameters regardless of the size of the firm. Real activity will never exactly match a given plan, but over time it will develop a good sense of the acceptable range for each indicator. The right combination of key measurements can provide a multidimensional picture of a firm's financial situation and help to identify and respond to trends. It is important to revisit the business plan quarterly to review and adjust targets. The ongoing business plan should include the establishment of cash reserves the firm can draw on in an emergency, and specific plans for the most productive use of cumulative profits being produced by successfully completed projects.

ONGOING ISSUES

Over time, basic management issues remain fairly constant in terms of finance, marketing, and human resources. Individual responsibilities for those issues will no doubt shift based on changes in staff and personal workloads, but ongoing concerns will include: maintaining the right mix of people and resources, maintaining a healthy financial and cash flow situation, and guiding new business efforts so that the firm identifies and pursues the most appropriate client relationships. There will always be operational issues in creating schedules and an ongoing need to find scaleable solutions for studio organization.

If the organization grows, that growth must never obscure the underlying mission of the firm. Whether small or large, every studio is part of a unique service industry. Design is really about people and communication. It's about quality relationships and respect—within the design team, between the design team and the client, and with clients' customers worldwide.

18

Transition

COLIN FORBES

This piece was written at the time of Mr. Forbes' impending retirement, in 1993. He and we feel it is still valid, in spite of the passage of time.

MOST DESIGN FIRMS, whether graphic, product, or architectural, have grown from the creative and entrepreneurial energy of an individual or two or three partners. Historically, only one or two out of thousands of firms have ever continued into a second generation. The design-driven offices of George Nelson, Charles and Ray Eames, and Eliot Noyes disappeared with the death of their founders. Practically the only design firms to survive beyond the first generation have been marketing-driven companies like Lippincott & Margulies and Walter Dorwin Teague. Yet if you consider dominant names in other service industries, Arthur Andersen or Peat Marwick in accounting, for example, or McKinsey or Deloitte in management consultancy, they have all reached their second or third generation. The size and success of these organizations make it hard to relate their experience to relatively minuscule design firms, but I believe we still have something to learn from them. The challenge is to run what we believe to be an ·excellent design-driven firm into a second generation.

As the first generation of the Pentagram partners, including myself, start to think about retiring, there are critical transitional issues facing our firm. In my opinion these issues are our constitution, personalities, and critical mass, and of these, by far the most important are constitution and personalities. There are two quotes, one from a management consultant and the other from a venture capitalist, which at first glance are contradictory but in fact support my view. The first is: "An above average person will fail in a poor structure where an average person can succeed in a goodt structure." The second is: "I would rather back an A man with a B idea than a B man with an A idea."

THE PENTAGRAM CONSTITUTION

Pentagram's constitution is based on the equality of its partners. Although we are incorporated, we use the term "partners" because it conveys the spirit of the relationship. The idea of equality goes back to our first company, Fletcher/Forbes/Gill, in which the three partners decided on equal equity and equal incomes. However, each partner's profitability was openly decided, which contributed to a competitive element.

During these early years, the partner who worried first about cash flow, the need for more studio space, or what might happen in five years, got the job of planning the progress of the firm permanently. That happened to be me. We were fundamentally a roundtable organization, but I was the one who led efforts to develop the shareholder agreements and the constitution with lawyers, to refine the financial reporting with the accountants, and to map out a five-year plan.

Our London lawyer was instrumental in drafting the agreements between us. He said at one of our early meetings, "You must be generous toward an incoming partner. The talented thirty-five-year-old that you need to help the business continue to thrive will not be able to buy in at ten times earnings." Therefore, we agreed that incoming partners would buy shares at asset value only, with no allowance for good will, and that the firm would assist with financing over an extended period. The lawyer also said, "You must create adhesion—the advantage must go to the remaining partners and not to a leaving partner." Therefore, a partner leaves with the auditor's valuation of the current asset value only; retirement pension schemes are our individual responsibilities. We have always taken the attitude that partners should be financially self-reliant because the variety of ages means that the requirements vary too much.

My position was further entrenched when, with the addition of two more partners and the formation of Pentagram in 1972, I instituted our six-monthly partners' retreats, which eventually formalized into our policy meetings. It seemed natural that I would chair all of the partners' meetings, and I continued to do so for eighteen years. Through these meetings we have learned to communicate with each other (although never enough) and to connect with the community. I believe the meetings are one of the major reasons the partners have stayed together. They have been part of our continuing education because they provide a forum where we can learn from one another and from our guests. They have taken place at remarkable venues such as Leeds Castle, the American Academy in Rome, and the St. Francis Yacht Club in San Francisco.

By 1978, two more partners had joined in London, and I moved to New York to establish the office there. In 1986 the San Francisco partners joined and introduced a new location. As we have continued to grow, our democratic philosophy kept us in good stead, but my role in all of this had been concentrated for three major reasons. First, I was unique in having strong relationships with the U.K. partners; second, I had negotiated the entry of each one of the U.S. partners; and third, I had always chaired all of our meetings. I should credit the fact that I have been blessed with exceptional mentors and consultants, but, maybe without undue modesty, I could say that I have had the good sense to choose and to listen to them.

When I announced in 1991 that I wanted to resign my long-term chairmanship, a number of interesting observations immediately arose from my partners. The most important seemed to be that one learned through leadership, and there were a number of partners who felt that they had been excluded from that experience. I had been advised that I should go on as chairman until the last minute and that the issue would resolve itself when I left. But I didn't accept that; I felt we needed a transition period during which we should agree on a Pentagram constitution to carry us through the next decade. I had also been advised that the chairman's tasks had to remain in one hand and that rotation of leadership would be a disaster. Whereas that may be sound advice for a conventional corporation, in my opinion, it did not take into account the personalities and motivations of my partners, and indeed, designers in general.

The following describes the structure that I proposed after listening carefully to my partners and which has been accepted. The basis is the division of responsibility to allow the chairmanship of the meetings to rotate and to establish permanent elected committees to be responsible for the major functions.

The real authority for policy decisions remains the full assembly of the partner-shareholders; however, we have had to establish executive committees to get things done. One partner is elected to be policy committee chairman to organize and lead the six-monthly policy meetings and to deal with any matters affecting the whole group that are not included in the roles of other committees. This position rotates after three meetings (eighteen months) by tenure such that each partner shall, in turn, serve as policy chairman. Therefore, by definition, the policy chairman will always be a senior member who has fully become part of Pentagram's culture.

Through our experience we had learned to divide nonprofessional work into three distinct areas: accounting, communication, and administration. The first two have impact on the offices internationally, but the third is primarily local. We therefore established two international sub-committees, a finance committee and a communications committee, each comprised of one representative from each of the three offices. In order to channel information and simplify meetings with outside advisers, we have also elected a chairman for each of these committees.

The committee members are nominated locally by each office and then approved by the group. In order to minimize rotation, there is no limitation on the term of membership, so unless someone is patently incompetent or uninterested, the committee appointments are virtually permanent.

The finance committee has the task of coordinating the financial affairs of the group with our financial advisers and lawyers. They discuss the details of matters like profitability by each partner and office, the distribution of our income and major capital investment, and then report to the full partnership when decisions need to be made. Likewise, the communications committee coordinates our substantial publishing program including the books, *Pentagram Papers, Pentaspeak,* and other initiatives pertaining to public relations and business development.

After the first six months with this structure in place, some partners still had concerns about leadership of the group as a whole; it seemed increasingly difficult to get the partners internationally to develop both working and social relationships. A group of partners met on an ad hoc basis to address this problem, and they proposed that there should be an elected steering committee to be responsible for long-term strategic planning for Pentagram as a whole and for finding solutions to internal conflicts. Like the others, the steering committee has one elected member from each of the three offices, and they elect a chairman for that group.

Although the structure appears to be complicated, it provides a necessary balance of involvement in leading the firm and yet ensures that the specialized jobs are done by the right person. The transition has not been simple. With changes, one is bound to make mistakes; things have fallen between the cracks, and we have had to arrive at new definitions of responsibility. Even though the policy committee—the full partnership—has ultimate power and can change or decide anything, it is very difficult to keep each partner at the same level of understanding of complicated legal and financial issues. Therefore it is perceived, and may be in reality, that the executive committee members have more power than the other partners.

It is an understatement to say that most designers are not naturally good managers and there is a necessary learning curve. Designers must learn to be managers and to take executive responsibility or their company policy will be set by administrators.

PERSONALITIES

The next big issue is personalities: who we will choose to elect as Pentagram partners and how they fit with and use the organization. Seventeen people cannot be the same or even truly equal; however, there are four criteria that are important in my view.

1. A partner must be able to generate business. Other partners do not want to become salesmen. Help is available on a collaborative basis, and the advantages include an expanded depth of work to draw from, the knowledge and expertise of other partners, and shared central support, but there should be no doubt as to where the ultimate responsibility lies.

2. A partner must have a national reputation as an outstanding professional in the chosen discipline. This is a subjective decision, but the partners have a sense of their standing in the field and the quality of work with which they wish to be associated. It is too easy to "water the wine."

3. A partner must be able to control projects and contribute to the profits of the firm. There is considerable generosity about difference of earning because of different contributions in other areas. However, one cannot share income with a person who does not have similar potential and, probably more important, a similar attitude toward desired income. Nor can one share with a person who cannot manage a project or a team.

4. The last, and certainly not the least, is that a partner must be a proactive member of the group and care about Pentagram and the partners. We spend our working lives together; we should like each other.

It sometimes helps to mix metaphors to make a point: I often say that this is not a shopping list; it is necessary to fire on all four cylinders. As stated by the venture capitalist, you need A people.

Our traditional source for new partners remains successful independent designers with small practices. However, we have established a precedent of developing new partners through an associate program. This additional route provides training in a way that is not available elsewhere and may suit the needs of a larger organization. Maybe Pentagram will also need partners in disciplines other than design. I do not know the answers, but I do know there will be change.

CRITICAL MASS

The last factor, which I believe helps an organization survive, is a critical mass. We have grown to a count of seventeen partners with more than twenty years' history. There comes a point when a sufficiency has been invested in building an international reputation, developing management skills, and a fund of case histories so that the organization has a value beyond the individuals. Growth will enable Pentagram to reinforce its traditional way of doing business: maintaining the balance between commercial and cultural and our aspiration to be the "thinking designers."

A larger firm has greater prominence in a crowded marketplace of hundreds of small design firms. This is evident when projects are on a national or international scale. For example, even a design enthusiast in Japan probably only knows of the six largest or most prominent western firms. A firm the size of Pentagram also has the resources to support a sophisticated and varied communication and publication program. The collective financial resources of a large group make it possible to invest in better facilities and resources or enter into new ventures.

These are the same reasons that bring the international service firms like McKinsey & Co. or Price Waterhouse. I believe that Pentagram's new structure will provide an opportunity for us to adapt to our larger size. Ultimately, if Pentagram is to fulfill its potential, there is a need for the members of the group to have a vision of what the organization should be—not only within the design industry, but also in the larger international business community.

Napoleon was once asked to comment on what quality he most valued in his generals. "I want them to be lucky," he said. There are changes to be made, risks to be taken, and conflicts to be resolved, and Pentagram needs to be lucky.

EXIT STRATEGIES

Although there is obviously goodwill invested in the name Pentagram in our kind of business, the goodwill leaves with the partner. To enable younger partners to contribute working capital and continue a business, it is necessary for the retiree to be satisfied with payment of net asset value. In addition, each person should individually invest in their retirement out of a relatively high income in working years.

19

Principles of Managing the Corporate Design Department

PETER L. PHILLIPS

"WHY DON'T I get any respect?" This is not only a phrase made famous by comedian Rodney Dangerfield, but also the common lament of thousands of managers of corporate design departments worldwide. "Why doesn't management value what I can offer?" "Why is the design function considered a service group rather than a team member?" "Why are there very few vice presidents of design?" "Why is my budget always the first to get cut?" These are routine questions I am asked as I meet with design managers at my client companies.

Design managers spend a lot of time lamenting their lowly position on the corporate totem pole. Frankly, they also wish they could get paid more for what they do. After all, they understand how important design is to the success of the enterprise. The problem is they don't work hard enough to make others understand how important the design function really is.

Design managers have to stop saying, "ain't it awful," and work at repositioning themselves in the corporate hierarchy. They need to demonstrate that they understand the business of *business*. They need to demonstrate that they know how to contribute to operating the business. They need to learn how to ask probing business questions and then how to solve the business problem with design thinking. They must learn how to talk about design, without talking about "design."

The worldwide market for graphic design services is upwards of $34 billion, according to James Woudhuysen, associate director at the Henley Centre for Forecasting in London and professor of design management at De Montfort University, Leicester, England. Woudhuysen suggests that design mangers become more proactive in this large and growing international marketplace. The interesting thing is that the expenditures for design are probably the least understood in boardrooms worldwide. I would suggest that senior management has little awareness of how much it all costs. It gets buried in other budgets. Design managers must make management aware that they are dealing with enormous budgets that could have incredible paybacks if managed properly. The design manager must position himself as an asset manager.

Woudhuysen's statistics place the design market fourth on the list of marketing services expenditures, after sales promotion, media advertising, and direct mail, and ahead of ten other categories including public relations, market research, and audiovisual communications.

Woudhuysen argues, "It is a marketplace which, in my view, will grow in the future, given the continued importance of graphic design to the maintenance of product, service, and especially corporate brands. The need, as never before, is to 'think big' in graphics and to recognize the political and cultural influence which the graphic design profession can bring to bear. The need is thus to get serious and to get real in design; to seek genuine and universal benefits by its application."

WHAT'S WRONG WITH THIS PICTURE?

In order to illustrate some of the most common problems faced by design managers, let me describe three situations I have encountered in the past few years.

VIGNETTE #1: Harry is the head of design for a major manufacturer of low-cost consumer products. Although the company's headquarters is in Asia, their single largest market is in the United States. The company built an enormous share of the market by focusing on the low-end. Their products were among the least expensive in their categories. They also sold heavily through mass-market discounters. Although the products were inexpensive, they did function in a satisfactory manner.

But the world changed. Due to increases in manufacturing and selling costs, it was no longer profitable for the company to produce products at their traditional low price to the consumer. The dilemma management faced involved changing consumer perception to assure the new higher prices at retail would be accepted.

Senior management held countless high-level meetings to try to develop a strategy for effectively repositioning the company in the marketplace. They hired a well-known management-consulting firm to help them write the plan.

Harry, the intrepid head of design, was aware of the dilemma and the high-level meetings, but he was not a participant. He anxiously awaited the results so he could determine how the new positioning would affect his design organization.

What would you advise Harry to do?

VIGNETTE #2: A major, global, high-tech company in the race to keep competitive and still be a market leader acquired a smaller company to create a new division and offer some innovative new products. As part of the purchase agreement, the smaller company's founder and president was made president of the new division and promised a great deal of autonomy in running the division. He was a brilliant engineer and manager and knew that he had only one year to show a profit or be replaced.

The new division head went to a former college classmate of his who ran a small design firm and commissioned him to develop a division logo, product logos, packaging, and communications collateral material. The design manager of the parent corporation did not find out this work was going on until after it had been completed. The new division's materials bore absolutely no relationship to the parent corporation's house style and, frankly, were outstanding examples of mediocre design.

The corporate design manager had a meeting with his boss and complained that the new division's material was not acceptable and that his group should have been involved from the beginning. The design manager's boss patiently explained that the new division president had to move quickly, was promised autonomy, and had no time or budget to go back and do the work over again. He suggested that the design manager just let the whole thing drop.

What went wrong?

VIGNETTE #3: Clarence is the design manager for a U.S. based company that has been expanding into the international marketplace over the past five years. Nearly all of the company's design work was done by Clarence's corporate design group, made up entirely of American designers. About the only design work not under the corporate group's control was the look and feel of the advertising, which was handled by a New York ad agency.

Company sales and marketing people, based in Europe and Asia, were expected to implement all design work created in the corporate headquarters without question. There were no trained designers on staff in the partner countries and the U.S. ad agency's work was the only advertising they could run. From time to time, when sales and market share did not grow abroad as planned, high-level meetings were held with the respective managers from each country. They often pointed to both the advertising as well as the design of packaging and sales collateral materials as being inappropriate for their countries' markets. Management looked at this as a weak excuse at best, but agreed to invite Clarence in to hear their complaints and other issues regarding design. They also invited the account manager from the advertising agency to attend. Both Clarence and the advertising agency were convinced their design work was excellent, strong, and compelling. Management agreed that there was probably nothing wrong with the design work and so were supportive of both Clarence and the agency.

As the day of the meeting approaches, how would you prepare yourself if you were Clarence? How would you handle this situation?

These three vignettes highlight the management techniques most commonly overlooked by corporate design managers in the design function: recognizing the role of design in the business, establishing and maintaining mutually valuable relationships, and implementing efficient work with processes.

As a first, proactive step in repositioning your corporate design function, consider the following model:

THE VALUE YOU OFFER

Let's start with you—the design manager. All managers of corporate functions need to periodically do a self-assessment. Make a list of your strengths and your weaknesses as they relate to your ability to manage the resources of people, money, time, and materials to accomplish the primary mission of your company. Rate

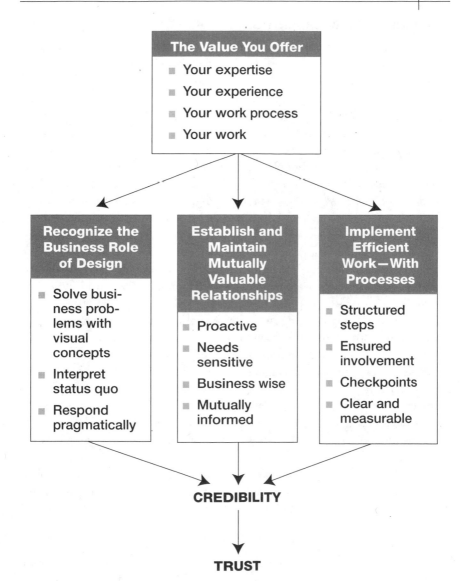

yourself on your skills in planning, organizing, coordinating, and communicating. How are you at establishing job objectives, motivating people, and making and communicating decisions?

If you have been objective and honest, you will have a clear picture of the areas in which you might improve. If you sincerely want to reposition the design function, first you have to understand how you and the function you manage are perceived today.

RECOGNIZE THE BUSINESS ROLE OF DESIGN

When I was managing corporate design departments earlier in my career, the first thing I would do is change the name of the group. Invariably, the department had been traditionally known as the Art Department. I believe art and design are two different things. I think of art as the free expression of an artist. Design is a problem solving discipline, not free expression. The term art department conjures up a group of nice enough people who draw well. Corporate design group has a more professional, business-like aura. As I used to tell my colleagues, artists create beautiful pieces of art, but you need a designer to tell you where to hang it! The point is to focus on problem solving, not aesthetics. Vice presidents of sales, marketing, manufacturing, or any function are not kept awake at night worrying about which typeface is best for their printed material or the colors, imagery, layout, etc. They are worried about making deadlines, manufacturing and moving product out the door, making their budgets, and keeping their jobs. Become very aware of the business needs of the company you work for and then step forward with solutions that involve the considerable skills of your design function.

In vignette # 1, Harry, being aware of the crises, should have developed a plan that: (a) demonstrated he understood the problem, (b) offered options to control costs by altering the design and production of product graphics and collateral materials, (c) explained that his group could effectively translate the new positioning strategy, whatever it might be, into a compelling visual manifestation of that identity. In doing all of this, Harry should not actually show design work or use too much technical jargon in talking about cost containment. The strategy is to not be the "art guy." The strategy is to be a valued partner in solving business problems.

Assemble your key staff. Identify the most critical business problems your company is facing today. Then develop a plan to present to management that shows you can solve business problems with design.

ESTABLISH AND MAINTAIN RELATIONSHIPS

Take a hard look at your company's organization chart. Identify the most critical people and make an effort to get to know them. Visit other departments. Learn as much as you can about their operations, their worries, and their methods. All of this knowledge will be of enormous help as you move forward. You will also begin to be recognized by your peers. When you visit other departments, resist the temptation to talk about your group. Listen to them as they tell you about their function.

Read everything written about your company. Know your company as well as the CEO knows the company. After you visit other departments, develop a profile of each group and make an assessment of how the design function could help them, and then offer that help.

In vignette #2, the corporate design manager did not take the time to get to know the new division president. He neglected to see that the man had a short time frame to prove himself and keep his job. He didn't make any effort to understand the perceived needs for design of this new division. As a result of all this, the company not only ended up with mediocre design from one division, but the design manager also lost credibility as a valuable contributor to the corporation.

IMPLEMENT EFFICIENT WORK-WITH PROCESSES

Establish some cross-functional work groups. By involving key stakeholders in the work of the design function, you become partners and allies. These groups do not design or get involved in design direction, but rather give you valuable input concerning business problems they are facing. Cultivate support from the highest possible management level. This will help you open doors to a variety of other senior managers. Establish, and publish, a strategic objective for the design function that maps to the corporate mission statement. Use the company newspaper or bulletin boards to inform the enterprise of your various activities. Above all, be a valued contributor, not an obstacle.

In vignette #3, Clarence clearly had not implemented any work-with processes with non-U.S. operations of the company. He was satisfied with his group's work in the United States and failed to recognize potential cultural or national issues in other parts of the world. Instead of being called to defend his work, Clarence should have taken the time to contact the country managers and ask for their input early on.

The most common mistake design managers make is to become too focused on design, rather than how design can support the corporation and add to the bottom line. Design managers must position themselves, and their departments, as business partners. They must talk about design as an asset of the corporation—an asset that they manage. Perceived as a well-managed corporate asset, the design function gains credibility and trust throughout the organization.

DEPARTMENTAL MANAGEMENT IS ALSO CRITICAL

So far, I have been talking about positioning the design function within the larger organization. But management of the function itself is equally critical. Once you have made a promise, you must be prepared to deliver on that promise. In general (there are notable exceptions) the most talented and creative designers working in a corporate environment today have had little business training or experience. The leading design schools seem to never include in their curriculum any management or business education. As a result, designers tend not to think about bottom lines, production efficiencies, return on investment, or marketing. It is the design manager's responsibility to impress upon his or her staff the importance of learning more about business and the design's role in helping that business be profitable. The best design managers I know spend a considerable amount of time researching and identifying appropriate professional development programs for their staff. They lobby to be sure their staff is included in key business meetings concerning the design projects they will be working on. The design manager must also take the time to discuss each project at length with each designer prior to work beginning on the project, and help the designer understand the business objective and the business constraints. Returning to the vignettes, the staff designers must understand the business crises the corporation is facing, be proactive in recognizing emerging business problems, and address the needs of various cultural and regional operations. A design solution that works brilliantly in the United States might be a disaster in Asia or Europe.

Many design departments are woefully understaffed relative to the number of projects the group is expected to execute in any given year. This condition leads to well-meaning design managers who try to take the burden of going to endless meetings away from designers. This can be a fatal error. If a designer is to solve the business problem through design, then the designer has to understand the problem in great depth. The designer also needs to focus on developing critical work-with skills. Especially important is to help the designer learn how to tactfully keep his or her internal client out of the aesthetic aspects of design. Design by committee never works, but nearly all internal corporate clients I have ever met cannot resist the temptation to make comments like, "what if we made the logo bigger, put it in the bottom center, and changed the color!" Designers must be trained to keep the discussions focused. The design manager must help by making it clear that designer-client meetings are not group meetings to design the artifacts. The internal client has the business need, the designer has the skill to use design principles effectively to meet the need.

One technique I have found successful is to agree to a simple norm at the outset of meetings with internal clients; no one present can use the phrases "I like" or "I don't like." I might like brown and you like blue, but the point is that neither of our personal preferences has anything to do with the business problem or need. Rather, each person must argue with points that can be substantiated, such as "Brown will work best to solve the business problem because…," or, "Blue will not work as well as brown because…" Once you get people away from their personal likes and dislikes and focused on the merits of various design elements in addressing the real business problem, you have a much better chance of being successful and of being recognized as a credible and respected partner.

Following all of the corporate downsizing of the past decade, design managers have been increasingly forced to utilize independent, external design resources. The principles of working with these agencies are the same. Agencies must be selected not only on their credentials as producers of good design but also for their ability to interact with internal corporate clients as business problem-solving partners.

Unlike accounting, law, purchasing, and other corporate functions, design is viewed as subjective. The design function must counter this view with hard, objective, factual arguments. Design functions and design managers will not earn the respect they are looking for or be truly valued in the corporate environment if they continue to ignore the real role they should be playing in the business. Their contribution will ultimately be measured on their success at helping the business to grow and prosper, not on the number of awards they win for beautiful design.

20

Large Project
Management

EVA DOMAN BRUCK

THE GREATEST CHALLENGE in producing a complicated and long-term assignment is finding ways to manage it so that there is enough time left to design it. Considering the overall span of time for the project; the potential need for more people, equipment, and outside resources; as well as systems for tracking and reporting information, materials, and costs that such projects generate, it is a formidable challenge.

Michael Bierut, a principal in Pentagram's New York office, says, "A large project is basically a series of interrelated small projects. The end users don't relate to the epic sweep and grandeur of the effort; they usually only see a few items at a time." Deborah Sussman of Sussman/Prejza in Los Angeles suggests, "You need to have the 'gut' for large projects. There are so many people who have an impact on what you do. In our environmental projects, there are usually architects, engineers, landscape architects, interior and lighting designers, fabricators, builders, and, of course, the client, which may include the state, city, local, private sectors, and all the layers of people in each."

PROPOSALS, PROGRESS REPORTS, AND MINUTES

Before you need to worry about how to administer a large project, you will be required to prove that you are capable of doing so to the prospective client. Large projects imply large budgets; lots of people; many meetings and presentations; a complex process of production, fabrication, and installation; and serious record keeping requirements.

In addition to the description of deliverables, working methodology, and conceptual framework that are usually included in any proposal, a large-scale project document should outline information concerning numbers and types of personnel that will be dedicated to the project, including designers, production artists, writers, project/client managers, fabrication specialists, and so on. It's always reassuring to include related project experience, especially if of similar scope or scale. Outside resources such as researchers, photographers, illustrators, and other design and nondesign specialists that will be brought in to work on the project should be named, and, if possible, include brief professional descriptions for each of them.

Schedules and timetables for individual project tasks, presentations, targeted completion dates, and project billings need to be identified. Knowing that no one reads long-winded proposals, charts, and graphs can be very effective in illustrating this kind of information.

While it is not necessary to list equipment and resource allocation in a proposal, you will want to have the appropriate computers, printers, scanners, software, and other necessary tools dedicated to the project.

Proposals usually do not include a description of the project documentation you plan to provide, but such information is essential to a well-run assignment. The purpose of providing the client with regular updates is not to make you a slave to paperwork. It is actually an effective way to communicate to your client matters which are irksome and obstructing the project's progress but which you may be reluctant to voice—particularly if your client contact is the source of the difficulties.

Progress reports are also a good place to identify items due from the client, such as add-ons, extensive changes, and delays. A clear, concise, and regularly disseminated status report is easy to produce using a word processing program. Column headings may be as simple as "Item," "Status," "Next Steps," "Due Date," "Who." Everyone associated with the project, including your contact's supervisor, should be sent a copy. Naturally, confidential information should be treated carefully and disseminated discreetly.

Large projects tend to be sponsored by government agencies or institutions, and their record keeping (and showing) requirements are usually intensely demanding. Depending upon how the deal is structured—flat fee or on a cost/use basis with a cap (i.e., not to exceed...) the budget report usually includes line-by-line listings of personnel, materials, services, etc., as well as columns showing amounts for "Budget," "Actuals," and "Variance." Even if line itemization is not routinely required, always be prepared to have your books examined. Keep time sheets, job sheets, and accurate backup for vendors and all outside resources.

Meeting minutes are an additional form of project reporting, and, while it may seem an added burden, it is often useful to have the chance to interpret events from your point of view. If there is ever a serious misunderstanding during the course of a project, thorough documentation may be your best protection.

Sussman recounts, "We try to be as organized as possible, but projects can be so unpredictable … we do block out and schedule at least three months ahead to get a sense of how things may unfold. Ironically, we often find that we produce design faster than clients are prepared to respond." She continues, "We have weekly meetings with our five associates to go over operations and managerial issues, and then talk about key events and problems of current projects. While we don't usually write meeting minutes, we do always try to issue work change orders for significant items."

Leslie Smolan of Carbone Smolan in New York City says, "Meeting minutes and progress reports are found to be useful when the client is missing deadlines. Sometimes we are pushing them as hard as they are pushing us. There are financial consequences for us as well as the client if turnaround is not quick enough. We do issue change orders, with or without numbers, when additional work is requested. Also, we put things in writing because we know that no one remembers details after the fact."

DAY-TO-DAY MANAGEMENT

Once you have spent the time and effort preparing the project proposal, you will begin to have a sense of just how big this breadbox is going to be. Now is the perfect time to figure out how you are going to get your arms around it. Perhaps the most crucial decision to make at the onset is who will be selected to manage the day-to-day aspects of the project.

If you are a principal with marketing, creative, and client responsibilities for other projects as well as this one, a project manager will become necessary for you to continue to run your firm and oversee a variety of projects. Some design offices place project management responsibilities on the project's chief designer, usually a senior level designer who reports directly to a principal. Besides cost savings, there are significant advantages to this arrangement. It provides the client with a central design and management contact, it places comprehensive responsibility (design, schedule, budget) on one person, and it is also a way of identifying candidates for the firm's future management. Be sure to provide administrative assistance for scheduling appointments, meetings, cost tracking, word processing, and so on, so your chief designer doesn't get bogged down with minutiae and become unable to fulfill design responsibilities.

There are some disadvantages to combining the design and project manager roles. Great designers are not always great administrators. A senior level designer may be able to handle several projects, assuming he is not too thinly spread because of time-consuming administrative tasks. It may be cheaper to hire a project manager than to have a top level designer fulfill the role. That is not to say, however, that the senior designer of a project should be relieved of all administrative responsibilities. There needs to be strong communication between the project designer and the project manager. Since designers are usually most privy to the intricacies of the design process, they must be accountable for information that is to be transmitted to the project administrator.

"While I oversee entire projects," says Smolan, "a selected design director has the day-to-day responsibilities for the assignment. There is a level of discussion about design where, with a nondesign manager, something gets lost in the translation." She adds, "If necessary, we prefer to bring a junior level designer into the role of project manager, which we call production coordinator...who can also spec and set type, proofread, and manage production traffic. We are wary of keeping on a single skilled person because of the inevitable downtime which is endemic to most long-term projects."

Designer Cheryl Lewin recalls, "When I had my own studio, I had always been the manager and designer on all of my projects. Clients tended to come to me for design services and I always made sure to make the project management side invisible. Unfortunately, doing that much by yourself can become all consuming. Now, I am more involved with managing the process, organizing people and resources, and communications between departments. While I am no longer on the boards, I see my work being applied to a larger arena in a much bigger business. I find it very satisfying."

At Sussman/Prejza, "We have five associates—all with design backgrounds who, with a design director, both design and manage projects. It is necessary to have a team with the skills and experience to design projects, but you also have to provide the necessary administrative staff to help manage them."

When affordable and appropriate, a professional project manager or coordinator can be a tremendous asset to a large project. They can relieve design professionals of most administrative chores, thereby allowing the greatest efficiencies of skills to tasks. Scheduling, tracking vendors, cost accounting, correspondence, status reports, and all other project communications are the responsibility of the project manager.

An experienced manager may even be able to locate and screen freelancers, vendors, and other outside resources. The manager should be able to do most of his or her own writing. With the right technical information, the manager should be able to build and maintain spreadsheets for cost accounting and scheduling, and communicate effectively with the design team and the client's team. A project administrator must have good judgment, self-motivation, and organizational skills. He or she also needs to be endorsed with enough authority to gather information and carry out decisions.

QUIRKS AND TIPS

"We find that we have to resell the project over and over during the course of the assignment. It seems to become our periodic role to convince the client to move forward," notes Leslie Smolan. Keep clear lines of communication on both sides. Sometimes there are bottleneck people—those who seem incapable of moving projects forward; work around them. It helps to understand the political processes at work, all the players, and their roles in obtaining approvals. The bigger the project, the less it is about design, and the more it is about moving through an organizational and political process.

Break down the project step-by-step and component-by-component. Analyze it in small pieces for personnel requirements, equipment, scheduling, and other items. Consider a customized accounting software package that links project scheduling, labor allocation, and cost tracking via network. This should help minimize additional bookkeeping.

Michael Bierut's observation cuts to the essentials and final conclusion of this topic: "I had always been involved in large projects, so I never thought they had any particular mystical qualities. At Pentagram, we manage a book cover about the same as a large project. In both instances, depending on the clients' behavior, intelligence, and commitment to the work, they can either make a project a dream or a nightmare. It is really a joy when someone with sufficient authority has decided to trust the designer and is capable of accepting some elements of unpredictability—and I'm not talking about novelty—but in those thoughts that might make the design memorable or breakthrough."

21

Successful Creative Briefs: Linking Business Objectives and Creative Strategies

EMILY RUTH COHEN

for Aquent

CALL THEM WHAT you will—"creative briefs," "design briefs," "marketing briefs," "communications briefs," or even "objectives and strategies statements"— the actual name is less important than helping creative and marketing professionals to fully understand and appreciate their potential value to any design initiative within your organization. Whatever your role in the creative development process, you have no doubt heard about these briefs; perhaps you even use them on a regular basis. The reality is, however, that many designers and their clients have yet to completely embrace the creative brief as a vital part of the design process to share valuable information, build consensus, align expectations, and set clear objectives.

Having worked with hundreds of creative professionals to hone their business skills in order to improve communications and relationships between themselves and their clients, I am confident that the creative brief—when properly developed and adhered to—is one of the most valuable tools in the design process, providing a vital connection between business objectives and creative strategies. For clients, account managers, and creatives, a clear and well-prepared design brief can help make a project, just as a long-winded and unfocused brief can lead

189

to its ultimate demise. While briefs should be customized to each individual discipline, company, and project, there are some common techniques that you can use to help ensure that your organization is not only creating impactful briefs but also getting the most out of them.

THE CREATIVE BRIEF: WHAT IS IT AND WHO DECIDES WHETHER TO USE ONE?

The creative brief is a written document that summarizes—comprehensively and concisely—both the business and creative requirements for a specific project or relationship. It is not a proposal, RFP, or initiation form, but instead the brief details overriding business objectives. A brief digs deep into a project and identifies the main factors that drive the entire creative strategy.

When developed by clients or designers working independently of each other, cut and pasted from pre-existing irrelevant documents, or written on the fly without any significant customer, market, or competitive research, a creative brief can become more of a hindrance than a driving force in the overall design process. If half-heartedly put together without the input of key stakeholders, it can actually confuse a project's overarching goals while sabotaging any real chance for success.

But if properly developed, a brief can mean stronger business results and a more cohesive and efficient creative process. "A well-written design brief is a written agreement, or contract, between the parties involved with the project," writes Peter L. Phillips in his book *Creating the Perfect Design Brief: How to Manage Design for Strategic Advantage*. "A design brief is also a road map, if you will, that defines the various steps that will be followed from the inception of the project to its completion. Design briefs must include a considerable amount of both business strategy and design strategy." As Phillips himself admits in his book, he is "quite taken" with the title "innovation brief"—a term commonly used in Europe—because he likes what it implies about design being an innovative or strategic business process.

Some industry professionals believe creative briefs should be used for any design project, no matter how small; others advocate using them only for larger-scale or longer-term initiatives because of the time and expense that can be involved to create a useable brief. Examples of these large-scope projects include advertising campaigns, branding, logo development, naming, packaging, integrated communications programs, and Web site projects. While the decision whether a given project might benefit from a creative brief is ultimately up to the client and the design team, an outside consultant is sometimes brought in to help evaluate a project's overall mission and to see if using a brief would add any significant value to the design process.

THE ONE-SIZE-FITS-ALL BRIEF OFTEN FAILS TO FIT ANYONE

Jennifer Miller is one such consultant. Her diverse career includes experience as a designer, as director of experiential and Internet marketing, and as creative director for a large ad agency. Miller now helps Aquent clients evaluate and improve their creative operations and processes. In this role she sees creative briefs in all shapes and sizes; she's a strong proponent of using three different levels of briefs depending on the scope of an initiative. "The first level is for the largest projects with overarching messaging and the most long-term objectives," Miller explains. "This brief should be developed at the beginning of any new client/creative relationship and it should be referred back to as necessary for any future initiatives. The second level brief is for mid-sized projects, and the third level is a rapid request form to be used for more tactical projects. Most creative initiatives I've come across could likely fit into the latter two levels, yet I often see companies mistakenly using one brief for all of their projects. This often results in individuals completing disjointed briefs that are either left mostly blank or containing information that is not especially pertinent to the specific goals."

That's why Miller says it's important for the individual tasked with writing a brief to understand that the document cannot cover everything, from high-level strategy to print specs. She believes the most effective brief begins with a templated format that can be automated, easily completed, and customized to meet specific client needs.

DEMONSTRATING THE BRIEF'S VALUE—AND YOUR OWN— TO THE CLIENT

If you are a designer faced with a client who fails to see the value of a creative brief, you may want to consider selling this "service" as part of your overall marketing strategy and in your promotional materials—on your Web site and in your initial sales pitch and proposal. Tell the client in every communication that the brief is an integral part of your process. If clients know about the brief in advance, they can allow time in their budget and schedule for it. Include a description of what the brief is and its purpose as a deliverable during the planning phase and you'll likely get more clients to sign on for this step of the process.

When the designer is not directly involved in developing the creative brief, miscommunication and misunderstandings can arise. On the other hand, when designers participate and lead in the process of creating a design brief, they express and reinforce the value of their insight and contribution. They also reiterate their role as the client's partner—rather than a vendor, an artist, or someone who simply executes ideas—and ensure buy-in to the entire process. Clients who include designers in the research and development process gain from the designers' insight and industry expertise. Both benefit from a mutually agreed upon set of expectations, objectives, and success criteria.

A creative brief also provides an opportunity to determine ROI (return on investment), a term clients love but designers hate because it's often difficult to measure. But if designers ask clients the right questions, they can gather great information, testimonials, and case studies to add to their resumes. Clients also can use this information as proof of the project's success and, thus, better define the value of their contributions and defend themselves to management.

If you are a designer handed an already finished creative brief, you must decide how to best interject yourself into the brief's development process without disregarding—or alienating—the client. Instead of discounting work already done, simply rename the document (for instance, as an objective and strategy document) and build upon what's there, adding your own thoughts to make it even more useful. This way, you demonstrate that you appreciate your client's efforts, and you prove your own value and willingness to collaborate. Many designers fail to be seen as total partners because they work on a "one-off" project basis without selling more integrated, bigger-picture strategic thinking. Whether based on your clients' initial information or created jointly with them, the creative brief is one way to incorporate strategy into the relationship and be seen as a valuable, long-term asset.

WRITING YOUR BRIEF: WHO TO INCLUDE AND WHEN TO BEGIN

Anyone with a true stake in the project should play an active role in the brief's development, including the entire creative team and the client's key stakeholders. Identify those responsible for writing the brief, and most importantly guiding and managing the project both internally and externally. Also include those individuals who contribute both internally and externally, as well as those who have the necessary insight into the project and the clout and expertise to make all critical decisions during the process—a.k.a., the approvers.

In some cases, designers receive the creative brief from their client; other times they write it in a vacuum without any client input. As a designer, if you're given a completed brief, you're not going to digest and absorb the information. If you try to create it on your own, there's a good chance you're not going to deliver what the client wants; as a result the client won't fully buy-in to the project.

Briefs are best written at the start of any relationship, prior to the development of a specific design solution, but after the research and discovery phase. The process of developing a creative brief generally includes the following steps: identifying key stakeholders, decision makers, and those individuals on your team who will be part of the process; reviewing any relevant background material provided by the client (including existing market research, business plans, audience profiles, branding guidelines, etc.); conducting a planning meeting with the client and stakeholders; conducting research to dig deep into individual issues and preferences before arriving at a collective decision; discussing conclusions and key information gathered from the research; discussing creative strategies; obtaining stakeholder buy-in to conclusions; and finally, drafting and issuing the brief for feedback and final approval.

The brief should provide a clear set of expectations and summarize everything you've learned during this process, including findings and related recommendations. It's your opportunity to align the client's business objectives with your creative strategy. Depending on how extensive the research is, and how long any feedback and approval takes, the entire creative brief process can take anywhere between one week to three months.

Miller says that the brief can originate with the client, but only after a long strategy discussion between the client and the creative team. "We advocate that everyone meet to get on the same page, even before the discovery phase or any work gets underway," she says. "This workshop session should include a discussion about overall objectives and also any recent trends in design and marketing so that all key participants are working with the same market information. It's a strategy summit, allowing each "side" to share their expertise with the other "side." The discovery and research phase follows, and from there the actual brief gets developed for a specific initiative. Aligning on overall strategy *before* the brief is written is critical to its ultimate usefulness—and success."

"Typically, in my experience, the account person crafts the brief since they are closest to the client," says David Haskell, senior copywriter at Boston-based Digitas. "Ideally it's a working session with the account person and the entire creative team to reach consensus on the brief's content. Afterwards, one person on the team writes the actual brief based on the meeting's results, and this document then goes to the client for input and buy-in."

It's always best to present the brief to your clients in person so you can walk them through it point by point. Otherwise, there's a good chance they won't thoroughly and completely read it. By reviewing the document with key stakeholders, you can make sure that they review it carefully, and that everyone agrees on the content and direction. Be sure to schedule enough time for the writing and review of the brief—the entire brief development process can sometimes take weeks if not longer to complete, depending on the project's scope. It's also crucial to provide clear deadlines for feedback and approval on the brief, and identify who will actually sign-off on it.

CONTENT GUIDELINES FOR A COMPELLING BRIEF

Although there is no one "right" way to develop a creative brief, there are certain guidelines you should consider following when beginning the crafting process (keeping in mind that to be most constructive, any content should be customized for each specific project or relationship).

Key categories of the brief might include:

- **Background information on company, product, or service.** Introduce the project and any background information that will drive its progress or success (i.e., new products, positioning strategies). Ideally, the designer should already have a good understanding of any client's organization, product, or service before the creative brief process has begun so this section should be kept brief.

- **User and target audience groups.** Identify the gender, age, geographic location, characteristics, priorities, occupations, and cultural considerations for each group. Find out what motivates and inspires each group, and identify differences and similarities between the sub-groups.

- **Brand attributes, promise, and mission.** Brand equity, assets, and strengths. Primary and secondary brand attributes. Differentiators. Expected brand perceptions and adjectives.

- **Competitive landscape.** Refer to the client's Web site or research you've already collected; analyze the competitive landscape, chart strengths and weaknesses, and determine how these are relevant to what you will be developing for the client. Best practices—inspirational (i.e., What does the client like and why? How is it relevant?).

- **Business objectives (success criteria).** Pinpoint the client's goals in developing a particular piece or service (i.e., Is the initiative meant to increase awareness, generate sales leads, educate existing clients, improve employee morale?).

- **Creative strategies.** Existing brand guidelines: what is relevant and what isn't? Logo, color palette, typography, imagery, content requirements, information hierarchy, visual and editorial themes, tone and image. This is the section to turn subjective opinions into objective strategies (i.e., If they ask for an "out-of-the-box" solution, how would they define this further?).

- **Functionality specifications.** (for Web projects)

- **Comparisons.** How should the audience perceive the brand/product/service?

- **Contribution and approval process.** Which contributors and approvers get involved at what stage of the project and what are they expected to contribute and/or approve?

- **Testing requirements.** Define how you test during the project and, after it's completed, measure its success.

- **Timelines.** Shelf life, launch of target dates.

- **Budget.** This demonstrates the client's financial commitment to the endeavor. How much are they willing to invest?

MAKE THE BRIEF VISUALLY APPEALING AND EASY TO INTERPRET

The design of the brief may be as important as the overall content because if it's not easy for clients—or designers—to read, then they most likely won't. Sheri L. Koetting, principal of New York-based MSLK Design (and a client of mine), is a fervent believer in an easy-to-scan chart format for creative briefs. Sheri cites a brief her firm presented to one of their new clients (see sample brief at end of article). "After meeting with the client, we realized that they really didn't understand their design goals for logo and packaging design. We needed to help them focus. They were trying to do too much, so one of the things we did in our creative brief was propose a radical design direction and a more middle-of-the-road design tweak," says Koetting. "We set up the two options in side-by-side columns so it was easy for the client to compare the benefits of the two different solutions. Because they could clearly see that we had done a thorough job researching the two options and that the more evolutionary, less radical option wasn't going far enough, they selected the more radical design, which is the one we were hoping they would chose."

MSLK has always used briefs to set design objectives and make strategy recommendations "because we believe that 99 percent of the solution is how you define the problem," Koetting adds. "That's why in our initial presentation with this client we felt it was important to include information detailing the value of defining a problem from the very beginning."

While the impact of MSLK's design is still unclear because the project is ongoing, their relationship with the client has been strengthened due to the successful collaboration. "After partnering with us on this one initiative, they trust and respect our opinion in a wide range of key decisions, not only their design needs," Koetting explains. "They see us as a key contributor, a touchstone to bounce ideas off of. For MLSK, this is the type of design firm we've always strived to be—focused on more than aesthetics and adding significant value to our clients."

THE TIMELESSNESS OF BRIEFS—EVEN IF THEIR FOCUS OR NAME CHANGES

During David Haskell's twenty-five years in advertising he has seen creative briefs used fairly consistently. "Even dating back to the 1940s, you'll find that many agencies had something resembling a creative brief," he says. "And while the format has stayed the same for the most part, the brief's primary focus has evolved. For a number of years, the unique selling proposition was the most important element, but the key objective has become helping clients stand out in a cluttered marketplace and attract customers bombarded with messages at every turn. It's not enough to have a unique or high quality product; it's about getting noticed, and many of today's briefs are addressing this market reality."

Haskell adds that the creative brief's ultimate usefulness ties back to how well the form is filled out and how knowledgeable the person completing it is. He believes that it may be better to go without a brief entirely, rather than using one that merely regurgitates generic language or is written with no genuine attempt by the author to offer detailed strategic information. To illustrate the importance of descriptive naming for the document itself, Haskell relays an anecdote involving Leonard/Monahan, New England Agency of the Year in 1987. "They called their brief a *Client and Agency Creative Brief*. It was widely accepted and very effective because everyone knew just by the name that it was not 'owned' by either party, but instead jointly produced by both teams."

SHARING IDEAS AND EDITING CONTENT: ESSENTIAL STEPS IN THE CREATIVE DEFINITION PROCESS

Top information design strategist Sylvia Harris (also one of my clients) helps implement communication programs for large institutions in the New York area. Sylvia uses briefs in varying amounts depending on who the client is. "I usually write the brief myself and then have my client review," she explains. "In my opinion, the greatest value of the brief is that everything is written down. I find that design teams often make assumptions at the beginning of a project, sometimes right, and often wrong. By putting thoughts on paper and sharing them with your client, everyone can agree from the beginning and nothing is left to interpretation or assumption. It's a way to create consensus among stakeholders. All the key players can start at the same place. They may not end up at the same place, but at least they are beginning from a unified position."

As with any written document, editing is critical in order to hone the brief's content. "Creative briefs should be brief," Haskell says. "A concise brief forces you to discipline yourself, to focus messaging from the get-go. Because the brief is a yardstick of the process that helps measure overall project effectiveness, the sharper the brief, the better results you'll see."

Harris agrees with Haskell about the importance of making briefs succinct. "Clients don't have time to wade through lengthy briefs and most designers are visual and would prefer to not read long, wordy documents. I find that most people glaze over after a page or two." She recommends including hot links in the brief for those individuals who may want a more detailed explanation for the various sections. That way, those who don't want to read longer explanations can ignore this and it's there for those who want it. She also stresses the importance of the brief as a means to define project "mandatories" that can or cannot change without being so precise as to risk stunting the creative process.

A GOOD BRIEF CUTS TO THE CHASE . . .

Michael Hunter, marketing director for the Whirlpool brand, concurs that brevity is essential when writing a brief. "Economy of words is key," he says. "You are defining the space within which the creative team should design, and then you need to let them do their job. The objective is to set goal posts for them without infringing on their territory."

Hunter references one of Mark Twain's quotes, "I didn't have time to write a short letter, so I wrote a long one instead," to illustrate his point that it's more challenging to write a short brief because more time is needed to polish the content—and that means more time up front defining and refining objectives and strategies to make them specific and targeted.

In Hunter's experience, there's a direct correlation between design and strategy. If the creative is off that means the initial strategy—and the creative brief—missed the mark. Hunter's marketing manager normally drafts any briefs and then shares them with him to get his input. The revised brief then gets submitted for review to the account and planning team within the agency.

. . . YET IS OFTEN HARD TO FIND

Jennifer Miller says she rarely comes across a creative brief that is structured well. "That's because most don't have enough segmentation of information," she explains. "Also there's not enough initial communication between those requesting the work (the client) and those executing the project (the creative team). The brief really encapsulates the ability of the involved parties to effectively pass along information. That is the single biggest factor for success or failure in any creative initiative."

CONCLUSION

Because the creative brief is intended to be a comprehensive strategic map for the entire design project, it's essential that all key team members be involved from the outset. For the designer, the brief can reinforce you as a strategic partner in the process. For clients, failing to include the creative team likely means they won't be fully immersed in the project or your objectives. By collaborating with the designer from the beginning of a project, clients will ensure the designer's buy-in and understanding, gain from his creative expertise, and have a clear, mutually agreed upon outline of goals and success criteria.

There is no rule of thumb when crafting a creative brief. "If there were just one correct format to use in creating the perfect design brief, all of our lives would be far less complicated!" writes Phillips. "It is also important to remember that there are a variety of design disciplines, and each discipline requires slightly different information in a truly useful design brief."

No matter which format you decide upon, make sure your brief is a user-friendly, visually-appealing document that people will actually make time to read. Each design organization must create its own specific set of standards, processes, and guidelines when developing a brief. As the first tangible results of any collaboration between client and designer, the creative brief can be a meaningful barometer of the interest—and ability—of both groups to forge a working relationship that encourages teamwork, honest discussion, and clear, open lines of communication. In the end, I think what matters most is that creative and marketing professionals understand the potential value of this important business tool to any design initiative and toward building a solid, mutually rewarding partnership.

What Makes a Creative Brief so Valuable?

When crafted properly, a creative brief:

- Links business objectives to creative strategies

- Guides the approval and decision process

- Mediates disagreements

- Provides a clear set of expectations and defines measurable objectives (metrics) to measure the progress and success of a project

Quick Tips to Keep in Mind

■ The brief should be introduced into any process early on so its full value can be explained and appreciated

■ You don't need one for every project—use only for large scale or important projects

■ The client is not your enemy, but your partner

■ If your client has given you a creative brief, rename the document but retain the process using elements from their existing brief, but revised to incorporate your new insights and knowledge

■ Allow enough time to develop and edit the brief

■ Provide clear deadlines for approval and feedback

■ Keep it simple and as short as possible

■ Use bulleted sound bites vs. narrative copy

■ Use charts and columns

■ Provide reasonable expectations—don't aim too high or low, don't over promise and under deliver

■ Customize the brief—don't use templates and don't leave any blanks

■ Adjust your presentation style to meet the unique personality of key decision makers

■ Conduct post-mortems/debriefs and include all key decision-makers and the entire design team

22

Sales Tax

DANIEL ABRAHAM AND MARCI BARBEY, CSA
Reprinted from *AIGA Design Business and Ethics*,
"Chapter 5: Sales Tax."

This review of sales tax practices in New York and California was commissioned by AIGA based on success in clarifying the issue in these bellwether states through legal and administrative proceedings. The intention of this chapter is to provide information to anyone in any state, using the New York and California examples as support in clarifying one's sales tax liability in one's own state.

As tax agencies are more aggressively enforcing the sales tax laws, more are eager to audit for possibly overlooked revenue. Graphic designers can best protect themselves from unexpected tax liability by learning when they are and are not required to collect sales tax on the work they provide for clients.

Sales tax is a state—and occasionally a local—matter, which prevents AIGA from pursuing a single national clarification of the issue. Statutes and the practice of the taxing authority will vary somewhat from jurisdiction to jurisdiction. In addition, graphic design services are seldom addressed explicitly in state sales tax laws. The many things that graphic design embraces—design services, illustration, printing specifications, and delivery of printed matter—are viewed as different forms of property and are treated and grouped differently for tax purposes from state to state. While AIGA offers a general guide to sales tax principles, dealing with sales tax should be worked out in consultation with an accountant.

You should be aware, however, that many accountants, even those "familiar with sales tax issues," may have no idea whatsoever what the sales tax issues are with regard to this poorly defined area of graphic design, and may suggest the safest course (but most expensive to designers): that designers charge tax on everything. A better course will be for designers to contact an accountant, and armed with this document, raise their consciousness on this issue, and then get their advice on how this affects your personal situation.

Current cases that help to narrow the liability of designers for sales tax will be posted on *www.aiga.org*.

A KEY DISTINCTION: IS YOUR WORK TANGIBLE OR INTANGIBLE?

The basic divide that determines what is subject to sales tax is the sometimes-blurry line between the tangible and the intangible. Transfers of tangible goods are generally taxed, unless specifically exempted by statutes or regulations; services and intangible property are generally exempt from tax, unless statutes or regulations specifically render them taxable. Graphic designers typically provide services that are in most cases nontaxable, and grant or license to clients rights to reproduce their work. Licenses are considered intangible personal property, and transfers of such are generally not subject to tax. Graphic designers may, however, also provide their clients with tangible personal property such as finished printed matter or a disk that contains the intangible personal property—a reproduction rights transfer—that is the substance of the contract. Tangible personal property is generally subject to tax, while tangible printed matter should be presumed taxable. Treatment of disks or other layout transfers may vary widely from jurisdiction to jurisdiction.

The designer, then, must consider what is being *done*, and what is being *transferred*, in the various elements of each client contract, and separate out a job's taxable elements from its nontaxable elements as precisely as possible in all contracts or invoices, according to the laws of the home jurisdiction.

SERVICES

Services, as noted above, are usually not subject to tax unless specifically included in a statute or regulation. This is the general category under which to group charges for time and labor; billable time for producing concepts and designs, scanning and manipulation, time spent on press, time spent building and encoding a Web site and similar billables should be calculated as services and so noted in all contracts and invoice terms.

INTANGIBLE PROPERTY

Copyright licenses are intangible *property*, as opposed to the intangible *services* of time and labor. Graphic designers, unlike illustrators, tend not to treat their client commissions as copyright licensing transactions. The images that a graphic designer creates, however—whether the logo which is clearly a free-standing image, or the larger image created by arranging type, illustrations, and photographs in a brochure or package or poster design—are copyrightable works of graphic art that the designer licenses to the client. This is not the place for a lengthy examination of the copyright-ability of graphic design. But the designer who registers designs when appropriate and who, registration or no, makes clear to the client that the client is acquiring a *license*, not purchasing *ownership* of either the original design itself or the boards or disks on which the design is embodied, is better able to retain control of the design and its integrity. Regarding sales tax, a clear paper trail indicating that the design is a copyright property being licensed to the client makes it clear to a taxing authority that the portion of the job not tax-exempt as "services" is a nontaxable transfer of intangible property.

TANGIBLE PROPERTY

Printed matter, such as brochures, stationery, or posters, is taxable as tangible property if the designer sells it to the client. If, however, the designer simply acts as the client's agent in dealing with the printer, with the client paying the printer directly, the transfer to the client will still be subject to tax; in this instance, the printer, not the designer, will have to collect it. The issue that arises when the designer transfers tangible personal property to the client in addition to performing services and licensing the design is how, and where, the line will be drawn between the intangible, nontaxable portion of the transaction, and the tangible, taxable portion. Taxing authorities are typically concerned that in a transaction of this nature, the bulk of the value will be loaded into the nontaxable portion of the transaction as an exercise in tax evasion—which is why a clear paper trail, differentiating the *value* of the intangible services (however calculated) and the licenses granted, from the taxable *costs* of the tangible printing and production, is essential to avoid unnecessary tax liability.

WHAT IS LESS CLEAR: IS GRAPHIC DESIGN TANGIBLE?

While most states do not tax intangible services or copyright transfers, the state laws and regulations may not be clear as to whether or not "graphic design" falls within provision of services and copyright license transfers, or is merely a production adjunct of the printing trade. Many state laws are woefully out of date, having been drafted long before the adoption of the current copyright law, in the era of engraving houses, hot type, and keylining, and do not even recognize the existence of the graphic designer independent from a printing or typesetting establishment. As an auditor's knowledge of the industry may well consist entirely of regulations that describe the industry as of twenty or more years ago, it falls entirely on the designer to provide clarification *within* the relevant laws and regulations, no matter how out of date, to explain why graphic design should be exempt from collection of tax in the event of an audit.

THE NEW YORK EXAMPLE

Nowhere in these classifications does the graphic designer, as such, clearly appear. Under New York tax law, then, a designer's services and licenses are potentially exempt from tax, but the designer must know in which category to classify different jobs.

New York exempts grants of the right to reproduce an "original image" from sales tax and also exempts "the services of an advertising agency or other persons acting in a representative capacity." Thus creation of an original work, such as a logo or creative services of a consulting nature, appears to be excluded.

New York does not, however, extend that exemption to what it terms a "license to use." Licensing of "original work"—i.e., created by the licensor—is a transfer of reproduction rights under New York law and not subject to tax if it is used as is. If, however, one is merely licensing the use of another's work, that is a "license to use" and subject to tax. It is also considered a taxable "license to use" if the licensee retouches or alters the work. The taxable "license to use" may apply to the designer who licenses an image from an archive or stock house, where the archive or stock house is not the creator of the work. If the designer manipulates the image in the sense of retouching it, the license paid by the designer is also a taxable "license to use" rather than a license of "reproduction rights."

Nonetheless, designers generally license original work to the client. Even if the original work of an annual report, book jacket design, or brochure design incorporates illustrations or photography which are someone else's original work, the end result which the designer licenses to the client is an original work in itself, in the form of a collective work which arranges the type, images, colors, paper, etc., into a different whole. The designer may have to pay tax on a "license to use" stock image that he or she manipulates to create the original design licensed to the end client, but the designer's end design, if reproduced as is, is a license of reproduction rights and not taxable. If the client, rather than the designer, adapts it and manipulates it, then it would appear the end client is licensing to "use" rather than to "reproduce," and must pay tax.

This would seem to be a strong incentive for designers and clients both not to have the client "adapt and apply" a design, but rather license it for straight reproduction. Not only does the client avoid paying tax, as does the designer avoid having to collect it, but the designer retains a greater level of control over his or her work.

"Original work," even that incorporating the licensed work of others, is the property of the designer whether the designer is a sole proprietor, or whether the designer is a commercial entity such as a partnership or corporation. In the latter instance, the original work of authorship—"the design"—is a work-for-hire work of authorship owned by the commercial entity. True, the hackles on every creator's neck rise at the term "work for hire," but if a work of authorship is created by several creatives in a company, and the end result is licensed by the company rather than an individual, the work is a "work for hire" owned by the company, and the company is the author.

In New York, design fees are not taxable, but transfers of tangible personal property such as layouts, printing plates, catalogues, and promotional handouts are. If you actually hand over design in a tangible form, rather than allowing the client to transfer design electronically for specified uses (without leaving a disk or tangible product), you are less likely to be liable for tax on a tangible product.

The designer may sometimes act as an advertising agency, or as an "other person acting in a representative capacity," avoiding tax on fees charged in both cases. A designer may also, however, grant a license to reproduce an original image—as in the case of a logo—or may license, or sub-license, images that the designer has retouched or otherwise manipulated. In the case of the logo, the designer's grant of reproduction rights is clearly not subject to tax; in the case of manipulated images, to avoid tax liability under a "license to use," it would be necessary for the designer to be able either to classify the job as being done in the role of an "advertising agency or other person acting in a representative capacity," or as the grantor of rights in the original *derivative* image, of which the designer is in fact the author.

Explanations in New York Sales and Use Tax Law

165–018 (f) "Reproduction rights" (1) The granting of a right to reproduce an original painting, illustration, photograph, sculpture, manuscript, or other similar work is not a license to use or a sale, and is not taxable, where the payment made for such right is in the nature of a royalty to the grantor under the laws relating to artistic and literary property.

(2) Mere temporary possession or custody for the purpose of making the reproduction is not deemed to be a transfer of possession which would convert the reproduction right into a license to use. See Howitt v. Street and Smith Publications, Inc., 276 NY 345 and Frissell v. McGoldrick, 300 NY 370.

(3) Where some use other than reproduction is made of the original work, such as retouching or exhibiting a photograph, the transaction is a license to use, which is taxable.

Example 1: A person contracts with an artist for a right to reproduce one of the artist's paintings on a book cover. No other right is given by the artist for the use of his painting. The person who obtains the reproduction right to the painting may have copies made and returns the painting to the artist without alteration, change, or correction, and without having destroyed or publicly exhibited the painting. The transfer is not held to be a transaction subject to the sales tax, as a rental, lease, or license to use.

Example 2: A photographer takes photographs and furnishes the same to a magazine publisher for the purpose of reproduction. In the course of reproduction, the publisher retouches the photograph. After reproduction, the photograph is returned to the photographer. The receipts from such a transaction are subject to the tax as a license to use.

Example 3: A dealer collects photographs and photographic prints. He furnishes the prints to a magazine publisher for the purpose of further reproduction. After reproduction, the prints are returned to the dealer. The prints may or may not be changed or altered. The receipts from such transactions are subject to the tax. Since the dealer merely collects the photographic prints and does not have the right to grant the right to reproduce the original, the transaction is deemed a license to use tangible personal property.

165–033 (b) "Exclusions" (5) Fees for the services of advertising agencies or other persons acting in a representative capacity are excluded from the tax. Advertising services consist of consultation and development of advertising campaigns and placement of advertisements with the media without the transfer of tangible personal property. The furnishing of a personal report containing information derived from information services by an advertising agency to its client for a fee is not a taxable information service. However, if an advertising agency is engaged only for the purpose of conducting a survey or if a survey is separately authorized and billed to the customer, the taxability of such survey is determined in accordance with the provisions of subdivision (a) of this section and the other provisions of this subdivision. Sales of tangible personal property such as layouts, printing plates, catalogs, mailing devices, or promotional handouts, tapes, or films by an advertising agency for its own account are taxable sales of tangible personal property.

Example 4: An advertising agency is hired to design an advertising program and to furnish artwork and layouts to the media. The fee charged by the agency to its clients for this service is not subject to the tax. However, if the layout and artwork are sold by the advertising agency to the customer for his use, the advertising agency is making a sale of tangible personal property, which is subject to the sales tax.

THE CALIFORNIA EXAMPLE

Unlike New York, California does directly refer to designers in its regulations, but the understanding of the design industry reflected there has traditionally rendered most finished work liable to tax. California in the past has exempted what it calls "preliminary art"—conceptual work, sketches, and preliminary layouts—but subjected "total charges for finished art"—that which is used for actual reproduction—to sales tax. Until recently, California's sales tax authority consistently refused to recognize the concept of licensing or reproduction rights as applied to images, though it did recognize these rights with regard to written works of authorship.

In the recent decision of Preston v. State Board of Equalization, the California Supreme Court rejected the state's traditional application of sales tax to image-based transfers of rights. In that case, an illustrator successfully sued the board for applying tax to payments for the copyright licenses she transferred to various publishers, and to the royalties she was subsequently paid. As a result of this favorable decision, brought about largely through an amicus brief filed by the Graphic Artists Guild and strongly supported by AIGA, the California sales tax regulations have been extensively redrafted. The redrafted regulations discuss rights transfers in terms of "technology transfer agreements," a California concept which evolved during the development of Silicon Valley, and which exempts transfers of intangible rights to images but does impose a minimal sales tax when such rights are transferred even temporarily in a tangible medium. The regulations affected include California sales and use tax regulations 1528, 1540, 1541 and 1543, and new regulation 1507; the most important for designers are regulation 1507, which discusses the technology transfer concept, and regulation 1540, which applies that concept to design, but most designers will at some time or another have to familiarize themselves with regulations 1528 (photography), 1541 (printing), and 1543 (publishing).

In brief, images transferred in intangible form—e.g., by modem—are wholly exempt from tax, but when the rights to an image are transferred using tangible means such as flat art, boards, or disks, the rights transfer itself is exempt from tax. However, the transfer of the tangible medium remains taxable, even if the transfer is temporary. Calculation of the amount subject to tax begins with a rebuttable presumption. If payment is received in a lump sum without distinguishing between "conceptual services" (which include all preliminary sketches and presentation pieces) and "finished art" (the final used for reproduction), it is presumed that 75 percent of the job fee is for conceptual services, leaving only 25 percent of the fee subject to tax.

However, this presumption of a taxable 25 percent can be reduced in three ways. If the designer's contract or invoice states the fee for the copyright license separately from the sale price for permanent transfer of the tangible material or the lease price for temporary transfer of the tangible material, the copyright license is nontaxable and the sale or lease price is the amount on which tax is due. If the contract or invoice does not separately state the charge for transferring the tangible work, the designer can calculate this taxable amount by referencing the taxable amounts of similar work done in the past. The third option is to calculate the taxable amount at 200 percent of the costs of materials and third-party labor. Under this last option, if a designer has no third-party labor costs (e.g. is a sole proprietor without employees or other assistance) and does the work on a computer, the sole taxable amount would be 200 percent of the cost of materials (i.e., of the disk or CD on which the final files are recorded and turned over to the client). Thus, with good record keeping, the actual tax burden can be calculated so as to be reduced to almost nothing.

SALES TAX VENUE

Sales tax applies only to business conducted within the designer's home state, with two exceptions. A few contiguous states, usually adjoining, have reciprocal agreements; the designer living in a state that has one of these agreements should consult an accountant to determine if tax is due on transactions with clients in the reciprocal state. Also, if an out-of-state client has a substantial business nexus such as a store or branch office in the designer's home state, tax will apply if due. If the designer is having printing done out of state for an in-state client, the shipping of the completed printed matter from out of state will still be subject to tax if the designer, not the printer, bills the client.

THE DESIGNER'S ROLE IN COLLECTING SALES TAX

Clients, understandably, do not want to pay tax if they can avoid doing so and frequently attempt to evade sales tax by the simple expedient of refusing to pay or ignoring the line item on the invoice. The designer, however, is liable to the state for the tax owed, whether or not the client pays and so should stress to the client that sales tax is "charged" by the state, not the designer, who merely *collects* it on behalf of the state, as mandated by law.

CONTRACT LANGUAGE THAT CLARIFIES THE TAX STATUS

The contract or proposal should contain language permitting the designer to pass through to the client any sales tax he/she must pay on a project and protecting the designer in the event that any taxing authority assesses sales tax on audit. The following wording should be in all contracts for *nontaxable* transactions and grants of rights for one-time reproduction of designs only: "Client is liable for sales tax paid by [the designer] to vendors or freelancers for services rendered or materials purchased relating to the execution of this project. The client shall also pay any sales, use, or other transfer taxes that may be applicable to the services provided, including any tax that may be assessed on subsequent audit of [the designer's] books of accounts."

On projects where the client is being provided the grant of a right for one-time reproduction of the designs only, all mechanicals and disks sent to the client must be marked with a stamp or label that provides the following message to avoid appearing to be a taxable transaction: "Ownership and title of all drawings, artwork, electronic files, and other visual presentations at all times remains the property of [the designer]. Temporary transfer of possession is granted only for the purpose of reproduction after which all materials must be returned, unaltered, and unretouched to [the name and address of the designer]." The following wording should be in all contracts for taxable projects: "This estimate does not include sales tax. Sales tax will be charged for that portion of the job delivered in New York State when the job is invoiced."

RECOMMENDATIONS TO MINIMIZE SALES TAX LIABILITY

Most states fall somewhere between New York and California in their application of sales tax to designers. The statutes and regulations may or may not recognize designers as such, or the existence and intangibility of reproduction rights, but most states—including California, once the regulatory revisions are complete—exempt most aspects of design transactions except for the delivery of tangible printed matter. The designer who wishes to avoid needlessly collecting tax and unnecessary liability for sales tax if audited, must be aware of how his or her home state statutes and regulations are configured and adjust contracts and billing to clearly distinguish tangibles from intangibles and taxable transfers from nontaxable in a manner that conforms to them. Initial consultation with an accountant familiar with sales tax can provide the designer with a template for design transactions that will enable the designer to avoid unpleasant surprises.

To minimize your sales tax liability, you should consider the following practices:

- Differentiate on your invoices the fees for design services (consulting), intangible products (use licenses), and tangible products (boards and disks, which should be treated as a commodity rather than as a specialized product to which all of the value of your creativity accrues). This may not be sufficient. An even more explicit approach would be to execute separate contracts for tangible and intangible products and services.

- Clarify in your written agreement with the client that you are providing the rights to use your work but not the ownership of the work itself.

- Specify on your boards or disks that they are the property of your studio and should be returned.

- Have clients pay directly for tangible products, such as printing, so that you do not have to assume the sales tax collection role.

23

Insurance Basics for the Designer

RAY AND SCOTT TAYLOR

THIS ARTICLE DISCUSSES the types of insurance coverage that graphic designers should know about. Purchasing insurance is similar in theory to purchasing a car. When you set out to purchase a car, you start with a basic, stripped-down model. Then you may add options, such as air conditioning, power windows, and automatic transmission. These added options improve the quality of the car you buy. Insurance is similar in that you start with a basic policy that excludes many types of losses. As with a car, you can add coverage by purchasing different types of endorsements, or options, and thereby improve the policy that you end up purchasing.

BUSINESS OWNERS POLICIES

The list below highlights the benefits offered by various business owners policies:

- Office Contents pays for the replacement cost of office contents lost due to fire, theft, water damage, smoke, lightning, hail, mischief, or an automobile or aircraft crashing into your building.

- Business Interruption covers the actual loss sustained for up to twelve months as a result of direct damage to the premises listed in your policy by a type of loss listed above. Payment is given for continuing overhead expenses during the period of business interruption.

- Valuable Papers covers the cost to restore the design work to the state it was in just prior to loss by fire, theft, or water damage. It is designed to cover a current job, and you must reproduce the job in order to collect. Coverage is usually limited to your office location.

❏ Electronic Data Processing protects your hardware and software in the event the equipment is damaged by fire, theft, or water. Coverage can be expanded to include any extra expenses needed to recreate the lost data in the event of a covered peril. Coverage is usually limited to your office location.

❏ Bailee protects property damage to other people's property in your care, custody, or control. There is usually a sublimit for jewelry, furs, fine arts, antiques, and no coverage for breakage, scratching, and marring.

❏ Portfolio covers the cost of duplicating twenty-five images at a cost not to exceed $100 each in the event your portfolio is destroyed, lost, or stolen. The coverage is worldwide. Please note, this does not cover stock photographs.

❏ Commercial General Liability protects your legal liability against lawsuits for bodily injuries or property damages that occur within the United States and Canada to other people or other people's property. Important exclusions are listed below. (Rest assured the actual policy contains many more exclusions):

❏ Damage to those people considered to be employees covered under your workers' compensation

❏ Damage to those people eligible for disability benefits under a state statute

❏ Damage to anything pertaining to an automobile, watercraft, or aircraft

❏ Damage to other people's property in your care, custody, or control

❏ Claims resulting from an improper model's release, invasion of privacy, infringement of copyright or trademark, infringement of patent, or libel or slander

❏ Claims occurring outside the United States or Canada

❏ Any damage pertaining to pollution

❏ Any intentional act or criminal act

❏ Discrimination or sexual harassment

❏ Claims by someone other than an employee to recover damages paid to or sought from a former or existing employee

❏ Nonowned and Hired Automobile Liability protects the employer for bodily injury or property damage claims that arise from use of a hired, borrowed, or rented automobile. This coverage will respond only after the policy insuring the vehicle involved in the accident has paid its limit.

There is no coverage for damage to the vehicle being driven, for the graphic artist to whom the vehicle belongs, or for damage to property belonging to the graphic artist. Coverage is limited to the United States, its possessions, and Canada.

WORKERS' COMPENSATION AND STATUTORY DISABILITY BENEFITS

There are other insurance options that should be purchased in addition to the business owners policy or its equivalent. They are: workers' compensation and employers liability insurance, and statutory disability benefits in the states of New York, New Jersey, Rhode Island, California, Puerto Rico, and Hawaii.

When you purchase workers' compensation and employers liability coverage, you are eliminating two important exclusions in the standard commercial liability policy. A workers' compensation policy will protect you for the benefits required under a state statute in the event your employee gets hurt on the job. Most state statutes cover an employee for his or her medical expenses and a portion of his or her income for disability. If you have not purchased this coverage, you are personally responsible for this benefit. Failure to provide workers' compensation is punishable by a fine, and the shareholders of the corporation will be personally liable for any benefits.

Oftentimes, the graphic designer will hire temporary workers in order to save money and paperwork. Because the designer considers temporary workers to be freelance, he or she will not withhold taxes or buy workers' compensation. However, the IRS and the Workers' Compensation Board are two different administrative agencies. In the eyes of the Workers' Compensation Board, freelance workers can be determined to be employees. In the event of an injury, the courts will go to great lengths to protect an employee's workers' compensation benefits. For example, a written agreement between an employer and employee where the employee signs away his rights to workers' compensation benefits will not be upheld.

Furthermore, it is far cheaper for an insurance company to pay the state mandated workers' compensation benefits than to pay the same claim under the commercial general liability coverage. This is because a large portion of the damage awards are for pain and suffering and there is no jury to award these damages in the workers' compensation. Since the structure of the benefits is set by the legislature, a commercial general liability insurance carrier will usually try to have a claimant categorized as an employee to lower the payout. The employer's liability coverage will protect you for claims brought by someone other than an employee to recover for damages paid to or sought from a former or existing employee. Workers' compensation benefits are determined by the state in which an employee is hired, and most state insurance policies offer a discount to the policy holder if there are no claims. The major disadvantage to these policies is that they only provide the benefits of the state in which they are located. Policies offered by the private insurance carriers will usually provide benefits for all states except those few states that have monopolistic state-run funds (or any state in which your insurance carrier is not licensed).

Lastly, it is important not to hire children in violation of their working papers. When such a worker is injured while on the job, the standard policy will only pay a single workers' compensation benefit. Some states require that multiple benefits be paid as a penalty in such cases. The difference between the standard compensation benefit and the penalized benefit is the responsibility of the employer.

When you purchase statutory disability coverage you are eliminating an important exclusion in the standard commercial general liability policy. Coverage is mandatory in New York, Hawaii, Rhode Island, Puerto Rico, California, and New Jersey. The statute renders an employer responsible for a set dollar amount should an employee get hurt or sick while off the job. In New York and Hawaii, coverage is usually purchased directly through the state or payroll deducted and transmitted with your other taxes.

ADDITIONAL OPTIONS

Options that should be considered in addition to the business owners policy or its equivalent, workers' compensation and statutory disability benefits include:

- Umbrella liability—which covers the insured sums that exceed the underlying liability limits of the commercial general liability, auto liability, non-owned and hired automobile liability, etc.
- Foreign commercial general liability, foreign nonowned and hired automobile liability, foreign workers' compensation
- Stock photo library coverage
- Coverage on a per job basis for jewelry, furs, antiques, silverware, and objects of art
- Nonowned and hired watercraft liability and/or physical damage
- Nonowned and hired aviation liability and/or physical damage
- Nonowned automobile physical damage
- Errors and omissions—to cover an improper model's release
- Pollution liability
- Coverage for improvements and betterments to studios
- Glass
- Boiler and machinery
- Employee dishonesty

- Monies and securities inside and outside premises, for petty cash
- Pension plan liability
- Business automobile policy

LOSS PAYEE VERSUS ADDITIONAL INSUREDS

People are always asking about the differences between a loss payee and an additional insured. A loss payee is a person or organization that has a financial interest in property given or leased to you and for which you have agreed to provide the insurance. By adding a loss payee endorsement, both signatures are needed on a claim check in order to cash the check. The loss payee thereby maintains control of the insurance claim proceeds.

An additional insured endorsement extends your liability policy to cover a person or organization other than yourself. You are sharing your insurance limit with this other party. Since the insurance carrier is now protecting more than one business, there is an added premium for this coverage.

DEDUCTIBLES

All property insurance coverages carry deductibles that provide no payment for claims that are less than $200, less than $500, or less than $1,000, and the deductible clause serves to lower the premium that needs to be paid for the coverage and eliminates the costly expense of adjusting minor or small claims. Higher deductibles can be obtained from the insurance carrier, particularly when the items or property insured are much greater in value and, therefore, greater in cost. With higher deductibles, the cost can be reduced substantially.

VALUATION

In buying property insurance, one should insure as close to actual value or replacement value of the property so as to be able to replace the property in the event of a loss. Liability limits should be adequate or high enough so that if there is a serious bodily injury or property damage claim caused by use of vehicles or ownership of a business or property, there is enough insurance coverage to prevent your personal assets from being used to satisfy a judgment or debt obligation.

In buying insurance coverages, the graphic designer should try to purchase as much coverage from the same brokerage company and insurance carrier as he or she can, since various discounts are available when all insurance coverages are maintained through the same agency or insurance carrier.

PERSONAL INSURANCE

In addition to the business property and liability insurance discussed above, the graphic designer should simultaneously maintain adequate personal insurance coverages. Obviously, if the graphic designer owns a house or an apartment, home owners' insurance should be kept in force. If the designer owns valuable personal belongings such as fine art objects, cameras, and jewelry, he or she should have them insured under a floater to cover them in the event of burglary, theft, fire, or related losses. The graphic designer should also have adequate levels of disability income to enable the payment of continuing overhead expenses and to replace lost income during periods of disability. Consideration should be given to purchasing adequate levels of life insurance to protect the designer's family or combine with savings that can be used with a retirement plan. The designer should give consideration to creating pension plans such as a SEP (Self-Employed Pension), Keogh Plan, 401(K), or IRA (Individual Retirement Account), and the form selected should be what best suits his or her needs. The AIGA can provide Association group disability income insurance at favorable rates, as well as hospitalization and major medical coverages.

This article is a general description of business insurance coverage for a graphic artist, and discusses coverage that is in effect and available as of the date of this printing. Each individual must refer to his or her insurance policies for an exact description of coverage provided.

24

Managing Health and Safety in the Design Studio

MONONA ROSSOL

GRAPHIC DESIGNERS COMBINE photos, type, and illustrations to make pages, posters, packages, or textile design. Processes used in graphic and commercial art include computer graphics design, illustration and photo processes, and paste up of mechanicals.

Recently, an illustrator friend of mine was working on a job for a major university press. She called the head graphic designer at the press about a problem that could be easily fixed if he would cut and paste a section of Photostat. To her surprise, she found that this was not possible because the graphic designer had never cut and pasted anything in his life!

This story demonstrates the incredible change that has occurred in the graphic design field. Computers have taken over. They have made skilled paste up and mechanical production workers an endangered species. They also make it possible for small studios and home-based freelancers to compete with established studios.

Some people see a certain coldness in computer generated graphics. They prefer to use the old methods in the same way that some music lovers are rejecting CDs and returning to vinyl. This chapter will cover health and safety issues of the old methods as well as the new.

TRADITIONAL GRAPHIC ART

Traditional graphic art is an industrial process. Its workers, like other industrial workers, use toxic chemicals to create their product. Included are aerosol spray products, toxic pigments and dyes, lead containing inks and paints, and toxic solvents. Hazardous equipment may be used, such as eye-damaging xenon and quartz light sources, ammonia-producing diazo copiers, and ozone-emitting photocopiers and laser printers.

HAZARDOUS PRODUCTS USED IN TRADITIONAL GRAPHIC ART

- ❏ Toxic/Flammable Solvent Vapors: rubber cement thinner, some glues and adhesives, felt tip markers and pens, turpentine propanol, and other solvents

- ❏ Toxic Dyes and Pigments: air brush inks and dyes, textile dyes and paints, touch-up colors, color correction products, gouache, oils, water colors, sign paints, and colored pencils

- ❏ May Contain Lead and Cadmium: sign paints, artists paints, metal primers, boat and auto paints

- ❏ Toxic/Flammable Aerosol Mists: spray adhesives, spray fixatives, aerosol spray paints

- ❏ Photo and Photo Print Chemicals: black and white processing, color developing chemicals, imaging and proofing systems, typography, photostats, blueprint chemicals, and ammonia

- ❏ Ozone-Emitting Equipment: copy machines, laser printers, bogus air purifiers, and old carbon arcs

HAZARDS OF TRADITIONAL MATERIALS
Dyes and Pigments

Dyes and pigments are used in airbrush colors, textile processes, and paints. Most are synthetic organic chemicals. Historically, the first synthetic dyes were made from a chemical called aniline, which was derived from coal tar. Now there are dozens of different chemical classes of dyes. Most dyes and organic pigments are members of these chemical classes.

The vast majority of dyes and pigments never have been studied for long-term hazards, such as cancer and birth defects. However, when several members of one of the chemical classes are tested and shown to cause cancer, it is wise to assume that the rest cause cancer too. Under current labeling laws, untested dyes and pigments can be labeled "nontoxic" even when they are closely related to chemicals known to cause cancer! It is best to treat all dyes and pigments as potentially toxic.

It is suspected that the cause of elevated incidences of bladder cancer in industrial and art painters is related to their use of such dyes and pigments. Some dyes and pigments also are hazardous because they contain highly toxic impurities such as cancer-causing PCBs (short for polychlorinated biphenyls).

Another class of pigments is the inorganic metal-containing pigments. Included among these are pigments containing lead, cadmium, cobalt, chrome, nickel, manganese, and mercury. The toxic effects of these pigments are better known. Lead-containing colors are especially toxic and are banned in consumer wall paints. Paints that still are allowed to contain lead include artists' paints and printmaking inks, sign paints, boat paints, automobile paints, and metal priming paints.

Solvents

The term "solvent" is applied to many different liquids used to dilute paints, inks, marking pens, adhesives, aerosol sprays, and the like. All common solvents are narcotics at some level of exposure. Glue sniffers have proven that they can get high—even die—from inhaling vapors from any solvent-containing product, including glue, gasoline, or spray paints. Abuse of correction fluid killed three people in 1985!

There are no safe solvents. All solvents, natural or synthetic, are toxic. Exposure may occur either by skin contact with the liquid or by inhalation of the vapors they emit into the air. Solvents also can damage the skin, eyes, respiratory tract, nervous system, and internal organs such as the liver and kidneys. These kinds of damage can be acute, from single heavy exposures, or chronic, from repeated low dose exposures over months or years. In addition, some solvents can cause specific diseases such as cancer.

Studies of one of the least toxic solvents—grain alcohol—have shown that babies born to drinking mothers may be of low birth weight and have varying degrees of mental retardation. Because most solvents damage the brain and nervous system, doctors have suspected for years that solvents would similarly affect the fetus. Now a Canadian study has shown an increase in birth defects of babies borne to moderately solvent-exposed mothers. A follow-up study showed that the normal children borne to solvent-exposed mothers were more impulsive, hyperactive, and subject to learning difficulties.

Photographic Chemicals

Vast numbers of substances, many of them complex organic chemicals, are used in photographic processes. Many of these are known to be hazardous, while the hazards of many others are unknown and unstudied. In addition, manufacturers add new photochemicals to their products regularly. For these reasons, it is impossible in the scope of this chapter to discuss all photochemicals. But in general, these chemicals cause occupational skin and respiratory diseases.

Skin Diseases

Many types of dermatitis have been seen in photographers including hyper- and hypopigmentation of the skin, contact dermatitis, lichen planus (rough scaly itching patches), and more. Developing chemicals probably are primarily responsible for these skin conditions because so many are strong irritants and sensitizers. Skin burns can also occur from contact with acids such as glacial acetic acid for stop baths and caustics, such as sodium hydroxide, intensifiers (bleaches), and oxalic acid (in some toners).

Respiratory Diseases

Allergic asthma, increased susceptibility to colds, and respiratory infections are associated with photographic developing. These effects can be caused by irritating and sensitizing gases and vapors emitted by photochemicals. Emissions from common photochemicals include sulfur dioxide, acetic acid vapors, and formaldehyde.

Photoprinting Chemicals

Many photographic processes have been adapted to printmaking uses. Included are photolithography, photoetching, and photo silkscreen processes. These processes require precautions because the chemicals used are similar to those used in printmaking.

High intensity light from sources such as halide, xenon, or quartz bulbs are needed for these processes. Historically, carbon arc lamps were used; these also emit highly toxic gases and should be avoided.

Photoetching uses solvents to etch plastic. Some of these solvents, called glycol ethers, are highly toxic to male and female reproductive systems. Photolithography uses solvents and dichromate solutions. The dichromates cause allergies and cancer.

Photo silkscreen processes include both direct and indirect emulsion methods. Direct emulsions usually use ammonium dichromate as the sensitizer. Indirect emulsions use presensitized films developed by concentrated hydrogen peroxide and cleaned of emulsion with bleach. Concentrated hydrogen peroxide and bleach can cause severe eye and skin damage on contact. When used to remove emulsions, bleach emits chlorine gas which requires ventilation.

PRECAUTIONS FOR TRADITIONAL GRAPHIC DESIGN

The following is a list of general tips to keep your studio safe.

- Never use toxic chemical products in home studios. Working at home can result in contamination of eating and sleeping areas. Workers are exposed for longer periods of time at home than in workplaces. Children and pregnant women must not be exposed to even low levels of toxic substances.

- Plan studios that can be cleaned easily. Shelving and floors must be sponged and wet-mopped.

- Install ventilation systems appropriate for the work done in the studio. For example, provide a spray booth for airbrushing. Provide ventilation at a rate of roughly twenty room exchanges per hour for small darkrooms, ten room exchanges per hour for large darkrooms.

- Separate electrical equipment from sources of water and wet processes as much as possible. Install ground fault interrupters on all outlets within ten feet of sources of water.

- Install eyewash stations if chemical corrosives or irritants are used. (Emergency showers also are required if large amounts are used.)

- Mark exits and fire evacuation routes. Provide a fire suppression system or fire extinguishers that are approved for the type of chemicals stored and the equipment used. Know how to use the extinguishers.

Personal Hygiene

- Do not eat, smoke, or drink in studios, shops, or other environments where there are toxic materials. Dust settles in coffee cups, vapors can be absorbed by sandwiches, and hands can transfer substances to food.

- Wash hands carefully after work, before eating, using the bathroom, and applying makeup.

- Wear special work clothes and remove them after work. If possible, leave them in the workshop and wash them frequently and separately from other clothing. Wear aprons for photochemical work, and other protective clothing as needed.

Storage of Materials

- Purchase materials in unbreakable containers whenever possible. Do not transfer materials to other containers unless all the label information is transferred as well.

- Apply good bookkeeping rules to storage of flammable or toxic materials. Keep a current inventory of all the materials and post locations of flammable or highly toxic materials.

- Apply good housekeeping rules to chemical storage. Have cleaning supplies and spill control materials at hand.

- Organize storage wisely. For example, do not store large containers on high shelves where they are difficult to retrieve. Never store hazardous chemicals directly on the floor or above shoulder height.

- Store reactive chemicals separately. Check technical advice from the manufacturer of each product (e.g., the Material Safety Data Sheet, MSDS).

- ❑ Keep all containers closed, except when using them, to prevent escape of dust or vapors.

- ❑ Storage of flammable chemicals should conform to all state and provincial fire regulations. Contact your local authorities for advice. Store large amounts of flammable solvents in metal flammable storage cabinets or specially designed storage rooms.

Chemical Handling and Disposal

- ❑ Do not use any cleaning methods that raise dust. Wet mop floors or sponge surfaces frequently and empty waste cans daily.

- ❑ Dispose of waste or unwanted materials safely. Check federal and local environmental protection regulations. There are serious fines associated with improper disposal of products containing certain metals (barium, cadmium, chromium, lead, mercury and silver, selenium) or flammable solvents. It is best to try to substitute water-based products for solvents and to avoid products containing these metals. Otherwise, have this kind of waste picked up by a hazardous waste company. Pour nonpolluting aqueous liquids down the sink one at a time with lots of water.

- ❑ Do not store flammable or combustible materials near exits or entrances. Keep sources of sparks, flames, ultraviolet light, and heat, as well as cigarettes, away from flammable or combustible materials.

Substitution

- ❑ Avoid solvents and solvent-containing products when possible. For example, use glue sticks (some glues now allow artists to reposition copy) and waxers rather than rubber cement or spray adhesives. Choose water-based or latex paints, inks, and other products over those containing solvents.

- ❑ Choose products that do not create dusts. Avoid materials in powdered form such as dry photochemical dyes and pigments, or soft pastels.

- ❑ Avoid air brush or aerosol products whenever possible to avoid inhalation hazards. If they must be used, install a spray booth or other local exhaust system that captures and removes the spray mists.

- ❑ The most comprehensive substitution is to replace chemical processes with computer generated graphics.

Computer Graphics

Computer generation of graphics is certainly a safer method than traditional chemical processes. However, this method is not entirely free of hazards. For example, computers and their monitors emit radiation in the form of visible, infrared, and ultraviolet light and electromagnetic frequency radiation. The new flat screen monitors emit far less radiation. Video display terminals are associated with eyestrain. Keyboards, the mouse, and stylus use may lead to physical overuse injuries and stress.

Light

Natural light contains a wide spectrum of visible, ultraviolet, and infrared rays. Artificial light contains a more limited array of light waves. It is well known that ultraviolet rays can damage the skin and eyes, and even cause skin cancer. Both sunlight and unshielded fluorescent lights have been implicated in causing cancer. Inadequate lighting, glare, and shadow-producing direct lighting can cause eyestrain.

Electromagnetic Radiation

Computers and monitors emit low-level, pulsed, electromagnetic frequency (EMF) radiation. EMF radiation is emitted from all electrical appliances and was thought to be harmless for many years. Now some studies show an increased risk of developing cancer among children, workers, and animals exposed to EMF radiation. However, there still is no conclusive evidence that these effects are due to EMF radiation.

To be on the safe side, pregnant Canadian government workers have been given the right to transfer from video display terminal jobs without loss of pay. This is a humane and reasonable strategy in the absence of definitive data on EMF radiation.

Exposure can also be reduced by remaining out of the high-dose areas immediately adjacent to the back and sides of the computer. And many new computers produce less EMF radiation than older models.

Overuse Injuries

Repetitive tasks such typing from the keyboard and using a mouse or stylus put artists at risk of developing special types of injuries called cumulative trauma disorders (CTDs). These usually affect tendons, bones, muscles, and nerves of the hands, wrists, arms, and shoulders. Common injuries include tendonitis and carpal tunnel syndrome.

Ergonomics is the study of ways to prevent CTDs. Ergonomics is the science of making the best use of human capabilities by designing work environments using data from engineering, anatomical, physiological, and psychological principles. Today many tools, machines, and office and shop furniture have been redesigned with ergonomic principles in mind.

PRECAUTIONS FOR COMPUTER GRAPHICS STUDIOS

You can preserve your health in the office by changing your habits. To prevent CTDs, pay careful attention to your body for signs of fatigue, pain, changes in endurance, weakness, and the like. Use good work habits to resolve early symptoms, including: good posture, frequent rest breaks every fifteen to thirty minutes, alternating tasks often or varying the types of work done; warming up muscles before work; moving and stretching muscles during breaks; easing back into heavy work schedules rather than expecting to work at full capacity immediately after holidays or periods away from work; modifying technique and equipment to avoid uncomfortable positions or movements.

If you have symptoms of CTDs and they do not respond quickly to better work habits, seek medical attention. Early medical intervention will resolve the majority of overuse injuries without expensive treatment or surgery. Delaying treatment can leave you disabled for long periods or even for life.

There are some simple ways to improve your environment as well, which will help preserve your health in the studio.

Room Lighting

- ❏ Provide good lighting, especially for close work. Use diffuse, indirect, overhead lighting combined with direct light on the copy and tasks.

- ❏ Keep room lighting levels at a comfortable medium level. This can be more easily facilitated if the walls are painted a neutral color like gray rather than bright colors or white.

- ❏ Use incandescent lights. Avoid fluorescent lights whose flickering and incomplete spectra can tire and irritate some people.

- ❏ If there are windows, use Venetian blinds, translucent curtaining, or other methods to avoid glare on the screen.

Screen Lighting and Use

- ❏ Use monitors that have accessible contrast and brightness controls for easy adjustments.

- ❏ Use maximum brightness and contrast only for mixing colors. When working on an image, lower contrast and brightness to more comfortable levels.

- ❏ Avoid background colors that are light and bright. Use black, dark, or neutral colors when possible.

- ❏ Get your eyes and your prescription glasses checked frequently. If you wear glasses, have one pair that focuses your eyes at between two to three feet and keep the monitor at this distance. Get lenses that block ultraviolet light. If you need a colored lens, use a neutral gray that will not interfere with color perception.

- Take breaks every fifteen minutes or so to look away from the screen and focus on a more distant place.

- Avoid using a one-pixel brush when possible. If you have to use the one-pixel brush, increase the scale.

- Use light tables lit by incandescent bulbs of low wattage. If you make your own, remember to provide a vent for the heat created by incandescent bulbs.

Equipment

- Place computer backs toward a wall to reduce exposure to EMF radiation. Never face the back or sides of a computer or monitor toward yourself or others.

- Purchase monitors that can swivel and tilt easily.

- Chairs should adjust easily for height. Those that can be pneumatically raised and lowered with a foot lever are easiest to operate. Armrests are desirable.

- Tables or keyboard shelves should be adjustable. Keyboards should be positioned so that hands and arms are in a relaxed position when typing.

- Using a stylus can cause repetitive motion problems. Modifying their shape can be helpful. This can be done by putting the handle into a hole drilled in a rubber ball, or placing a lump of warm, hard plasticine or casting material on the stylus and squeezing it into the shape of your hand.

- Drafting boards should be adjustable, even to a vertical position. Select worktables that are at a comfortable level for your height.

Ventilation

Windows should provide enough ventilation for small studios and home studios in which computer graphics are the sole method of work. Larger studios require ventilation systems.

The American Society of Heating, Refrigerating, and Air-Conditioning Engineers estimates the amount of fresh air required for comfort and health at twenty cubic feet per minute per building occupant. Many office and commercial buildings do not provide this much fresh air. And no office building ventilation system is capable of providing proper ventilation for control of chemicals from traditional graphic arts processes.

Should you suspect there is poor air quality in an office or commercial building, a ventilation engineer or industrial hygienist may be needed to identify the cause. This may involve a survey of the system, tests of temperature, humidity, carbon dioxide levels over time, and others. If the ventilation system is at fault, fixing it may involve rebalancing the system or modification of the existing equipment.

Temporary relief from poor air quality can sometimes be accomplished with air purifying devices. But advertising claims for air purifiers often grossly overestimate their effectiveness. Before purchasing one, obtain professional advice from someone who is not selling the equipment. And do not purchase any air purifier that releases ozone.

Occasionally, people will experience air quality problems when new computer equipment is installed. Computers outgas small amounts of plasticizers and solvents used in the plastic casing, wiring, and circuit boards when they are turned on and get warm. Most people do not even notice these chemicals, but others will have symptoms that will only resolve after months or years when the computer stops outgassing.

GRAPHIC ART WORKPLACES AND THE LAW

Whether traditional chemical processes or computers are used, graphic design studios are just another workplace as far as the laws are concerned. Employees in these studios, like any other industrial workers, are protected by the Occupational Safety and Health Administration (OSHA). OSHA requires that employers provide graphic art workers with work and a workplace that is "free of recognized hazards."

OSHA only has jurisdiction over employees. Some graphic studio owners try to avoid the OSHA rules and paperwork by giving their jobs to independent contractors. But if these people work under the employer's direction, and especially if they work on the premises, it is likely the IRS will consider these people employees. Many an employer has found this out after a laid off or fired independent contractor has filed for unemployment benefits.

Should an employee become injured or ill on the job, workers' compensation usually provides benefits for the employee. At the same time, workers' compensation protects the employer from being sued for damages by the employee. There are only a few states in which employees can sue employers for workplace injuries under limited circumstances.

Some employers also allow unpaid assistants to work in the studio. These might include students, interns, volunteers, or workers' children. Should these non-employees incur injuries or illnesses in the studio, they usually can sue the shop owner.

While such assistants are not regulated by OSHA, the liability of the employer can best be protected by extending the same rights to them as OSHA accords to workers. This means that all the required protective equipment, training, and access to hazard information should be provided to all workers paid and unpaid.

What are Your OSHA Obligations?

The OSHA regulations apply to every phase of workplace safety such as walking surfaces, lighting, electrical equipment, air quality, fire safety, and much more. OSHA requires employers to provide a workplace free of "recognized hazards." To determine what these hazards actually are, you need to consult the regulations. The OSHA rules are found in the Code of Federal Regulations (CFR) Section 29 from numbers 1900–1910. Information about obtaining these regulations can be obtained from your local OSHA office (see the blue pages of your telephone book).

If hazardous chemicals and products are used in the graphic studio there are three rules that apply specifically to their use:

1. Hazard Communication (29 CFR 1910.1200)

2. Respiratory Protection (29 CFR 1910.134)

3. Personal Protective Equipment (29 CFR 1910.132)

The fewer the number of chemical products used on the premises, the easier these rules are to follow. In fact, one of the greatest benefits of conversion to digital and computer-generated graphics is that they do not involve chemicals that apply to these rules.

Hazard Communication

The Hazard Communication standard (29 CFR 1910.1200), or Right-to-Know law, requires that employers develop a program to inform and train all full- and part-time employees about the hazards on their jobs. Failure to comply can result in OSHA citations and fines. Required are:

- A written hazard communication program detailing how the provisions of the rule will be met. A prototype plan for small businesses can be obtained from OSHA.

- A written inventory of all potentially hazardous products on the premises must be developed.

- Material safety data sheets on all potentially hazardous materials must be on file.

- Labels on all containers of chemicals must be in compliance with the Hazard Communication Standard rules.

- Formal training by a qualified person must be provided for all employees who are potentially exposed to toxic chemicals.

- Ready access to MSDSs (material safety data sheets) and all written elements of the program must be given to workers during all working hours.

Canadian graphic artists are protected by a similar law called the Workplace Hazardous Materials Information System (WHMIS). It also requires collection of MSDSs and formal training of workers.

Respiratory Protection

Respirator use must comply with 29 CFR 1910.134, which requires employers to establish a respirator program. 29 CFR 1910.134(b) provisions (1) to (11) list the "Requirements for a minimal acceptable program." These include:

- A written program explaining how the employer will meet the requirements and how respirators will be selected

- Formal fit testing of workers by a qualified person using one of the approved methods done at least annually

- An annual check on the employees' medical status to assure that they are physically able to wear a respirator and safely tolerate the breathing stress caused by masks and respirators

- Procedures for regular cleaning, disinfecting, and maintaining all respirators. Respirators that are shared must be disinfected after every use.

- Procedures for formal, documented training of workers

Personal Protective Equipment

In 1996, OSHA changed the rules for personal protective equipment (29 CFR 1910.132, 133, 135–138). OSHA now requires a written program, documented worker training, and regular review of the effectiveness of the program. These requirements are not as onerous as they sound. A short statement about why protective equipment is needed and a list of things the worker needs to know about the equipment takes care of the written materials. Then checking each point off as it is explained to a worker and having the worker sign and date a copy of the list should suffice for training about gloves, goggles, etc. These procedures also protect the liability of employers and supervisors.

SUMMARY

There are scores of other OSHA regulations affecting employees in the workplace. However, self-employed workers who work alone do not come under OSHA's jurisdiction. The fact that home workers can bid on jobs without factoring in the cost of worker training and OSHA compliance programs is likely to make them even more competitive in the graphic design business.

Yet, home workers need safety training and precautions, too. Homes are often less than ideal workplaces. Space, lighting, ventilation, and other studio requirements must be provided at home. And unless great care is taken, the chemicals home workers use, such as those in spray adhesives, markers, paints, airbrush dyes, and the like, will put children and other family members at risk.

Whether in a large graphic design studio or a home office, safety and health must be the graphic designer's first priority.

SOURCE OF HELP

For advice on safety or regulatory issues, contact Monona Rossol at Arts, Crafts and Theater Safety, 181 Thompson St. # 23, New York, NY 10012-2586; (212) 777-0062; *www.artscraftstheatersafety.org*; ACTSNYC@cs.com.

Part 3
Rights

25

Copyright
and Licensing

TAD CRAWFORD

THIS CHAPTER ON copyright and licensing is an appropriate introduction
to the section on rights. This section tries to cover the most important intellectual property issues that the graphic designer may confront. Copyright is the
foundation for many of the rights created by the designer in the course of
doing work. Whether on behalf of the designer or client, the designer must
understand the attributes of copyright and how to protect and deal with copyrights. Licensing is the best way to be paid for creating copyrights—that is, to
license and be paid for many pieces of a copyright rather than simply selling
the entire copyright. The designer's perplexity as to when copying the work of
others is a forbidden infringement is addressed in chapter 26, "Infringement,
Influence, and Plagiarism," while chapter 27 on "Understanding Permissions"
explains the guidelines for when permissions are needed. Chapter 28, "Web
Design Contracts and Issues," explores significant risks faced by designers creating Web sites. Chapters 29 through 31 delve into trademarks, another important form of intellectual property, which the designer may create for clients.
How to avoid trademark infringement is explored in chapter 29, "Other People's Trademarks—Using Them Without Problems." Chapter 30, "Trademark
and Trade Dress," offers guidance not only to the laws pertaining to trademarks but also the closely related doctrines that apply to trade dress. Chapter
31, "Trademarks in Cyberspace," reviews some of the issues that the vast corporate migration to the Web has been causing in the trademark realm. Finally,
Chapter 32, "Use of Fonts," discusses the legal issues arising from the designer's
use of typefaces.

COPYRIGHT AND THE GRAPHIC DESIGNER

I have found that a significant number of graphic designers seem less interested in copyright and licensing than photographers, illustrators, and authors. While some designers feel they are not adequately compensated and are concerned about the protection of copyrights that they create, other designers believe that they are creating client-specific work that has no other potential application. If they are paid well enough, they assume that the client should own the copyright and that is the end of the matter. This is an unfortunate attitude, because it discourages understanding the ways in which copyright may be of value to graphic designers and their clients. If some designers are paid extremely well for work that only their client could use, these designers may be satisfied to transfer the copyright to the client. However, other designers may be creating designs that can only be used by a particular client but not receiving fees sufficient to compensate for unlimited uses. In this situation, or for designs that have obvious reuse potential in other markets, the designer would be wise to license limited rights and retain rights that the client does not immediately need. If the client later wants to make additional uses, the contract between designer and client can provide for reuse fees. On the other hand, if the designer wants to license the design to other markets, such as merchandising, the designer has retained the rights and is free to do this. And, of course, what designers transfer to clients are copyright licenses. Copyright gives the designer the power to bargain; it gives the client the power to protect the designs.

So copyright is, in fact, immensely important for the graphic designer. While many designers seldom consider copyright, the designs they license to clients are protected under the copyright law. It is copyright that allows a designer to control whether or not a work may be copied. If the designer permits a work to be copied, it is the copyright that gives the designer the right to negotiate for fees or royalties. If the client of a designer is to be protected from the theft of designs by competitors, it is because the copyright law gives such protection. Also, an understanding of copyright is necessary if the designer is to obtain for the client appropriate licenses of copyright from suppliers such as photographers, illustrators, and authors.

WHAT IS COPYRIGHTABLE?

Pictorial, graphic, and sculptural works are copyrightable. Included in these categories are such items as two- and three-dimensional works of fine, graphic, and applied art; photographs; photographic slides not intended to be shown as a related series of images; prints and art reproductions; maps; globes; charts; technical drawings; diagrams; and models. Audiovisual works form another category of copyrightable work and include works that consist of a series of related images intended to be shown by the use of a machine such as a projector or a viewer, together with any accompanying sounds. A motion picture is an audiovisual work that also imparts an impression of motion, something the other audiovisual works don't have to do.

Work must be original and creative to be copyrightable. Originality simply means that the designer created the work and did not copy it from someone else. If, by some incredible chance, two designers independently created an identical work, each work would be original and copyrightable. Creative means that the work has some minimal aesthetic qualities. A child's painting, for example, could meet this standard. Although the Copyright Office has sometimes shown a limited understanding of the artistry of graphic design, especially when elements unprotected by copyright laws are arranged to create a new design, most graphic design should be copyrightable.

Ideas, titles, names, and short phrases are usually not copyrightable because they lack a sufficient amount of expression. Ideas can sometimes be protected by an idea disclosure agreement. Likewise, style is not copyrightable, but specific designs created as the expression of a style are copyrightable. Utilitarian objects are not copyrightable, but a utilitarian object incorporating an artistic motif, such as a lamp base in the form of a statue, can be copyrighted to protect the artistic material. Basic geometric shapes, such as squares and circles, are not copyrightable, but artistic combinations of these shapes can be copyrighted. Typeface designs are also excluded from being copyrightable. Calligraphy would appear to be copyrightable if expressed in artwork, especially insofar as the characters are embellished, but not to be copyrightable if merely expressed in the form of a guide, such as an alphabet. Computer programs and the images created through the use of computers are both copyrightable.

FEDERAL COPYRIGHT DURATION

The copyright law enacted in 1978 ended the often-confusing dual system of state and federal copyright protection. Designers now have federal copyright as soon as a design is created—without putting copyright notice on it or registering it with the Copyright Office. Copyrights created after January 1, 1978, as well as those already existing in work not published or registered, will last for the designer's life plus seventy years. If the designer is an employee, the copyright term will be ninety-five years from the first publication of the design and will, of course, belong to the employer.

EXCLUSIVE RIGHTS

The graphic designer, as the copyright owner, has the exclusive rights to reproduce work; license work; prepare derivative works, such as a poster copied from a design; perform work; and display work (the owner of a copy of the work can also display it). Anyone who violates these rights is an infringer whom the designer can sue for damages and prevent from continuing the infringement. If the designer would have trouble proving actual damages, which include the designer's losses and the infringer's profits, the law provides for statutory damages that are awarded in the court's discretion in the amount of $750 to $30,000 for each infringement. The infringer can also be required to pay attorney's fees. However, to be eligible for consideration for statutory damages and attorney's fees, designs must be registered with the Copyright Office prior to the commencement of the infringement.

FAIR USE

Fair use is a limited exception to the exclusive power of the designer, or client, if the designer has transferred rights to the client, to control the uses of designs. Fair use permits someone to use work without permission for a purpose that is basically not going to compete with or injure the market for the work, such as using a design in an article about the designer's career. The test for whether a use is fair or infringing turns on the following factors: (l) the purpose and character of the use, including whether or not it is for profit; (2) the nature and character of the copyrighted work; (3) the amount and substantiality of the portion used, not only in relation to the copyrighted work as a whole but also, in some cases, in relation to defendant's work (and this can be a qualitative as well as quantitative test); and (4) the effect the use will have on the market for, or value of the copyrighted work.

TRANSFERS AND TERMINATIONS

The copyright law explicitly states that copyrights are separate from the physical design, such as a mechanical or, more recently, a digital storage medium. Selling the physical design would not transfer the copyright, because any copyright or any exclusive right of use of a copyright must always be transferred in a written instrument signed by the designer. Only a nonexclusive right can be transferred verbally, such as when the designer sells a design to one client (for example, a wallpaper company), but doesn't make the transfer exclusive so that it can also be sold to another client (for example, a placemat company). Both exclusive transfers of copyrights or parts of copyrights and nonexclusive licenses of copyrights can be terminated by the designer during a five-year period starting thirty-five years after the date of publication or forty years after the date of execution of the transfer, whichever period ends earlier. This right of termination is an important right, but it does not apply to works for hire or transfers made by will.

COPYRIGHT NOTICE

Copyright notice is now optional but not unimportant. The designer has a copyright as soon as a work is created and is not required to place copyright notice on the design at the time of publication. However, placing the copyright notice on the work, or requiring that it appear with the work when published, has certain advantages. The copyright notice is Copyright, Copr., or ©; the designer's name, an abbreviation for the name, or an alternate designation by which the designer is known to the public; and the year of publication. For example, notice could take the form of © Jane Designer 2008. If notice is omitted when a design is published, an infringer may convince the court to lower the amount of damages on the grounds that the infringement was innocent, that is, the infringer wasn't warned off by a copyright notice. In addition, copyright notice informs the public as to the designer's creative authorship of the work. The best course is simply to place the copyright notice on the design before it leaves the studio and make certain that copyright notice accompanies the design when published, even if, in some cases, the copyright notice on publication may be the client's rather than the designer's.

WORK FOR HIRE

Work for hire is a highly problematic provision of the copyright law. If a designer does work for hire for a client, or if a designer hires a supplier to do work for hire, the party doing work for hire loses all rights and can't even terminate the rights transferred after thirty-five years. A work for hire can come into existence in two ways: (1) an employee creating a copyright in the course of the employment; or (2) a freelancer creating a specially ordered or commissioned work if the work falls into one of several categories and both parties sign a written contract agreeing to consider the art work as a work for hire.

This means, for example, that partners in design firms do not own the copyrights in what they create. Assuming the partners are employees, the firm owns those copyrights just as it owns the copyrights created by any other employee. If a partner wants rights to what he or she has created, a special contract will be necessary. Also, a salaried employee may request a written contractual agreement that allows the employee to retain some copyright ownership.

For freelancers, the categories of specially ordered or commissioned works that can be work for hire include: a contribution to a collective work, such as a magazine, newspaper, encyclopedia, or anthology; a contribution used as part of a motion picture or other audiovisual work; and a supplementary work, which includes pictorial illustrations done to supplement a work by another author.

In my opinion, commissioned design rarely falls into a category that can be work for hire under the copyright law. Even if it did, I would advise designers against agreeing to it unless unusually generous compensation were being given (enough to cover all conceivable future uses in any medium whatsoever). Also, I believe that work for hire should almost never be used when designers are commissioning photographers or illustrators. Whether the designer is working for a client or is the client hiring a photographer or illustrator, work for hire demeans the creative process. It says, in effect, that the party who created the art is not the artist. It takes every conceivable right forever, when the value of these rights can hardly be ascertained and is almost never paid. It is a clumsy, antagonizing way to achieve usage rights. Corporate attorneys often rely on work for hire because they lack sophistication in parceling out the limited rights that their employers actually need. Or, in some cases, conglomerates may use work for hire with the intention of building inventories of stock images for resale.

Often the term work for hire is used loosely to mean a buyout or the transfer of all rights. It is important to understand that work for hire is defined in the copyright law, but neither buyout nor all rights have a universally agreed upon definition. For example, all rights might mean the transfer of all conceivable rights in every medium, or might simply mean the transfer of all rights in the first medium in which the design is used. Buyout might mean the transfer of all conceivable rights plus any physical objects incorporating the design, such as mechanicals or a digital storage medium, or might mean a lesser transfer of rights without ownership of any physical object. Because of these ambiguities, designers should spell out the rights transferred by type of use, media of use, duration of use, geography of use, and any other description that makes clear what the parties intend. Ownership of any physical objects contained in the work should also be clarified, and may have a bearing on whether sales tax has to be charged.

But, whether the contract refers to work for hire, a buyout, or all rights, the issue facing the designer remains the same. Unless generous compensation is given to cover all conceivable future uses, the designer should seek to transfer only limited rights to the client. This will ease the designer's task in dealing with suppliers, since the designer won't have to negotiate for rights that may be considered too extensive. If the client demands extensive rights, obviously the designer will have to budget for acquiring extensive rights from any suppliers and should explain this cost to the client. Moreover, the designer might explain that such a cost is often unnecessary, since the client's desire for work for hire or all rights is often for the purpose of preventing the client's competitors from using the design or images in the design. The client can be protected against such competitive use by a simple clause in the contract stating, "The designer agrees not to license the design or any images contained therein to competitors of the client." This might be accompanied by the client's right of approval over some or any licensing of the design and incorporated images. The designer would then have to include similar restrictions in contracts with suppliers.

Designers must be careful to make certain that their contracts for rights with photographers and illustrators conform to the rights that the designers have contractually agreed to give their clients. Ideally, therefore, designers will resist clients that demand work for hire—both for themselves and for the allied creative professionals who will be asked to work on the design project. The designer will be wise to use a written limited rights contract so that both parties know exactly what deal is being agreed to.

REGISTRATION

Almost all designs can be registered, whether published or unpublished. But why would it be desirable to pay the registration fee if copyright protection already exists simply by creating the design? There are several reasons: (1) almost all designs must be registered in order to sue, except if the design is not of United States origin; (2) registration is proof that the statements in the Certificate of Registration are true, such as the designer is the creator of the design; and (3) registration is necessary for the designer to be entitled to the statutory damages and attorney's fees discussed earlier with respect to infringement.

Registration allows the artist to make a record of the design and have that record held by a neutral party—the Copyright Office. Because registration is so significant if a lawsuit is necessary, the deposit materials that accompany the application are especially important. It is these deposit materials that will show what the designer, in fact, created. Groups of unpublished designs can be registered for a single registration fee using an alternative form of deposit, such as slides or copies of the designs. This greatly reduces the expense of registration, since the designs will not have to be registered again when published. The Copyright Office is in the process of including online registration and making changes to streamline their system. Up-to-date details about this can be found on the Web site.

THE COPYRIGHT FORMS

Most designs would be registered on Form VA (which stands for visual arts). If a designer wants to register a work with both text and design, Form VA should be used if the design predominates and Form TX if the text predominates. Because these classifications are only for administrative purposes, rights will not be lost if an error is made in choosing the correct classification.

Form VA is a simple two-page form with step-by-step directions explaining how to fill it out. A filing fee of and copies of the work being registered should be sent with the application form to the Copyright Office, Library of Congress, Washington, DC 20559. There is also a Short Form VA which is even simpler than Form VA and can be used when the designer is the only author, the design is not work for hire, and the work is completely new. Registration is effective as of the date when an acceptable application, deposit, and fee have *all* arrived at the Copyright Office. Although the certificate of registration will be mailed later, this will not change the effective date. If there is an error in a completed registration or if information should be amplified, Form CA should be used for supplementary registration.

GROUP REGISTRATION

Unpublished works may be registered as a group under a single title for one registration fee. This will dramatically reduce the expense of registration, and no copyright notice need be placed on unpublished work. The following conditions must be met to allow for group deposit: (1) the deposit materials must be assembled in an orderly form; (2) the collection must have a single title identifying the work as a whole, such as "Collected Designs of Jane Designer, 1998"; (3) the person claiming copyright in each work forming part of the collection must be the person claiming copyright in the entire collection; and (4) all the works in the collection must be by the same person or, if by different people, at least one of them must have contributed copyrightable material to each work in the collection. No limit is placed on the number of works that can be included in such a collection.

It is important that a work registered when unpublished need not be registered again when published. But, if new material is added to the work or it is changed into a new medium—creating a substantially different work from that registered—it would be wise to register the work again to protect the changed version.

DEPOSIT

One complete copy of an unpublished work or two copies of a published work must be sent to the Copyright Office with the registration form and fee. If a work is first published outside of the United States, only one complete copy of the work need be deposited. The Copyright Office regulations give details of the deposits required for different categories of art.

Sometimes an alternate deposit may be made in place of the actual work itself. Expense may be avoided by depositing something in place of copies of a work. For both published and unpublished works, generally only one set of alternate deposit materials needs to be sent in. Combining this with the group deposit provisions, the benefits of registration may be gained inexpensively. Alternate deposit is for pictorial or graphic works if: (1) the work is unpublished; (2) less than five copies of the work have been published; or (3) the work has been published and sold or offered for sale in a limited edition consisting of no more than three hundred numbered copies. If the work is too valuable to deposit, a special request may be made to the Copyright Office for permission to submit identifying material rather than copies of the actual work. Alternate deposit materials must be sent in for three-dimensional works and oversize works, which are those exceeding ninety-six inches in any dimension. If this mandatory requirement of alternate deposit would create a hardship due to expense or difficulty, a special request may be made to the Copyright Office to deposit actual copies of a work.

For works that are pictorial or graphic, three-dimensional, or oversized, the materials used for alternate deposit can be photographic prints; transparencies; photostats; or drawings, similar two-dimensional reproductions, or renderings of the work in a form that can be looked at without the aid of a machine. The materials used for alternate deposit should all be of the same size, with photographic transparencies at least 35 mm (mounted if 3-by-3 inches or less, and preferably mounted even if greater than 3-by-3 inches) and all other materials preferably 8-by-10 inches (but no less than 3-by-3 inches and no more than 9-by-12 inches). For pictorial and graphic work, the materials must reproduce the actual colors of the work.

THE VALUE OF COPYRIGHT

The value of copyright for the designer is undeniable. Knowing how to register work enhances this value by strengthening the designer's position in the event of a lawsuit. If a designer feels a work will be so successful as to be a target for infringement, that work should undoubtedly be registered. Because group registration for unpublished works is easy and inexpensive, office procedures might well be structured to include registration in appropriate cases. To be knowledgeable about copyright is not to take an antagonistic stance with respect to clients since clients will also benefit from the designer's care in protecting designs.

When client and designer enter into a contractual arrangement, whether verbal or, preferably, written, allocation of the copyright is one issue to be resolved. With respect to the rest of the world, that is, potential infringers, the designer and client both want the same result—maximum protection for the copyright. There is no conflict or competition here. Certainly neither client nor designer benefits if the copyright is not protected in the best possible way.

LICENSING

The value of copyright leads to the concept of licensing. If the designer understands that his or her work consists of many different rights, only some of which are needed by the client, then the designer will often want to retain rights. In some cases only the client will have any interest in using the design again, in which case the initial contract could provide for reuse fees. On the other hand, if there are unrelated uses for the design, then the designer may be able to license rights to additional users.

A license defines exactly what rights are being transferred to the client. For example, the license might be to use the design as a poster in the United States for a period of five years. Payment might be by a flat fee or, more preferably, by an advance against royalties. Royalties allow the designer to share in the success of the product. If an advance is paid, the designer has a guaranteed income, which may grow if royalties are earned beyond the amount of the advance. If royalties are to be paid, the licensing agreement should provide for accountings and the right of the designer to inspect the books and records of the client. The designer would want samples of the product and would also want to be able to ensure that certain quality standards are achieved. The client would be expected to make best efforts to promote the product and might even specify certain promotional steps or a budget. The designer would not want the client to be able to assign the agreement without the designer's consent. Of course, the designer would want to reserve the copyright and all rights not granted.

Both the grant of rights to the original clients and the grant of rights to a subsequent client for the same design are licenses. By licensing, the designer honors the creativity that goes into the design and retains a future connection to the design. That connection may result in residual income. In *Business and Legal Forms for Graphic Designers* (Allworth Press) the Project Confirmation Agreement and the Licensing Contract to Merchandise Designs each deal with many of the typical issues arising from licensing rights and are worth reviewing in this context.

PROPOSED LEGISLATION

Federal legislation has been proposed to deal with "orphan works." The legislation proposes to allow a person to use a work without permission if the person has "performed and documented a reasonably diligent search in good faith to locate the owner of the infringed copyright." If the owner cannot be found after such a search, then even though the use is technically an infringement, the penalties for the infringement are minimal or nonexistent. If an owner discovers the infringement, the highest compensation that the owner can obtain is "reasonable compensation" and the infringement can continue. The owner is not allowed to seek damages, costs, or attorney's fees. If the infringement is "without any purpose of direct or indirect commercial advantage and primarily for a charitable, religious, scholarly, or educational purpose," and the usage ceases after the owner complains, then the owner will not even have the right to ask for reasonable compensation.

This scheme is in many ways like the compulsory license contained in Section 118 of the copyright law. The compulsory license allows educational broadcasting stations such as PBS and its affiliates to use "pictorial, graphic, and sculptural works" without permission of the copyright owner. Any usage has to be accounted for and, if owners can be found, very modest fees must be paid for the usage. I had extensive experience with the Section 118 compulsory license acting on behalf of organizations such as the Graphic Artists Guild and the American Society of Media Photographers. It's fair to say that almost no fees were ever paid to copyright owners pursuant to the compulsory license. The accountings would show the nature of the visual work, but the copyright owners were rarely located for the payment of fees. Essentially, the usage became free.

This is the problem with the Orphan Works bill. No matter how many times the bill uses the word "reasonably," it simply doesn't come to terms with the actual situation facing creative artists. For example, a "reasonably diligent search" under the bill would involve going through "the records of the Copyright Office" as well as other sources with information as to copyright ownership. However, only a tiny fraction of visual arts works are ever registered with the Copyright Office, so searching the records there will be of almost no value. And what is meant by other sources? By and large, these don't exist. So most "reasonably diligent" searches will not locate the copyright owner.

This means that the work may be used without payment. What if the copyright owner discovers the use and comes forward to complain? The bill envisages a negotiation to determine "reasonable compensation." What if the user and owner can't agree on the right amount for "reasonable compensation?" The owner can then take the matter to litigation. Here the bill actually requires the copyright owner to bear "the burden of establishing the amount on which a reasonable willing buyer and a reasonable willing seller in the positions of the owner and the infringer would have agreed with respect to the infringing use of the work immediately before the infringement began."

Unfortunately, in the real world, very few artists have the resources to pay the exorbitant legal fees necessary to pursue a copyright claim. What artist in his or her right mind would commence such an action when the artist is limited to only recovering "reasonable compensation" and cannot collect damages, costs, or attorney's fees? And, in addition, the artist must carry the burden of proof with respect to what "reasonable compensation" should have been.

In fact, the Orphan Works bill is simply an appealing description for what should be called free use or, less politely, theft. Everyone roots for an orphan to be adopted, but what if we called the bill the Protection of Copyright Theft Act? Then we would be hoping that stern justice would be meted out to the immoral thieves. Also, while the Section 118 compulsory license only applied to educational broadcasters, the Orphan Works bill would apply to all users. The potential magnitude of the unrecompensed taking of creative work is staggering.

Moreover, the copyright law has long provided for fair use of works under certain conditions. A fair use does not require the permission of the copyright owner, but the fair use guidelines avoid the dangers that are so apparent in the Orphan Works bill. It would be far better to work within this long-established and tested framework than to create a radical departure from prior law that will leave most creative artists impotent to redress the unpaid use of their works.

SOURCES OF COPYRIGHT INFORMATION

Legal Guide for the Visual Artist (Allworth Press) contains an extensive discussion of copyright. The Copyright Office makes available free information and application forms such as Form VA for a work in the visual arts. The extensive information and forms available from the Copyright Office can be obtained online by visiting *www.copyright.gov*. Forms from the Copyright Office can also be requested by writing to the Copyright Office, Library of Congress, Washington, D.C. 20559 or calling the telephone hotline: (202) 707–9100. The public information number for the Copyright Office is (202) 707–3000.

26

Infringement, Influence, and Plagiarism

TAD CRAWFORD AND STEVEN HELLER

SHOULD THE DESIGNER'S standards of professional behavior be rooted in law, ethics, or both? That is the subject of the following dialog. Designers are often influenced by contemporary art and design and borrow elements for their own creativity. When does this borrowing become more than influence? When is it plagiarism, and, if so, is plagiarism the equivalent of copyright infringement? Can the design profession police itself and set its own standards? Or are aesthetic standards too subjective, too vague, so that policing must be left to the heavier hand of the law?

Steve: There is a perilously fine line between infringement, influence, and plagiarism. How would we define these terms to make them manageable?

Tad: In general I think that designers are more likely to consider a work to have been plagiarized than I would as an attorney. This reflects a refinement of vision but also relates to the disparity between what most designers consider plagiarism and the standard for copyright infringement.

Plagiarism is a moral term, while infringement is a legal term. As every law student learns (to his or her disappointment), there is often a gap between the moral and the legal. Also, the test for infringement under the copyright law may be very difficult for the designer to apply to his or her own work. That test is whether an ordinary observer who looks at an original work and an alleged copy will believe one to have been copied from the other. If the similarity is great enough, it will not be necessary to prove the alleged infringer had access to the original work to do the

241

copying. Designers pride themselves on not being ordinary observers, and this may explain why the designers are likely to see plagiarism. From a lawyer's point of view, what the designer considers plagiarism, a bad thing, might merely be influence, presumably a good thing. Do you think there is a higher standard to which designers must adhere, a standard derived not from the vision of an ordinary observer but from the vision of a designer versed in aesthetic issues?

Steve: Unlike the fine arts, which also has its share of sanctioned and unsanctioned thefts, graphic or advertising design is a commercial art, and like clothing or furniture design, it adheres to the knockoff principle. Styles, fashions, and even languages are built on the universality of certain forms. Then you have to factor in the intellectual property issue, which I understand is a dicey term: How can a creator protect his or her creation in the marketplace? This creation could be the basis for a livelihood or reputation, and if it is knocked off or trivialized, then this has an adverse effect on the creator. But highfalutin talk aside, I think that styles can be copied, but ideas should somehow be preserved. As a lawyer, would you agree with these distinctions? And if so, how do you insure such rights?

Tad: No, I really can't agree. Neither style nor ideas are copyrightable. We have to keep in mind that copyright gives its owner a monopoly for the term of the copyright, subject to the fair use exception (see chapter 27). It would be counterproductive to creative endeavor to give anyone a monopoly on a style or an idea because it would prevent others from working in that style or with that idea. The classic legal distinction is based on the dichotomy between an idea and the expression of an idea. The idea is not copyrightable, but the expression of the idea is copyrightable. So, for example, the idea to create a book cover using a certain combination of type faces and a negative image of someone's eyes (the idea for the cover of *Looking Closer 2*) is not copyrightable, but the actual cover as created by Michael Bierut is copyrightable. In terms of the idea-expression dichotomy, style would fall on the side of ideas. Of course, any specific work is copyrightable, even though the style in which the work is created is not copyrightable. Do you think that some ideas should be copyrightable, such as original ideas?

Steve: Originality is a difficult concept. Is David Carson's work original, or as an interpreter of the Zeitgeist, is his design a refinement of other experiments? Push Pin Studios incorporated Art Nouveau and Art Deco into their decidedly contemporary designs. Is there any lack of originality there because they invoked styles that existed in history? While originality is difficult to define, it needs defining. And in the process I believe that standards of design behavior must be established. Ethically speaking, don't you think that a designer's unique ideas should be protected from abuse? Legally speaking, what elements of a design are undisputedly protected?

Tad: In part, this is the question of whether design is copyrightable. Often, design is created from many elements that are not copyrightable. Ideas are not copyrightable. Typefaces; colors; common geometric forms, such as circles, squares, or triangles; useful objects; and systems are not copyrightable. Yet a creative combination of elements not protectable by copyright certainly is copyrightable. This means that original design *can* be protected from abuse under the copyright law, although there may be some minimal designs that cannot be copyrighted. However, the copyright law may be an unwieldy way to approach issues of creative plagiarism. To litigate is expensive and a great waste of energy. Don't you think that the profession itself should define its own standards, which, presumably, would be on a higher level than that of the ordinary observer?

Steve: Well, this goes back to the earlier question of ethics. The profession is not in a position to either establish or enforce such dicta. Moreover, as the sands of time shift, young art and creative directors take commissioning roles, and many of these people don't know who came up with what first. So often, designers themselves are the ignorant culprits, and clients go innocently along for the ride. In the best of worlds there would be some arbitration group, but everyone would have to subscribe to their rulings. I don't see that happening.

Needless to say, we've been talking in generalities. What about clear cases of pilfering or, to be more generous, over influence? What about the case of the *Swing* magazine cover (November 1994) where the image is a head wrapped in words and wearing sunglasses, set against a blue background that is virtually identical to a cover of *PC Format* (May 1995)? Presumably one copied the other, and the duplication is so brazen that it is embarrassing to look at it. How do you adjudicate something like that? But before answering, let me add a wrinkle. The presumably original *Swing* cover is itself a rip-off of a 1966 poster for *Caspar Magazine* by Frieder and Renata Grindler in the Museum of Modern Art poster collection and reproduced in their catalog *The Modern Poster*. In each case, a little bit has been altered (it is not simply a pickup); so is this just the nature of commercial graphic art?

Tad: When we speak of blind justice, we might consider one aspect of the rules about copyright infringement. If two designers create an identical work, each without having seen the work of the other designer, there is no copyright infringement, regardless of who created it first. We also have to keep in mind the public domain, which is where all creative works go after their copyright expires or is lost. By public domain, we mean free to be copied by anyone, which would include most works by United States citizens published more than seventy-five years ago. If the cover of *PC Format* has been scanned and slightly altered, it will clearly be an infringement. If the idea for it has been stolen, it will depend on how closely an observer would say that the expression, as opposed to the idea, had been stolen; then it would be copyright infringement. At the same time, both works could be infringing the 1966 poster if it is, in fact, still protected by copyright, which would have to be established by exploring its particular copyright status. I should note that if a work is composed of infringing and non-infringing materials, the non-infringing materials are protected by copyright. But what are we to make of the fact that so many designers and illustrators are urged by their instructors in school to maintain reference files? Are such files intended to be for influence or for scanning and unauthorized reuse?

Steve: "Swipe file" is the common term for research or reference resources, which are mainstays for the average illustrator and designer. Strictly speaking though, a good illustrator or designer wouldn't actually steal the material therein or reuse it verbatim. Alterations are required, unless the designer is either so ignorant that he or she doesn't know any better or so corrupt that he or she doesn't care. I hope that when teachers encourage students to make these files, they are also warning them about the limits of such use. Even the New York Public Library picture collection—the greatest swipe source in New York—cautions users that copyrights may be in question. But in actuality, illustrators and designers are not taught about ethics in school. Most teachers ask students to make dummies or comps using existing printed material. I can only speculate whether or not this reinforces bad behavior, but students are usually the most influenced by the work they see in annuals and books, anyway. So here's a hypothetical situation: A young designer is told by his or her boss or client to appropriate a certain look. They are shown a particular design, say a poster by Pentagram or a type design by Neville Brody and told, "this is how our job should look." There are various degrees of copying here. At what point would you say, "Stop, there is a legal problem here"?

Tad: Scanning has made appropriation so easy that educators should be rigorous in warning their students. The schools are obviously the best place to create and deepen awareness of professional standards, although professional groups like the AIGA and the Graphic Artists Guild also play important roles. Some instructors give their students misinformation about legalities. For example, one bit of wishful thinking is the frequently repeated, and incorrect, test for infringement: As long as you change 25 percent of an artwork, you can copy it freely. This isn't true, since a part of a work can certainly be infringing if an ordinary observer would find it to have been copied. Taking your examples of a poster by Pentagram or a type design by Neville Brody, the legal standard would again be whether the ordinary observer believes the new work copied from the existing work. However, I think that stealing style is hardly desirable, since it implies a lack of creative force, unless, of course, the theft is itself a commentary such as a parody. In this context, it's also worth mentioning that using images without permission in the course of creating in-house dummies also raises ethical questions, particularly if there is no intention of giving an assignment to the creator of the dummy. If knocking off a particular style goes beyond what we might call influence, as I think it does, I would say that the unauthorized use of art for in-house dummies is plagiarism and unethical. What do you think?

Steve: Whew! That's a toughie. Every creative act is built in some way on other creative acts. In the case of dummies, however, there is direct use of another's creation. But practically speaking, before expenses are incurred it is necessary to present the job in some concrete form. In the old days it was called comping. Commercial artists had to draw or trace everything. In the computer age designers comp from scanned pictures, and some of these are available from stock houses. But, I see your point. When one is using another's ideas to establish a particular context, they are, in fact, stealing the work. But in my hypothetical, I am asking what happens when an existing designer's work is the basis for a cultural or commercial style. Neville Brody invented a language, based on other graphic languages, that became the code for a new generation. Once that code is released in the air, doesn't it become public domain? Another example is the Pentagram's poster by Paula Scher for the Public Theater; it is a synthesis of existing design languages (i.e., Victorian typography and street placard imagery)filtered through the designer's vision into a distinct identity for the Public Theater. But, who is to say that she has cornered the market on the underlying language? Can't others use bold gothics and primary colors? Even if these "influenced" designers don't know of the original historical source and take their inspiration directly from the Public Theater posters?

Tad: Your examples help draw a quixotic line in the aesthetic sands. Design certainly informs culture, which in its myriad diffusions casts the spell of influence. I don't think of that kind of influence as plagiarism, and it certainly isn't copyright infringement. However, if a designer instructs an assistant to create a work like another work, even though it may not be copyright infringement, it seems to me to raise the ethical question of whether it is plagiarism. This might also be true if the instruction is to create a work in the style of another artist without specifying a particular work. To return for a moment to the issue of comps, it is worth mentioning that the unauthorized scanning of an image for use in a comp is an infringement of copyright. If designers feel they can get away with this, "getting away" with something is quite a remove from doing what is right. Any designer would be outraged if his or her portfolio were used by another design firm to obtain a project. Shouldn't this same solicitude apply to unauthorized use of the work of other creative talent?

Steve: Isn't preventing scans of others' work for comp use just as unenforceable as tearing the "It is illegal to remove" sticker from a mattress? So here are two questions for you: One, can a prohibition on this kind of scanning be enforced? And two, which is an extension of this question as well as another question entirely, how can plagiarism be proven? Or put another way, what standard does the court use to decide whether or not something is actually either stolen or an airborne idea?

Tad: Prohibition is probably a good word to use because prevention of something done so easily in private would be like the enforcement problems with people who wanted to drink alcohol during Prohibition. However, the fact that something is difficult to prove doesn't make it legal. Moreover, a disgruntled or zealously ethical employee might decide to blow the whistle on an employer making unauthorized use of art and photography. This isn't a consensual crime because one party is absent and definitely not consenting. To move to your larger question: Copying is often inferred from the infringer's access to a work and the substantial similarity of the work alleged to be infringing. So the party suing may not have to show the infringer actually stole the work as long as the infringer had access (i.e., if the work has been published or distributed, the infringer probably had access), and the work was substantially similar. The standard for judging substantial similarity is the ordinary observer test discussed earlier. The idea-expression dichotomy is used to determine if what is taken is copyrightable and therefore, capable of being infringed. Designers and other creators cannot protect ideas but only the expression of those ideas. Another point worth making is the substantial amounts involved in copyright infringements. The owner of an infringed work may get his or her damages plus the infringer's profits. If these infringements are hard to prove, the aggrieved party may be able to ask the court for statutory damages, which are an amount between $750 and $30,000 for each work infringed. The $30,000 can be increased to $150,000 if the infringement is willful, that is, done with knowledge that the work is protected by copyright. The victor in a copyright suit may also be able to ask that the loser pay attorney's fees and court costs, which can be substantial amounts. To be eligible for statutory damages and attorney's fees, the work must be registered prior to the commencement of the infringement. All of these dollar amounts suggest another reason why it is better for the profession to have high ethical standards that exceed the requirements of law. Whatever the benefit of knocking off people's work, I think there is a greater and practical benefit to having the highest standards and never needing to worry about exposure to expensive and time-consuming litigation.

Steve: Sometimes what appears to be infringement to the casual viewer is not really the case. I'm referring to the image used for the poster for the film, *Show-girls*, which shows a woman whose leg and torso is curvaceously framed by dark areas, which appear like an open coat or dress. It is sensual and surreal, but was it original? In fact, it was based on a photograph that was used as the cover for a book, *The Nude*, less than a year before the poster came out. What seemed like a clear case of plagiarism was sanctioned by the original photographer who sold the image rights to his creation to an ad agency, which then had the right to have another photographer alter the image. Okay, I realize that this is done all the time—novelists sell their books to the movies to adapt into screenplays, etc. But something's not right. I can't really put my finger on it. The photographer was presumably well paid—so its not theft, per se—but it certainly trivializes the originality of the work.

Tad: If I understand the facts, it would seem that there is no copyright issue. In fact, it is a good illustration of how the value of copyrights can be maximized through licensing multiple uses. If an identity symbol is successful, why should multiple applications create an issue? For example, if a corporate identity program is expected to have multiple applications, why should it be surprising that a highly original image finds more than one use? That is the basis for stock photography houses and the concept of reuse fees following the licensing of limited rights. Yet, I think that you are on to something here, a subtle essence about what it means to create design and be a designer. If something disturbs your eye as an art director, but not mine as an attorney, it seems that we've returned to the place where we started. The very sophistication of the designer's vision calls for standards that exceed the mere requirements of the copyright law. Where these standards are forged is and will be in the heart—and eyes, and mind—of every designer.

27

Understanding Permissions

LEE WILSON

ONE OF THE realities of copyright that is often very difficult for would-be copyright users to understand is that copyright owners control almost absolutely both how and whether their works are used by others. There are only a few exceptions to this rule; the most important exceptions in the U.S. are called compulsory licenses. (For instance, if your song has been recorded previously with your permission and the recording was distributed in the form of phonorecords to the public within the United States, anyone can issue another recording of the song, subject only to the obligations imposed by law to notify you in advance of releasing the new phonorecord, to pay you royalties at a prescribed rate, and to furnish you with monthly royalty statements. This provision of the copyright statute is referred to as the "compulsory [mechanical] license" provision. There are also three other, less important and more obscure, uses specified in the U.S. copyright statute for which compulsory licensing is prescribed.)

Other exceptions to the rule of absolute control by the copyright owner are those uses that are "fair" uses of the copyrighted work. We already know the name for any use that is made without specific permission and that is neither governed by the compulsory license provisions of the copyright statute nor a legitimate fair use of the copyrighted work—any such use is called copyright infringement. In fact, it's safe to say that many infringements result from a would-be user's inability to understand the word "No"—or the reluctance, for whatever reason, to ask for permission to use the copyrighted work in the first place. The ability to ask correctly for permission to use a copyrighted work is an art—in some situations it may require a certain degree of diplomacy. That's because the more you need to obtain permission to use a work, the more you may need to call

249

on everything you know about copyright and tact in order to make your request properly and enhance your chances of getting the permission you need.

It's important to understand that, other than in a very few instances involving musical compositions, there are no fixed fees prescribed by the copyright statute or the Copyright Office or otherwise for the right to use copyrighted works. This lack of universal standards for what is charged for permissions means that each request for a permission leads to a negotiation with almost no parameters—in some cases, the only standard for what a copyright owner can charge for a copyright license is what the traffic will bear.

It's also important to understand before seeking permission to use a copyrighted work that a copyright owner's agenda may not include accommodating yours. If you request the right to use a copyrighted work in the same format as that which the copyright owner markets, you are likely to be denied permission to use the work. And even if the work is not presently being used in the form in which you want to use it, the copyright owner may have plans for a similar use, or a more profitable license may have been offered by someone else. These are reasons not to assume that you will be given the right to use the work in the way you request— but the only way to find out what you *will* be permitted to do is to ask.

Permissions to use copyrighted works are called permissions or licenses. A "permission" often denotes that the right to use a work has been granted without the payment of a fee; "license" often denotes that some money has changed hands. Although this is the way these terms are sometimes used, the words themselves mean the same thing and in this book the terms are used interchangeably. There are two sorts of licenses—non-exclusive licenses and exclusive licenses. An exclusive license is a permission to use a copyrighted work that has been granted to one person with the limitation that no other similar license to use the work will be granted to anyone else; exclusivity of use usually costs more. A non-exclusive license is a permission to use a copyrighted work that has been granted to one person with*out* the limitation that no other similar license to use the work will be granted to anyone else. The person granting the license is called the "licensor"; the person to whom the license is granted is called the "licensee."

An important factor in negotiations for any license is what portion of the copyrighted work is to be licensed. Many proposed uses of a work require permission to use the entire work; in the case of other proposed uses, permission to use only a part of the work is sufficient. And how long the work is to be used is another factor that can determine whether the copyright owner will or will not license the work for the proposed use and, if payment is to be made for the license, what the license fee will be. A third factor in negotiations is territory— over what geographic area will the licensed work be used or in what segment of the market for that work? A work may be licensed for "the entire United States" or for "the world" or for "the state of Oklahoma." It may be licensed for use as part of an anthology of American paintings or for a television commercial or as an article in an encyclopedia. Any combination of geographic area and market segment may be specified—that is, it may be licensed for use in a television commercial for the entire United States or for the state of Oklahoma.

Non-exclusive licenses of copyright do not have to be written to be effective. You can say "I'll let you use my photograph of a sunset as the background for your public-service television ad, Jamal, and I won't even charge you for the use." This would give your friend the right to use the photograph in the way you specify. However, Jamal may want to remember that non-exclusive licenses of copyright granted in this way (i.e., verbally) are also terminable at will—that means that he is at your mercy as to how long you will allow him to use your photo because you can terminate the permission at any time. It's far better to get a written document outlining the terms of any license, even a non-exclusive one, in order to make sure that everyone involved understands just what has been agreed. Unlike non-exclusive licenses, exclusive licenses of copyright have to be in writing to be effective.

THE COPYRIGHT CLOCK

The first determination you must make in seeking permission to use a copyrighted work is whether the work is still protected by copyright. This seems too obvious to mention, but skipping an examination of the copyright status of the work you want to use can end up costing you whatever time you spend seeking a permission you don't need. Always devote your first efforts to figuring out whether the work is protected by copyright or has fallen into the public domain. This exercise can do more than keep you from spending time requesting permission to use a public domain work. It may be that you will be able to trump a copyright owner who is reluctant to grant permission to use a work by simply biding your time—if you find that copyright protection for the work is running out and will expire soon, perhaps you can simply wait until copyright protection expires and save yourself the effort of asking for permission to use the work. Read the Copyright Office's publications "Duration of Copyright" and "How to Investigate the Copyright Status of a Work" for information on determining the copyright status of a work. Both of these publications include information that will be invaluable in any effort to determine whether a work you want to use is still protected by copyright. (The Copyright Office website can be accessed at: *http://www.copyright.gov/*. Clicking on the "Circulars and Brochures" or the "Factsheets" subheads under "Publications" will take you to a long list of very useful publications available to download for free. This is a resource you will want to remember as it is always available, always authoritative, and can help settle many copyright questions as soon as they arise.)

WHAT DO YOU NEED?

The second determination you must make in seeking permission to use a copyrighted work is exactly *what* rights you need. Do you want to reprint the entire scientific paper or would being able to reproduce the chart on page eleven suffice?

Do you want to be able to use the photograph as the cover of your book, or is it better as an illustration in one of the chapters? Do you want to use the entire text of a famous speech on your poster, or will one well-known sentence from it suffice? Attention to this question can even eliminate the need for a permission altogether—perhaps the portion of the copyrighted work that you really need to use is small enough to qualify your proposed use as a fair use of the work. For example, maybe you need to quote only two sentences from *The New York Times* review that praises your first documentary in the prospectus that you're writing to raise money for the second one; using the entire review would be superfluous and would require that you obtain the right to reprint it, but you don't need permission to quote only a very brief section of the review.

Narrowing your request to obtain only the rights you actually *need* can also save you money; using an entire musical composition as the soundtrack for your short animated film will cost you more than using only a few bars as incidental music in one scene. It may even be useful to come up with two possible approaches to using a work: what is the minimum you need and what is the maximum you could use? If the copyright owner agrees to grant permission for the minimal use of his or her work, ask what it would cost to make the maximum use of it. Or, conversely, if permission to make maximum use of the work is too expensive or is denied, find out whether it's possible to get permission to use the work minimally.

WHOM DO YOU ASK?

Your skill as a researcher can be an important factor in whether getting permission to use a copyrighted work is a relatively straightforward task or a months-long wild goose chase. Before you can ask for permission you must find where and to whom to send your request. It may be all but impossible to trace the copyright owner for an unpublished work, but a published work will almost certainly bear some information about the publisher and/or the copyright owner. Somewhere on the physical object that embodies a published work, there will be publication information that can lead you to the owner of copyright or the owner of the exclusive right to publish the copyrighted work, which are different statuses from the viewpoint of the copyright owner, but are functionally the same from the viewpoint of a would-be user of the work, like you.

With a poem or play or book or any other published literary work, write or call the "Permissions Department" of the publisher of the work to request permission to use it. If the publisher isn't the owner of copyright in the work, it will certainly have been licensed to publish it and, depending upon the nature of the use for which you request permission, will grant or deny your request or forward your letter to the author of the work for his or her consideration.

Copyrights in popular songs and other contemporary musical compositions are usually owned by music publishers. If you call one of the performing rights societies that collect royalties for broadcast uses of musical compositions (BMI, ASCAP, and SESAC) with the title of the composition and the name of the songwriter or composer, you can determine the name of the publisher of the composition, from whom you should request permission to use it. (Contact information for BMI, ASCAP, and SESAC is at the University of Texas at Austin's "Getting Permissions" Web site, the address for which is given below.) Record companies own the recordings of songs that are released on CDs and cassettes; write the record company if you want permission to use the *recording* of the song, as opposed to the song itself, *in addition to* the publisher who can grant permission to use the *song*, including all or a portion of the lyrics.

For works of the visual arts, such as paintings or sculptures, you should contact the artist directly or, in the case of a deceased artist, the artist's estate. Galleries and museums may be good sources for such address information. However, don't assume that because a painting is owned by a museum or an individual collector that the copyright in the painting or sculpture is also owned by the museum or collector. Although the owner of a painting or sculpture is, of course, allowed to display it, ownership of a work of art does not automatically bestow on the owner of the work the right to exercise any of the other exclusive rights of copyright. Requests to use photos should be addressed to the photographer or his or her licensing agency.

Finding the owners of copyrights in other sorts of works may be more difficult. If you can't find the information you need about the owner of a copyright, you may be able to get it online. If you know the title of the work or the name of the author, start with the Copyright Office. Go to *http://www.copyright.gov/records/* to search the registration and ownership records for books, music, films, sound recordings, maps, software, photos, art, multimedia works, periodicals, magazines, journals, and newspapers recorded since 1978. The Copyright Office allows members of the public to search its records, but this requires that you go to Washington or hire a copyright search service to search for you. A better method of determining the ownership of a copyright may be to hire the Copyright Office to search its records for you; at $75 an hour, having the Copyright Office search for you isn't cheap, but the results of such a search may be more reliable than a do-it-yourself effort. You can find out more about searching the records of the Copyright Office in the Copyright Office publications, "How to Investigate the Copyright Status of a Work" and "The Copyright Card Catalog and the Online Files of the Copyright Office," both of which are available online or can be mailed to you without charge from the Copyright Office.

Another excellent source of information is the "Getting Permission" source list maintained by the University of Texas at Austin at *http://www.utsystem.edu/ogc/intellectualproperty/permissn.htm*. This site offers links to an assortment of organizations that can grant permission to use all sorts of copyrighted works or, if they can't grant permission, can give you the information you need to find the right person or company to ask for permission. There are many online sites that give information about copyright clearance. Like the UT-Austin site, many of them are operated by universities perhaps because universities are concerned, justly, about the liability inherent in the unauthorized use of copyrights by their faculty, staff, and students.

The age of the work can be important in determining whom to ask for permission because the owner of an older work may be hard to find, even if you have a name and address for the owner. Lots of things can happen during the term of copyright in a work—publishers may be bought by other publishers, authors may sell copyrights or die and leave them to their heirs, contracts that give someone the right to use a work may expire, etc. If you have a copy of the work you want to use that indicates a publisher or copyright owner, you may be in a better position than someone who has no leads as to where to start in a search for the owner of a copyright, but neither can you assume that the copyright owner or publisher named on the copy of an older work still controls the copyright in it. View such information as a starting place and in any situation where there may be a later edition or version of a published work, try to find the later edition so your information about the copyright owner will be as recent as possible.

The prominence or obscurity of the owner of copyright in a work can determine how difficult it will be for you to get permission to use the work. You won't have the same trouble locating a copyright owner who is a big company or prominent person. But that same prominence may make it harder to get permission to use the copyrighted work—a work that has been exploited by and is owned by a successful publisher or a well-known author may be more valuable than a more obscure work and less likely to be licensed for use by someone else.

28

Web Design Contracts and Issues

DON BRUNSTEN

PRACTITIONERS OF WEB design face the same legal concerns that confront practitioners of other design disciplines. Web design firms also face a set of emerging legal problems they unfortunately can call their own. For the purposes of this article, the term "Web design firms" embraces the spectrum of Web-related services provided by independent firms with design or programming expertise, from basic graphic design and operation of Web sites, to consulting on interaction design or user experience, e-business processes and applications, online corporate identity and branding, or strategic planning on Web trends and opportunities.

The work of Web design is today carried out across a foggy legal landscape. Copyright and trademark issues abound in the use of relatively common technologies, such as deep links, frames, in-lines, or mash-ups, which may connect the content or brands of unaffiliated companies, and there is a similar and growing exposure in being connected with the development of Web sites built around user-supplied content, of which YouTube is the most notorious current example. Likewise, patent issues keep popping up over seemingly routine functional features like frames, menus, navigation systems, and e-commerce interactions. Functionality is also the touchstone for Web-related claims under civil rights laws, as in the recent Roommates.com case, where the Web site's user interface/form system amounted to a civil rights violation because online users searching for potential roommates were asked to express a racial preference. Web site functionality also implicates privacy and financial laws covering online transactions processing, as well as laws mandating reasonable access to online services for the disabled.

With the principal types of intellectual property ("IP") claims—copyright, trademark, or patent—the federal courts are taking an increasingly expansive view of who, among the many players contributing to the development or implementation of a Web site or Web application, may be held responsible for any resulting infringement. The key supporting evidence for design firm liability is often found in agreements, conduct, practices, or communications giving the appearance that the design firm had some measure of *control* over the choice of a Web site's legally problematic features, content, or functionality. In short, the design firm can be left sharing, or holding, the liability bag, even if the firm's control may not extend to all aspects of Web site design or any continuing Web site management. In IP law, there is no rule of proportionality between the size of the project, or of the size of the design fees, and the level of the design firm's legal exposure. Sometimes small projects for small clients lead to the biggest headaches, damages awards, and legal bills.

Of course, there also are plenty of potential legal problems directly between a Web design firm and its client that have nothing to do with aggrieved third parties. In this category, obligations to test, maintain, or service Web sites, together with alternative or contingent forms of compensation for services, are perhaps the most common traps for the unwary design firm.

With these various risks in mind, we'll review some of the key methods available to Web design firms to reduce their exposure and expand their bottom line.

THE DESIGN FIRM'S STANDARD CLIENT CONTRACT

A central building block in any action plan is the design firm's standard form client contract. The AIGA has promulgated a standard form with a supplement for interactive design projects. There are also good standard forms available from other sources. Every design firm using a form, like the one from AIGA, needs to go through an initial set-up of the template, as the form's provisions vary depending on the design firm's business model. From there, the basic template has to be fine-tuned from project to project and client to client.

Given the ongoing hazards in the practice of Web design, the design firm's standard contract needs to embrace, among other things, the following concepts:

- ❑ Ideally, the standard contract would have a blanket exclusion of any duty by the design firm to indemnify (i.e., reimburse) the client for anything, including but not limited to IP claims brought by third parties that are arguably related to design features the design firm included in the client deliverables. This sort of blanket exclusion may be a deal breaker for larger or more sophisticated clients. As an alternative, the design firm can feel reasonably comfortable with a standard contract imposing substantial limits on its duty to indemnify the client. These limits should include a dollar cap on indemnification (it's not unusual for the cap to be the amount paid for services, or perhaps the profit margin for the services in question); a right to re-design deliverables to mitigate damages; a right to control the legal defense of any claims the design firm may be obligated to indemnify; and an exclusion of the duty with respect to any claim based on decisions or content that originated with the client, were approved by the client, or otherwise were not within the design firm's exclusive control. Remember, above all, that the design firm is not protected if the contract simply avoids the subject of indemnification. In that scenario, state statutes or case law may read into the contract an implied right of the client to indemnification.

❑ Another important contract goal is reciprocal indemnification, in other words, requiring the client to reimburse the design firm for liabilities and legal fees if a third party should directly sue or threaten to sue the design firm. Reciprocal indemnification used to be something of an afterthought, but we are seeing more instances of Web site-related infringement actions directly naming the independent design firm as a defendant. Even when the case against the design firm is weak, the firm's legal defense costs are inevitably substantial.

❑ Unsurprisingly, clients do not want to pay for crosschecking the deliverables against trademark or patent searches. Client reluctance to pay for (or accept the time delay for) IP due diligence underscores the need for a complete contractual exclusion on the design firm's duty to indemnify the client for trademark or patent risks (except for trademarks or patents actually known to the design firm at the time of services). Once again, larger and more sophisticated clients often refuse to accept that kind of exclusion. Design firms, hungry for big projects, tend to go along with the contractual demands from those clients, or negotiate some compromise that still leaves the firm exposed. The design firm is then left to pray it doesn't get sued later over a trademark or patent of which the firm had no knowledge. A few design firm clients my office has worked with made lemonade out of lemons by offering, along with design services, trademark and even patent due diligence work, and turning those activities into a significant new profit center. Attorneys, of course, were used to handle the legal work.

❑ Without limiting the basic indemnification conditions described above, the standard form client contract should also deal with known trouble spots by expressly providing that any sort of connection, navigation, or e-commerce technology—for example, frames, links, in-lines, mash-ups, shopping carts, and e-commerce transaction processing tools—are incorporated in the deliverables at the client's sole risk, and the client's acceptance of the deliverables confirms that those features have been included at the client's direct instruction and request. The nature of patent exposure, especially, demands this kind of contract protection. Under U.S. patent law, knowing infringement carries with it far heavier penalties (e.g., triple damages) than innocent infringement. Suppose neither the client, the design firm, nor anyone else conducts a reasonable patent search before launching the client's Web site. Some patent law decisions hold that such head-in-the-sand conduct is tantamount to prior knowledge of any patent later alleged to cover some feature in the Web site. A very recent U.S. Supreme Court case suggests the high court may be pulling back from quite such a far-reaching view of patent liability, but there is almost only one solid "out" from patent liability for an independent design firm: a previously signed client contract that openly acknowledges the possibility of patent infringement and says, clearly, that the client has accepted the sole responsibility and obligation to check for possible patent conflicts.

❑ The standard client contract must specify a clear process by which the client is obligated to affirmatively approve all elements and processes included in the design firm's deliverables and that the client's failure to make timely objections will result in approval by default. This is a highly underappreciated type of contract provision that helps design firms get paid, move projects along, and remediate the appearance of design firm control over the particular features of the deliverables.

❑ Continuing the theme of "control," there is a nearly ubiquitous "independent contractor" provision in off-the-shelf form agreements. This provision primarily is intended to support the designer's ownership rights in IP, and preclude withholding tax and other pitfalls of an employer-employee relationship. Unfortunately, independent contractor status can also, in the brave new world of Web design, create an unwelcome vector for IP infringement exposure. The legal hallmark of an independent contractor is the right and practice of exclusively controlling the final results of the contracted services, as well as controlling the personnel and assets used to produce those results. When an infringement case arises, the client will argue that the allegedly offending feature or content in its Web site was put there by the design firm, which the parties have stipulated is an "independent contractor" and thus solely responsible for the exact form of the Web site deliverables. Of course, the notion of controlling "final results" is ambiguous in a collaborative process like Web design; a design firm is hired to produce something (often through multiple iterations) closely corresponding to the client's specifications and vision, and reflecting the client's feedback. This issue underscores the need, discussed in more detail below, for the design firm to consistently document client-supplied content, client specifications, input, requests, review, approval, and acceptance of deliverables.

❏ The standard contract should exclude any form of ongoing support services for the client's Web site. At most, the design firm should be obliged, for added compensation, to provide Web site deliverables testing (and perhaps certain defined enhancements) over a set period of time. Any testing obligations should also be limited to front end user experience issues, and exclude potential back end problems involving things like user privacy or financial information. Past the testing period, the deliverables should be contractually considered delivered "as is." If the design firm's business model intentionally takes on a wider brief, such as hosting or ongoing management of the client's Web site, that arrangement should be separately spelled out as an amendment to or an adaptation of the standard contract.

❏ Web design firms are typically compensated for services on some variation of a flat fee (for the whole project or per phase) or time and materials. But some design firms seek compensation based on traffic, click-throughs, or some other metric. This contingent form of compensation is a good thing as long as it is conceived as a bonus and does not significantly reduce the basic, up-front compensation for design firm services. Wherever contingent compensation is in play, the design firm must have the contractual right to independently audit the performance metrics in a cost-effective way, and should strive to have both measurement and payment of the success compensation guaranteed by a creditworthy third party, for instance, a reputable online, automated advertising brokerage.

THE CLIENT'S FORM CONTRACT

Design firms doing business with larger clients often have little choice but to refuse the assignment or accept the client's own boilerplate vendor contract. Signing off on the client's standard form contract for vendors can be a Faustian bargain. There is almost no end to the mischief in these pieces of paper. In the legal world, there is an old expression, "he who drafts, wins." Even where members of the design firm may have good personal relationships with their counterparts on the client side, when the chips are down, does a design firm want to be at the contractual mercy of the client? In my office, a common task is to help design firms remove or re-negotiate some of the more draconian or untenable elements of large corporate purchasing contracts. In a nutshell, the task is to drive the client's form contract as closely as possible to your own form, especially on the most serious potential liability issues.

As an example, the use of third party material is a recurring and sensitive issue when the design firm is operating under a client form contract. Today microstock sources like Shutterstock are handy, providing images under relatively loose licenses and often royalty-free. Another example of this emerging "bottom-up" phenomenon is the Creative Commons license, potentially applicable to all types of content from all sorts of sources. Meanwhile, larger image vendors like Getty or Corbis have tried to simplify and expand their licensing programs. But who in the design firm makes sure these supposedly "simple" licenses *completely match up* with the representations and warranties to which the firm has committed under the client's form contract? Consider that stock material is usually licensed non-exclusively, and the vendor often specifies in its online user agreements that the content may include digital watermarks or other forms of rights management technology that allows the vendor to crawl the Web to seek out and disable unauthorized uses of the content. If anyone reads the client's form contract carefully, it will likely be discovered that the design firm must exclusively own and transfer to the client all rights in anything embodied in the deliverables, and the design firm must guarantee that the client's use of the deliverables for any purpose will not be in any way legally or technologically impaired. Likewise, beware of vendor programs that allow for the purchase of "exclusive" rights in content. In the fine print, the vendors are not willing to represent and warrant that the "exclusive" rights are truly exclusive.

INTERNAL PRACTICES

Another shield, just as important as a good contract, is a set of consistently applied, day-to-day internal policies to address the legal exposure from the design firm's relationships. And by far the strongest position is to have the design firm's standard contract language and daily practice in alignment.

- Where the deliverables include frames, links, in-lines, mash-ups, or any other emergent technology that leverages content from unaffiliated Web sites, the design firm must seek out any user agreements or licenses posted on the unaffiliated site. The design firm should look at the online agreement or license at an early stage and then quickly pass the agreement on to the client for final authorization. If there is no such agreement, or it is unacceptable for some reason, there should be a direct negotiation with the unaffiliated publisher, culminating in a written license. Absent these conditions, the design firm should not include in the deliverables any form of connecting technology, save perhaps simple hyperlinks to home pages.

- If authorization to use an unaffiliated Web site's content remains a problem, some design firms suggest to the client that the deliverables include a prominent disclaimer making clear there is no endorsement for or from the unaffiliated Web site. This is a weak form of protection, at best. A disclaimer will do nothing to protect against copyright or patent claims (and possibly will make the situation worse) but in a trademark case, a court may take a conspicuously visible and clear disclaimer that reduces consumer confusion as a reason to impose less drastic or costly remedies for infringement.

❑ Here is very arguably the most valuable recommendation in this article: The design firm should make it an iron rule to contemporaneously document all suggestions, requests, specifications, designs, content—or proposed changes to those items—that come from the client. This documentation process is not always easy, as client meetings transpire on the phone or in a casual environment with plenty of spitballing from everyone involved. Even if only done within the firm's offices, a few minutes spent summarizing these conversations often turn into solid gold. The failure to document the process often becomes a source of bitter frustration. These records are frequently the decisive evidence in legal disputes over who is financially responsible for an infringement or similar design-related problem.

❑ Consider having an experienced attorney audit your firm's practices. This involves the attorney spending some time with the design firm, understanding the firm's projects, procedures, work flow, communications, agreements, and clients. This sort of preventive legal care is sometimes available at a relatively low package price, rather than at more expensive hourly rates. While the published guidance from AIGA and other authors in support of their standard forms is a great starting point, a knowledgeable attorney can deliver considerable long run value by, among other things, walking through the preparation of a few actual agreements for specific clients, with the twin goals of adjusting the standard forms to better fit the firm's way of doing business, and having the firm fully understand and internalize the standard forms' logic and correct implementation. Preventive care and training is almost assuredly less expensive than the resolution of *any* legal conflict arising from imprecise or poorly managed contracting practices.

INSURANCE

The familiar, comprehensive general liability policy purchased by many businesses does not, except in vary rare circumstances, cover the risks considered in this article. Errors and omissions insurance covering IP risks is the great, unmet need in the Web design industry. The policies are not widely marketed, and even when insurers make them available, they are expensive, have many significant exclusions from coverage, and require the design firm to maintain an expensive, ongoing due diligence program that includes reliance on IP counsel.

DESIGN FIRM MARKETING

Here's a final and often overlooked question: how does your design firm market itself? Increasingly, the practitioners of Web design (as we have broadly defined that term) do not call themselves or think of themselves as, "Web design firms." There are many valid reasons, including accuracy, for a firm to market itself under a different rubric, for example "strategic services," "branding consultancy," "e-commerce advisors," "information architects," or "user experience design." But in light of current legal trends, it's worth pausing for a moment to consider the problems that might arise if your firm is labeled, say, the "strategic consultant" for a Web site that primarily and heavily traffics in user-supplied, unauthorized uploads of copyrighted entertainment. The legal risk tail shouldn't wag the successful-marketing-of-your-business dog, but sometimes plain, old-fashioned "graphic designer" doesn't sound so bad.

29

Other People's Trademarks

LEE WILSON

ALMOST EVERYONE KNOWS that selling toothpaste or sneakers or brokerage services by using a trademark that belongs to someone else is a quick ticket to a federal suit for trademark infringement. The law allows marketers to protect themselves from interlopers who want a free ride on their commercial coattails; they do this by means of lawsuits to preserve the integrity of their trademarks, which represent them to the public. The penumbra of protection granted an established trademark extends to identical marks and to marks that, although not identical, are similar enough to confuse consumers.

Usually, the comparison to determine trademark infringement is made between marks used to market similar products or services. However, the more famous and unusual the trademark, the wider the scope of protection trademark law grants it; no one can use Kleenex® or Coca-Cola® or Exxon® for any product without encountering serious opposition from platoons of trademark lawyers who work for those companies, especially since the Trademark Dilution Act became effective in early 1996. (The Trademark Dilution Act formalizes and makes a part of the federal trademark statute a principle of trademark law that had been available as a ground for suit in only about half the states. It allows the owners of an existing "famous" trademark to ask the court to enjoin the use of the same mark by another company—even if there is no likelihood of confusion between the marks—on the ground that the defendant's use of the mark, even for noncompeting goods or services, "dilutes" the distinctive quality of the famous mark. This allows the owners of truly famous marks to stop the use of their marks by the marketers of noncompeting goods and services as well as by competitors.)

There are other ways to infringe a trademark besides adopting a name for a product or service that is confusingly similar to an established mark for a similar product or service. Because trademark owners are vigilant in protecting their trademarks, wariness in the matter of other people's trademarks is a very good idea. However, such wariness can lead to an exaggerated fear of trademarks that belong to others and unnecessary maneuvering to avoid any mention or depiction of them. Surprisingly enough, there are some circumstances when using someone else's trademark *is* safe.

Broadly speaking, the law gives a trademark owner protection against any action that creates confusion about that trademark in the minds of consumers. This means that the dividing line between safe and unsafe uses of a trademark is where consumer confusion begins. Determining whether a given use of someone else's trademark will lead to a lawsuit is simply a matter of determining, under all the circumstances, whether that use will confuse anyone.

There are two common varieties of use of someone else's trademark that are usually safe and one that is, by definition, almost never safe. An examination of each of these situations will demonstrate the considerations involved in using other people's trademarks.

INCIDENTAL USE OF TRADEMARKS

More than one graphic designer has called in a lawyer to evaluate whether the presence of a Coke® can sitting on a table in a photograph is enough to disqualify the photo for use in an ad that isn't supposed to advertise Coke products. Before the lawyer can answer the question, he or she will have to see the photograph in question and read the ad copy, because the two important factors in evaluating whether the Coca-Cola Company is likely to sue are the emphasis of the photograph and the context of the use of the Coke logo.

Trademarks are a part of our world; they so pervade every environment of modern life that it is next to impossible to walk down a street or visit a public place or sit in a room without being surrounded by trademarks of every sort. This means that any realistic depiction of a street scene or restaurant setting or home or office situation will include representations of the trademarks found in that environment. Even though the trademarks that appear in such depictions are the valuable property of the companies that own them, in a way they also belong to the rest of us because they are a part of our lives. The First Amendment protects commercial speech such as advertising as well as other sorts of speech. This means that, as a matter of free speech, we have a right to "mention" the trademarks around us, either verbally or visually.

Which brings us back to the Coke® can in that photograph. Although free speech gives us the right to talk about or depict the world we live in, including trademarks, trademark law limits that right to some extent by discouraging certain sorts of uses of trademarks. The law would allow the Coca-Cola Company to sue the ad agency and the agency's client for trademark infringement if anything about the photo that included the Coke® can implied that there was some connection between Coca-Cola® and the product advertised in the ad for which the photo was used. The same would be true if consumers could infer from the ad that the Coca-Cola Company somehow sponsored the ad or the product it advertised. As a practical matter, it is not likely that either of these grounds for suit would exist unless the Coke logo was legible and the can on which it appeared was a prominent element of the photograph; a background depiction of the can wouldn't create a problem, especially if the can wasn't an emphasis of the photograph.

Similarly, the context of the appearance in an ad of a "borrowed" trademark is important. If the Coke® can photograph depicted the scene around the pool at an upscale resort hotel in an ad for that hotel, implying, however obliquely, that Coca-Cola is a favorite drink of carefree, wealthy people who look good in stylish bathing suits, the Coca-Cola Company probably would not object to the incidental appearance of its name and logo in the ad. If, however, the Coke can appeared in an objectionable photograph or if that photograph were used in any unsavory context, the Coca-Cola Company would be inclined to take whatever action was necessary to halt further use of the photo, especially if the Coke can was prominent in the photograph. The Coca-Cola Company, along with everybody else in the world, knows that villains and heroes and every other variety of human being drink Coca-Cola soft drinks. However, it is understandable that no one in Atlanta except the lawyers who earn their keep by guarding the various valuable Coca-Cola trademarks would like to see an ad photo prominently depicting a Coke can lying on a heap of rancid garbage or a broken Coke bottle being wielded as a weapon in a bar fight. Similarly, an identifiable depiction of a Coca-Cola product used in an ad for a topless bar or cigarettes or a personal hygiene product could earn the animosity of the Coca-Cola Company. Any use of a trademark in an unsavory context can lead to a claim of product disparagement, which is comparable to a defamation suit brought on behalf of a trademark.

COMPARATIVE ADVERTISING

Strangely enough, there is one variety of calculated, obvious use of other people's trademarks that will seldom cause trouble if carried out carefully. This is the use of trademarks belonging to competitor companies in comparative advertising. Trademark law does not prohibit *non*trademark or informational uses of the trademarks of others but, rather, punishes uses that confuse consumers. Comparative advertising informs consumers by explicitly comparing the merits of one product with those of another. The competitor's product, which always suffers from the comparison, is mentioned specifically in the ad copy and its package is usually pictured beside the advertiser's product in a head-on shot. Such ads require by their very nature that the products compared be carefully identified before the distinctions between them are drawn; only a very clumsy ad would fail to make entirely clear whether Joy® detergent or Ivory® detergent "cuts grease faster in laboratory tests." The test for trademark infringement is whether the public will be confused by the use of the mark. Because the possibility of consumer confusion is eliminated in comparative advertising, so is the likelihood of any charge of trademark infringement.

However, only claims that are truthful and that can be substantiated are safe. Because exaggerated claims or claims that can't be documented can lead to false advertising suits or unfair competition claims, every statement in a comparative advertising campaign should be carefully documented and every element of the campaign should be carefully designed.

Comparative advertisements can safely make use of competitors' trademarks if they are carefully constructed. Using a photo of a competing product or mentioning the product by name in an ad that compares it to your client's product is not an infringement of the trademark rights of the other company if the ad truthfully compares the products named by the trademarks and if the character and arrangement of the visual elements and the content of the ad copy do not create any likelihood that consumers will somehow mistakenly believe that your company's product has some relation to the product of the other company.

Although properly designed comparative advertising does not usually lead to trademark infringement suits, there is one caveat. Whenever you use a trademark belonging to someone else in an ad, it is only prudent to state who owns that trademark in order to emphasize that the mark has no connection with the advertiser's product. This is easily accomplished by means of a "footnote" ownership statement. That is, a short statement should be included somewhere along the bottom margin or up the side margin of print ads and at the bottom of the screen in television commercials to the effect that "Dove® is a registered trademark of the Lever Brothers Company."

The competitor's trademark should be used in exactly the form it appears on the competitor's product; that is, if it is a federally registered trademark and bears the ® symbol, that symbol should be used in the ownership statement. If the mark is not registered, no such symbol will appear, or the ™ symbol will be used in conjunction with the mark. In this event, the usage as it appears on the product should be duplicated and the ownership statement should read something like this: "Crunchies™ is a trademark of the Toasted Oats Company and is not owned or licensed by the makers of Sweeties™ brand cereal." A statement that your client's competitor owns its mark should completely eliminate any valid claim that the comparative ad creates confusion regarding the ownership of the mark or the manufacturer of the product it names. However, because not just any such disclaimer will suffice, any such ad and proposed disclaimer should be reviewed before the ad is published by a trademark lawyer who can evaluate the possibility that the ad will result in an infringement lawsuit.

It is important to remember that the laws regarding comparative advertising in other countries may vary considerably from those in the United States. Be especially sure that any ad you prepare that mentions another company's trademark and will be published or circulated outside the United States will not furnish the owner of the other trademark with grounds for suit. Marketers use comparative advertising because it is effective—a comparative ad can lure consumers away from a product they are in the habit of buying on the strength of its convincing claims of the benefits of a rival product that is "new and improved" or simply "more effective in 75 percent of laboratory tests." This is enough to make the owners of the product that fares badly in such comparisons want to do whatever they can to stop the further publication of the ad. A lawsuit can do this. If a competitor finds your comparative advertising objectionable and the law in one or more of the countries where the ad appears supports that viewpoint, you will be vulnerable in any country where your competitor can, with a straight face, file a suit. Maybe U.S. law, with its predisposition to allow free speech in all possible contexts, can't be used as a club to stop your trumpeting the better performance of your product, but it may be possible to use the laws of other markets for just such a purpose, and every segment of international commerce counts. Japanese or Swedish or German money can fatten the bottom line for marketers just as well as American dollars. It's possible that somebody who works for your competitor wouldn't mind a long trip abroad at company expense to hire and supervise the lawyers who will be suing you under laws that you never heard of. Because you can't keep a tame trademark lawyer in your desk drawer to consult whenever you need advice, put his or her phone number on your Rolodex® rotary card file (this is an example of correct usage of a trademark) *and* on your speed dial.

TRADEMARK PARODY

When a company decides to market a product under a name that is a parody of another mark, it is engaging in trademark parody. Trademark parody is almost always a bad idea, for two reasons. The first reason is that one of the kinds of confusion that trademark owners can legitimately complain about in court is "dilution," which is a claim that someone's use of an established mark is eroding the mark's strength even though the complained-of use is made in connection with a product that is unrelated to the product named by the established mark. If this fact alone isn't enough to convince you that trademark parody is almost invariably a dumb idea, consider this: only very famous trademarks are parodied—a parody of an obscure mark just wouldn't work. This means that the parodist is picking on a company rich enough to finance a trademark infringement lawsuit out of its petty cash. And since the passage of the Trademark Dilution Act, suits for dilution are easier for owners of famous marks to file and win. (The Federal Express suit to stop the use of Federal Espresso for a coffeehouse is a good example of a parody use of a famous trademark that ran afoul of the Trademark Dilution Act's proscriptions soon after the Act became effective.)

Another factor in trademark parody that often contributes to the problems that parodists face is that the parodied mark is often the butt of a joke, which may be an off-color joke. Nobody likes wise guys. The owners of the parodied mark may be so enraged by the parody of their mark that they will rush to file a trademark infringement suit and ask for an injunction against the parodist. Courts are usually sympathetic to the interests of the owners of famous trademarks; as a result, trademark parodists are routinely enjoined from pursuing their bad jokes at the expense of the well-known marks they parody.

You can understand trademark parody better by considering a few trademark parody cases in which the parodists were ordered by the court to give up making jokes at the expense of the plaintiff trademark owners. The pairs of marks that were the subjects of these suits tell the story in themselves; if reading the list makes you wince, you're getting the right idea about trademark parody. Not surprisingly, all these defendants lost in court.

Plaintiff Company	Defendant Trademark
Coca-Cola Company	"Enjoy Cocaine" (used, on a poster, in a script and color identical to those used for the Coca-Cola® logo)
Anheuser Busch, Inc.	"Where There's Life . . . There's Bugs" (for a combination floor wax insecticide, in a parody of the Anheuser Busch slogan "Where There's Life . . . There's Bud")
General Electric Company	"Genital Electric" (used, on men's underwear, in a script monogram similar to the General Electric® script logo)
Johnny Carson	"Here's Johnny" (used, as the name of a line of portable toilets, in a parody of the phrase associated with the famous comedian; no trademark infringement was found, but the court found that Mr. Carson's right of publicity had been violated)

Not every trademark parody is ruled a trademark infringement. For example, the use in a florist's ad campaign of the slogan "This bud's for you" was held not to infringe the trademark rights of Anheuser-Busch, Inc. In its ruling, the court specifically mentioned the innocuous and pleasant nature of the florist's slogan. As a practical matter, all this tells us is that *sometimes* parodists win in court.

Because paying to defend a lawsuit is almost as much a misfortune as losing it, this is really no encouragement to would-be parodists. The best thing to do with famous trademarks is to steer clear of them, especially if your parody is smutty or would associate a famous mark with an unsavory product.

More than one trademark infringement lawsuit has been brought simply because the trademark owner was angry and felt like doing something about it. If this doesn't scare you, consider the fact that owners of famous trademarks have whole platoons of trademark lawyers who have to justify their existence by periodically going after evildoers. If they are short of true malefactors this month, you and your ad may look like very good targets. When it comes to using someone else's famous trademark in an ad without permission, discretion really is the better part of valor.

THE ETIQUETTE OF TRADEMARK USAGE

The only thing left to say about using other people's trademarks is that you should do so carefully. This boils down to the following four rules:

1. **Trademarks are proper adjectives; remember to use them as such.** It is a "Kleenex® tissue," not just a "kleenex," and you wear "Levi's® jeans," not just "levis."

2. **Trademarks should never be used as nouns or verbs.** You do not "Xerox®" a document, you make a photocopy of it, and it *is* a "photocopy," not simply a "xerox."

3. **Spell it right.** Most importantly, capitalize trademarks; it is "Coke®," not "coke," and "Cuisinart®," not "cuisinart."

4. **Give a mark its due.** If it is a registered mark, use the ® symbol in conjunction with the mark in at least the two or three most prominent uses of the mark in a text or an ad. If it is not registered, use informal trademark notice (i.e., the ™ superscript or subscript) if the owner of the mark does so on its products. (If the mark names a service, the trademark owner may use^{SM} to indicate this.)

If you are confused about the proper spelling of a trademark or whether it is federally registered and therefore entitled to be escorted by the ® symbol whenever it appears in print, you can research the mark on the International Trademark Association (INTA) Web site. Compiled to help journalists, proofreaders, and others with proper trademark usage, the INTA's Trademark Checklist exclusively lists trademarks federally registered in the United States (nearly 3,000 marks), along with the generic terms for the products and services they name and indicates proper spelling, capitalization, and punctuation. You can access the INTA's Trademark Checklist at *www.inta.org/tmchklst.htm*. If you can't find the mark you are investigating, call the INTA Trademark Hotline at (212) 768–9886 for proper-usage information or contact the Hotline at *tmhotline@inta.org*. The Hotline operates weekdays from 2:00 P.M. to 5:00 P.M. eastern standard time.

Your rights won't be affected if you fail to follow these rules in using other people's trademarks, but theirs may be diminished. A trademark that is used incorrectly can become "generic"; that is, the mark loses its ability to refer to a particular product or service and comes to indicate a whole class of products. If this happens, the original owner of the mark loses the exclusive right to use it. This happened to "aspirin," and "escalator," and "thermos" as well as numerous other once-valuable trademarks. In determining whether a mark has lost its significance as an indicator of *one* company's products or services, courts often consider whether a trademark owner has acted against infringers. You may have no legal *duty* to use the marks of others carefully, but they may have a very good legal reason—the preservation of their rights—to challenge any misuse of those marks.

Because a trademark represents the reputation in the marketplace of the products or services of the company that owns it, it may be that company's most valuable asset. It is understandable that trademark owners pay close attention when their marks are used by people they've never met and in ways they don't necessarily approve. That's why they spend time writing letters to people who misuse them and money to publish ads to explain proper trademark usage. The way to avoid trouble when using other people's trademarks is to handle them like you would handle other people's money—carefully.

I'LL SEE YOU IN COURT

The following are thumbnail accounts of actual trademark disputes between the owners of established trademarks and people who used identical marks for *unrelated* products or services. These accounts are proof that the owners of famous trademarks are serious—some would say overvigilant—about protecting their marks. Sometimes the owners of the famous marks won their suits against the accused interlopers, sometimes the courts sided with the junior user of the mark—either way, being the object of a lawsuit filed by a rich plaintiff is a memorable misfortune.

- ❑ The giant cereal manufacturer, the Kellogg Company, sued Toucan Golf, Inc., which marketed golf clubs and other golf products by using a depiction of a toucan and the words "Toucan Gold." Kellogg claimed that Toucan Golf infringed on Kellogg's Toucan Sam cartoon trademarks used to market cereals. The court did not agree.

- ❑ The online auction giant eBay has been active in challenging similar and parody names for unconnected trading sites. It sued BidBay, a rival auction site, sent a letter to AlternaBay, a gay auction site, and complained about a parody site called eGray.org, which was run by opponents of (then) California governor Gray Davis. A Lego-trading site named Brick-Bay.com changed its name to BrickLink.com after eBay said that Brick-Bay infringed eBay's trademark rights. The famous eBay has staked its claim to a large hunk of cyberspace and intends to keep it.

❑ The World Wrestling Federation (WWF) wrote a letter to the independent record label that marketed the recordings of Wesley Willis, asking it to stop the sale and distribution of an album called "The Wesley Willis Fiasco Live E.P." The album cover featured a logo similar to the WWF logo. The WWF letter claimed that the album logo infringed upon and diluted the WWF trademark and asked that all copies of the album be recalled and destroyed or surrendered to the WWF.

❑ The World Wildlife Fund sued the World Wrestling Federation to compel it to live up to a 1994 agreement not to use the WWF abbreviation, which the World Wildlife Fund registered when it was formed in 1961. The wildlife group wants the wrestling group to stop using any domain name that includes the WWF mark and to stop selling merchandise bearing it.

❑ The large online merchant Amazon.com sued Amazon Cosmetics and Tan Products, the owner of Amazontan.com, saying that the beauty products company was infringing its rights; the suit was dismissed on jurisdictional grounds. It also sued the operator of Amazon.gr, which called itself "Greece's Biggest Bookstore"; the Greek business was ordered by the court to stop using the Amazon name.

❑ The OCLC Online Computer Library Center, Inc. sued The Library Hotel, a boutique New York hotel near the main New York Public Library, for trademark infringement. It claimed that The Library Hotel was using the Dewey Decimal Classification® trademarks without permission. The hotel features theme-based rooms and each room is stocked with books that relate to its specific Dewey Decimal® theme. The suit was settled; the hotel was granted permission to use the OCLC's trademarks in its hotel and marketing materials and the hotel made a charitable contribution to promote children's reading.

30

Trademarks
and Trade Dress

LEONARD D. DUBOFF

TRADEMARK LAW WAS once thought to be important and relevant only to a select group of persons or corporations whose legal interests were handled by specialists. Today it is recognized that trademarks are far more pervasive than most people realize. Similarly, the body of law known as trade dress has been developed to protect the "look and feel" of a distinctive product or service.

TRADEMARKS

Trademarks, and the goodwill associated with them, are valuable assets to the businesses that own them, and any infringements are likely to be vigorously challenged. When, for example, Time Warner learned that an artists' organization in Sarajevo was publishing a magazine profiling survivors of the war in Bosnia-Herzegovina entitled *Life* with the *e* reversed in the spelling, it swung into action. Time Warner, owner of the *Life* trademark, was angered because the Sarajevan magazine appropriated the look and feel of *Life Magazine* and had a title that was confusingly similar to their magazine's protected title. The attorneys representing Time Warner insisted on having all of the infringing magazines destroyed, making it clear that trademark infringement is a serious offense.

Virtually every business, whether it deals in products or services, is involved with trademarks. Many established corporations, which aggressively compete in the marketplace for consumer dollars, consider their trademarks to be their business's single most valuable asset. From computers to rental cars, from magazines to crafts, it is the reputation associated with a trademark that may in the end become the decisive factor causing the consumer to choose one brand over another.

For some time, Queen Elizabeth II has permitted the House of Windsor name to be used in connection with products ranging from furniture to rugs. The Church of Jesus Christ of Latter Day Saints has also permitted the use of its name as a trademark in connection with educational products and home decorating items. Even the Vatican Library has realized the value of its name as a trademark and the effect that its endorsement of products may have on consumers. In fact, the Vatican Library has a licensing program permitting product manufacturers to include its official seal on authorized merchandise. Similarly, Colonial Williamsburg has had a licensing program which helps fund the colonial restoration's significant activities.

Oleg Cassini, the famous clothing designer responsible for creating Jacqueline Kennedy's look during her tenure as the First Lady and the first designer to use licensing, has said, "Many times I've thought about it, what keeps me going, and I think it is a pride of trademark. That may seem like a commercial thing. But two of the greatest names in fashion today are Chanel and Dior; and they died years ago. I have young people in my company, and I like to think my trademark will survive me."

The same rationale affects smaller, growing businesses, such as your graphic design business, and the clients it serves. As a result, disputes may arise regarding ownership of a mark in situations where a family business is placed in the middle of a marriage dissolution or an estate dispute.

Virtually every business will be involved with trademarks or infringement issues at some point. It is, therefore, important to have some rudimentary knowledge of this area of law in order to determine whether your graphic design business has a protectable intellectual property right or, conversely, whether you have, either intentionally or unwittingly, stumbled into a potential trademark dispute. Similarly, you should advise your clients about the importance of protecting the trademarks you create for them and be sure to avoid thrusting your client into a trademark dispute.

TRADEMARK INFRINGEMENT

Any name, symbol, logo, or combination of these items, that is not generic, when used in connection with a product or service, may be protected as a trademark. Registration is not a prerequisite to creating a protected mark, and even unregistered marks are protectable and enforceable. Section 43(a) of the Lanham Act grants the proprietor/owner of a protectable mark the right to prevent others from using a mark that sounds like, looks like, or is confusingly similar to the protected mark.

"Likelihood of confusion" is a rather broad legal standard and may permit an infringement claim, even if the challenged mark is not identical to the one protected. If a reasonable consumer would be confused and misled into believing that a product or service that bears the knockoff mark is manufactured, endorsed and authorized, or licensed by the owner of the protected trademark, then an injunction against further market confusion may be obtained. The trademark owner may recover defendant's profits, damages, and, in an appropriate case, the costs of the litigation. Thus, merely changing the spelling of a word or slightly modifying a logo will not avoid a claim of infringement. In addition, in certain circumstances, the trademark proprietor may also recover treble damages. The fact that the alleged infringer was ignorant of the protected mark is relevant only in determining whether the case is extraordinary, in which case attorneys' fees would also be available.

DILUTION

Pursuant to the federal antidilution statute, a famous mark can be protected even when there is no likelihood of confusion if the unauthorized use tarnishes the mark (as when a pornographic Web site uses a protected mark as an identifier) or when the mark's distinctiveness is "blurred" by the unauthorized use (as when an unauthorized use trades on the good reputation of the owner of the mark).

The federal antidilution statute entitles the owner of a famous mark to an injunction against another person's commercial use of a mark where such use begins after the mark has become famous and causes dilution of the distinctive quality of that mark. Willful intent to trade on the owner's reputation or to cause dilution of the mark may also entitle the owner of the mark to the same remedies as those set forth for trademark infringement, including damages, costs, and attorneys' fees.

Dilution is defined as "the lessening of the capacity of a famous mark to identify and distinguish goods or services, regardless of the presence or absence of: (1) competition between the owner of the famous mark and other parties, or (2) likelihood of confusion, mistake, or deception."

The statute provides that "a mark is famous if it is widely recognized by the general consuming public of the United States as a designation of source of the goods or services of the mark's owner" and sets forth a list of factors to be considered in determining whether or not a mark is famous. These factors are:

---

1. The duration, extent, and geographic reach of advertising and publicity of the mark, whether advertised or publicized by the owner or third parties;

2. The amount, volume, and geographic extent of sales of goods or services offered under the mark;

3. The extent of actual recognition of the mark; and

4. Whether the mark was registered under the Act of March 3, 1881, or the Act of February 20, 1905, or on the principal register.

Ownership of a valid registration under the Act of March 3, 1881, or February 20, 1905, or on the Principal Register is a complete bar to a state- or common-law antidilution action against an owner with respect to that mark. In addition, the following nonactionable uses of a mark are set forth in Section 43: fair use of a famous mark by another person in comparative commercial advertising or promotion to identify the competing goods or services of the owner of the famous mark; noncommercial use of a mark; and all forms of news reporting and news commentary.

The federal antidilution statute differs from many of the state antidilution statutes, which sometimes offer more protection. If you are working with a client who owns a famous trademark, you should advise that client to work with a skilled intellectual property lawyer in order to achieve maximum protection for that trademark.

TRADEMARK REGISTRATION

A mark can be registered federally, in which case the process involves dealing with the Assistant Commissioner of Trademarks in Arlington, Virginia, and ultimately having the proposed mark published in the *Official Gazette of the U.S. Patent and Trademark Office*. This weekly publication is reviewed by trademark lawyers who look out for marks that may conflict with those of their clients. Anyone who feels that a mark that appears in the *Gazette* should not be registered may oppose registration, and a hearing will be conducted to determine the rights of the respective parties. If no objection (or request for an extension of time within which to make an objection) is filed within thirty days after a proposed mark has appeared in the *Gazette*, then a Certificate of Registration will ultimately be issued. It is only then that the trademark proprietor may use the ® symbol in connection with a mark. Any other use of this trademark symbol is improper.

The symbols ™ and ℠ may be used in connection with unregistered marks, as well as state registered marks. When a person desires to protect a mark she or he believes might be used in the future, an "intent to use" application may be filed even before the mark is actually used. If the mark is ultimately used in interstate commerce, then the intent to use registration may be converted into an actual registration by filing the appropriate documents with the Patent and Trademark Office within the required time period.

United States Customs has been charged with the responsibility of policing American borders and aiding proprietors of registered U.S. intellectual property, including trademarks, by preventing the importation of material bearing infringing marks.

STATE TRADEMARK LAWS

A trademark may also be registered on the state level. Unfortunately, state registrations are geographically limited by the state's boundaries, although the legal remedies available against an infringer of a mark that enjoys state registration may be different from, and in some cases better than, those available under the federal statute.

For example, many states have their own form of antidilution protection. Essentially, this means that activities that might not be actionable under the federal statute may give rise to liability under state antidilution laws, which generally do not require that the infringed mark be famous.

TRADEMARK AVAILABILITY

It is essential to determine whether a name, symbol, logo, or combination of these is already protected and owned by another individual or business before using a particular mark. For this reason, graphic design businesses should commission a broad-based trademark search as a prerequisite to starting a new venture or identifying a product or service with a mark. Many law firms can actually conduct preliminary searches in-house. An experienced trademark lawyer can review the search results to determine whether the desired mark is potentially available and whether it would be prudent to commence using it. You may be able to conduct a preliminary or "knock out" search by going to *www.uspto.gov* and searching the trademark registry. Unfortunately, this search is very superficial since you must also be able to evaluate the results of this knock out search, and it only deals with marks that have been federally registered or for which applications have been filed. It does not cover other uses that give rise to trademark rights.

Some things may not be protected as trademarks. If the proposed mark is generic, for example, the word is the noun or verb describing the product or service (like "chair" to describe a chair or "car" to describe an automobile), then the mark cannot be protected. Some trademarks have become generic because of improper use. When, for example, the owner of a protected mark allows it to be used as the noun or verb describing the product or service and the mark becomes known as the name for that product or service, it will become generic. Examples of marks that were protected and became generic because of improper use are escalator, thermos, and aspirin.

On the other hand, if the proposed mark is merely descriptive, then it may qualify for protection once the mark has achieved a "secondary meaning." Descriptive marks that conjure up images of the products or services that they represent are said to have achieved this secondary meaning and, therefore, are afforded protection. Thus, *TV Guide* is descriptive; yet it has achieved secondary meaning and is protected. If the proposed mark is available, then there are a number of options that the business may select in order to protect it. As noted above, merely using a protectable mark in interstate commerce will give rise to protection under the federal trademark statute. It is, however, still a good idea to register protectable marks, because registration provides a trademark proprietor certain benefits in litigation as well as in public notoriety. In addition, a registered mark is presumed valid and thus the owner may not have to prove its validity in litigation when enforcement is sought.

TRADE DRESS

A relatively new body of law has emerged known as trade dress. Initially, this doctrine was used exclusively for protecting unique and distinctive packaging when the packaging helped to identify the source of a product or service. More recently, trade dress law has been extended to the protection of products or services themselves. When, for example, the Hallmark Greeting Card Company appropriated the look and feel of the distinctive greeting card produced by the Colorado-based Blue Mountain Company, trade dress law came to the rescue. Because the Hallmark cards were not substantially similar to those produced by Blue Mountain, the Hallmark line did not infringe the copyright in Blue Mountain's distinctive cards. The court relied on the then emerging doctrine of trade dress in holding that appropriating the look and feel of another's distinctive product or service is an infringement.

The U.S. Supreme Court endorsed this expansion of the trade dress doctrine by holding that the distinctive characteristics of a fast-food restaurant may be a protectable trade dress. In *Two Pesos v. Taco Cabana*, the court held that distinctive characteristics that are not functional and that are used to identify a product or service may be protectable, even though they do not enjoy copyright protection or are not traditional trademarks. All the plaintiff needs to prove is that the trade dress is not functional, that it is distinctive and notorious, and that the plaintiff is known by the characteristics claimed to be a protectable trade dress.

The trade dress doctrine has been used to protect the distinctive characteristics of an artist's style, a craft show's format, a jewelry rack's unique characteristics, and many other products or services that may not enjoy other forms of intellectual property protection.

Graphic designers who create unique product designs, packaging, corporate personalities, or the like may be able to rely on the trade dress doctrine for purposes of protecting their creative work.

There is no registration required for trade dress protection; rather, the law affords a remedy for the unauthorized misappropriation of the protected work, though registering a protectable trade dress may provide significant benefits. In *Wal-Mart Stores, Inc. v. Samara Brothers, Inc.*, the U.S. Supreme Court imposed a significant obstacle to the continued expansion of the trade dress doctrine. In that case, the Supreme Court held that in order to establish trade dress protection in a product design, the complainant must prove that the alleged trade dress has acquired secondary meaning. Secondary meaning generally must be established through expensive consumer surveys, but if the trade dress were registered as a trademark, then the presumption of validity might avoid the necessity of having to conduct the survey. There is thus a real advantage in evaluating whether or not your or your client's trade dress can be registered.

Graphic designers should consult with a skilled intellectual property lawyer in order to determine whether the product or service in question is protectable under any of the intellectual property laws, such as patent, trade secret, copyright, trademark, or trade dress. A skilled attorney can advise you on the best method of securing the rights to your creations and what steps you should take in order to properly advise your clients.

The importance of the trademark and trade dress laws cannot be overemphasized. They pervade virtually every business, and nearly every businessperson will encounter them at some time. It is for this reason that all graphic artists should be familiar with these bodies of law and work with an experienced intellectual property attorney on a regular basis. Carelessness in dealing with these forms of intellectual property can result in serious consequences. Today there are both a vast array of reference materials available and an increasing number of attorneys who are adopting intellectual property law as a specialty.

With the advent of the World Wide Web, e-mail, faxes, and inexpensive long-distance telephone service, the world is shrinking. It is thus possible for you to consult with your attorney on a regular basis, even when you are half a world away. As a graphic artist, your stock in trade is your distinctive creations, which will only retain their value if you can protect them. For more information on trademark, trade dress, and related areas of intellectual property, see *www.dubofflaw.com*; click on "Critical Issues."

31

Trademarks in Cyberspace

LEE WILSON

LIKE ALL FRONTIERS, cyberspace is largely populated by mavericks and rebels who like the cyber-atmosphere of "if you can imagine it, you can do it." Unfortunately, the very dearth of rules that makes cyberspace so intriguing to everyone who has something to say or sell electronically is also causing problems. Americans often complain about overregulation by local, state, and federal governmental agencies and authorities. But many who are familiar with the problems that can arise when Internet users and marketers compete for domain names would agree that, in some corners of cyberspace, more rules are needed.

The ownership of domain names has produced disputes since the very early days of the Internet. A domain name is the heart of an e-mail address. In the e-mail address johnjones@jonesventures.com, "jonesventures.com" is the domain name. Domain names tell Internet users where to find companies and individuals in cyberspace. They function like ZIP codes do for "snail mail"; they direct e-mail and other communications to the right cyberspace neighborhood to find the person or entity named in the first part of the e-mail address. They allow Internet users to visit World Wide Web pages.

The system of categorizing Internet user addresses according to type is familiar to most Net surfers. They are called Top Level Domain names, or TLDs. The original five major nonmilitary domains are: .com for commercial entities, .gov for governmental bodies, .edu for educational institutions, .org for organizations, and .net for networks. ICANN, the Internet Corporation for Assigned Names and Numbers (found at *www.icann.org*), subsequently introduced seven new domain-name categories in addition to the original five; they are: .biz, .info, .aero, .museum, .name, .pro, and .coop. As with the original five domain-name categories, not just anyone can use the additional domain-name categories; .biz is restricted to businesses; .aero is reserved for the use of airlines and similar organizations, .museum is limited to museums; .name is for personal names, .pro is reserved for doctors, lawyers, and accountants; and .coop is only for cooperatives. The additional domain-name categories eased the competition for domain names to some extent by allowing individuals and organizations more elbow room in cyberspace. This is the complete list of existing TLD categories, and their sponsors, available for general use, taken from the ICANN Web site:

Generic Top-Level Domains

- The .aero domain is reserved for members of the air-transport industry and is sponsored by Société Internationale de Télécommunications Aéronautiques (SITA).

- The .asia domain is restricted to the Pan-Asia and Asia Pacific community and is operated by DotAsia Organisation.

- The .biz domain is restricted to businesses and is operated by NeuLevel, Inc.

- The .cat domain is reserved for the Catalan linguistic and cultural community and is sponsored by Fundació puntCat.

- The .com domain is operated by VeriSign Global Registry Services.

- The .coop domain is reserved for cooperative associations and is sponsored by Dot Cooperation LLC.

- The .info domain is operated by Afilias Limited.

- The .jobs domain is reserved for human resource managers and is sponsored by Employ Media LLC.

- The .mobi domain is reserved for consumers and providers of mobile products and services and is sponsored by mTLD Top Level Domain, Ltd.

- The .museum domain is reserved for museums and is sponsored by the Museum Domain Management Association.

- The .name domain is reserved for individuals and is operated by Global Name Registry.

- The .net domain is operated by VeriSign Global Registry Services.

- The .org domain is operated by Public Interest Registry. It is intended to serve the noncommercial community, but all are eligible to register within .org.

- The .pro domain is restricted to credentialed professionals and related entities and is operated by RegistryPro.

- The .tel domain is reserved for businesses and individuals to publish their contact data and is sponsored by Telnic Ltd.

- The .travel domain is reserved for entities whose primary area of activity is in the travel industry and is sponsored by Tralliance Corporation.

Registrations in the domains listed above may be made through dozens of competitive registrars. For a list of the currently operating accredited registrars, go to the InterNIC site. Information about becoming an accredited registrar is available on the ICANN site.

- The .gov domain is reserved exclusively for the United States Government. It is operated by the U.S. General Services Administration.

- The .edu domain is reserved for postsecondary institutions accredited by an agency on the U.S. Department of Education's list of Nationally Recognized Accrediting Agencies and is registered only through Educause.

- The .mil domain is reserved exclusively for the United States Military. It is operated by the U.S. DoD Network Information Center.

- The .int domain is used only for registering organizations established by international treaties between governments. It is operated by the IANA .int Domain Registry.

(A list of existing country-code TLDs can be found at *www.iana. org/root-whois/index.html*.)

In 2004, ICANN solicited suggestions for new TLD names. Of those suggested, six regional or industry-specific names were approved. An example of an industry-specific name is .travel; .asia is a regional domain-name suffix. ICANN rejected .xxx for adult entertainment sites. There is, as yet, no process in place for applying for these new TLDs; however, ICANN is working on implementing a policy and procedure for new and future applications. You can find more information on this process at *www.icann.org/topics/gtld-strategy-area.html*. The new domain names are likely to be available by mid-2008. You can read about ICANN's policies for new names at *www.icann.org/topics/new-gtld-strategy-faq.htm*.

Even if these or other TLD categories are instituted, the Internet is likely to continue to be a crowded place. And because marketers have found ways to sell everything from coffee to books to the stuff from your hall closet online, the most crowded part of cyberspace probably will continue to be the commercial district, where all the .com addresses are located.

Internet addresses are actually a series of numbers. However, because people who want to locate an Internet merchant are much more likely to remember a verbal address than a series of numbers, domain names are alpha and/or numeric names that a computer can convert to numeric addresses. This means that the best domain names look like the names of the companies that own them; this sort of domain name creates an expectation as to who is at the Internet address it names. If you are familiar with a company and its product or services and its domain name resembles the name of the company, you know that its address on the Internet is your portal to whatever the company sells. Such Internet addresses are easy to guess and easy to remember. For example, because ibm.com is one of the elements of the Internet address for IBM, anyone can guess that that address belongs to that company.

And although multiple companies engaged in different sorts of business can share a name, or elements of their names, without confusion because people shopping for tires won't look for them in grocery stores, the same is not true for Internet addresses that are very similar. Because cyberspace isn't a physical space but is, rather, a conceptual place, the physical attributes of a product, such as where it is manufactured and in what stores it is sold, do not mitigate any similarity between product or company names. That is, the Internet—the information superhighway—lines up businesses, along with other entities, *only* according to their addresses. And no factor besides addresses determines the accessibility of those businesses and other entities.

To understand this critical distinction between company names and domain names, consider the Johnsons. There are many Johnson companies in the U.S. and they offer everything from paint to accounting services. The products of two of them can be found in literally nearly every household in the country; they are the S.C. Johnson Company and Johnson & Johnson, which is really a family of companies. The S.C. Johnson Company manufactures and markets Windex®, Ziploc®, Pledge®, and Glade® products, among others. Johnson & Johnson manufactures Band-aid®, Motrin®, Mylanta®, Neutrogena®, and St. Joseph® products among many others, including Johnson's® baby shampoo and other baby products. We distinguish one giant Johnson company from the other because we shop for household cleaning and storage products in different aisles of the supermarket from the ones in which we buy medicines and self-care products.

Further, because of the reputations of the different brands owned by these two companies, we shop for the brand names themselves rather than specifically for the products of one Johnson company or the other. This sort of differentiation is not possible in cyberspace. Neither company can use the dominant verbal element in its name for its Web address, so the S.C. Johnson Company uses *www.scjohnson.com* as its Web address and Johnson & Johnson's Web address is *www.jnj.com*. (The domain name johnson.com is the address for yet *another* Johnson company, the company that manufactures Johnson outboard motors.) In cyberspace you can't stand in front of a store, look through the front window, and see that home-cleaning products or over-the-counter medications and cosmetics are sold there. Instead, you have to depend on the only indicator of source possible—the domain name or Internet address for that business.

OBSTACLES ON THE SUPERHIGHWAY

So far, trademark disputes have been one of the biggest impediments facing Internet marketers. The gist of trademark law is that every marketer is entitled to his or her own reputation in the marketplace. Any interference with this—any act that causes consumers to confuse the products or services of one marketer with those of another—is trademark infringement. Anyone who understands trademark law would agree that domain names are more than just virtual street addresses.

Problems with domain names usually arise when one company registers a domain name identical or similar to the name of another company. It is reasonable that a company whose name has been adopted as the domain name of another enterprise would feel that its rights in its trademark—the embodiment of its commercial reputation—have been infringed. One variety of trademark infringement is confusion of sponsorship or affiliation. If, on account of similarities between a domain name and the name of an unrelated company, consumers are likely to believe that there is some relationship between the owner of the domain name and the company, the company's trademark rights have been infringed.

SUPERHIGHWAY ROBBERY

Trademark disputes have, in recent years, resulted when competitors and pranksters have registered domain names that are logically related to the names of established companies. Many such domain-name registrations were apparently made for the purpose of extorting fat buyouts from rich corporations. In the early days of the Internet, a journalist registered the domain name mcdonalds.com as a part of his research for an article for *Wired* magazine. Needless to say, McDonald's was chagrined to find that the most obvious domain name it could choose had already been registered. Some overeager capitalist at Sprint Communications registered mci.com; not surprisingly, MCI Telecommunications objected. The Princeton Review, a leading test-preparation company, registered kaplan.com, a domain name based on the name of its competitor, Stanley Kaplan Review, and planned to set up a Web site that compared the two companies' products, presumably showing the alleged inferiority of the Kaplan products. The domain name mtv.com was registered and used by a former MTV employee. The domain names windows95.com and nyt.com were registered by people who were not connected with Microsoft or the New York Times. Although several of these early "land grabs" resulted in lawsuits, all four disputes were settled out of court.

Similar problems have arisen when companies have registered domain names they had no intention of using. This has been done in the hope that some company that does want to use one of the registered domain names will buy it from the original registrant. This sort of kidnapping has been fairly common. And whenever new TLDs (Top Level Domain names) are authorized by ICANN, more cybersquatting is likely.

SUPERHIGHWAY PATROL

The Internet grew—and grew big—before there were enough systems to control its growth. However, it may be that domain-name disputes will soon become merely a relic of the early, lawless days when the Internet was new and land grabs were still possible. Now ICANN has acted to settle, if not obviate, most domain-name disputes.

In late 1999, ICANN adopted the Uniform Domain Name Dispute Resolution Policy. The policy has now been adopted by all accredited domain-name registrars for domain names ending in .com, .net, and .org and by some managers of country-code top-level domains. Among other important changes, the policy, which is employed by domain-name registrars, states that a would-be domain-name registrant must meet the following criteria when applying to register a domain name:

1. The statements made in the registrant's Registration Agreement are complete and accurate.

2. To the knowledge of the registrant, the registration of the domain name does not infringe upon or otherwise violate the rights of any third party.

3. The registrant is not registering the domain name for an unlawful purpose.

4. The registrant will not knowingly use the domain name in violation of any applicable laws or regulations. The registrant is responsible for determining whether the domain name infringes or violates someone else's rights.

These provisions should all but eliminate domain-name hijacking. In addition, they will reduce disputes between legitimate businesses by requiring a registrant to figure out, in advance of trying to register a domain name, whether the name will infringe the rights of anyone else. This would make a trademark search a prerequisite for applying to register a domain name.

In addition, the policy allows a registrar to cancel any domain-name registration if a court, administrative body, or arbitrator determines that the registrant is not actually entitled to the domain name.

There is also a procedure which allows an entity that believes its rights are being harmed by the use of a particular domain name to complain to the registrar. Any registrant accused of using a domain name to which it is not entitled must submit to a mandatory administrative proceeding conducted by an approved arbitrator.

To prevail, a complaining entity must prove to a registrar that a registrant's name is identical or confusingly similar to a trademark or service mark in which the complaining entity has rights, that the registrant has no rights or legitimate interests in the domain name, and that the domain name has been registered and is being used in bad faith. Bad faith is defined as:

1. Registering or acquiring a domain name primarily for the purpose of selling it to the owner of the corresponding trademark or a competitor of the owner for more than costs directly related to the acquisition of the domain name

2. Registering a domain name in an effort to prevent the use of the corresponding trademark by the owner, if the registrant has previously engaged in such conduct

3. Registering a domain name primarily to disrupt the business of a competitor

4. Intentionally using a domain name to attract traffic to a Web site by creating the likelihood of confusion between the registrant's site or products and the site or products of the complaining entity

In the early days of the Internet, the parties feuding over the right to a domain name sometimes sued the registrar. The policy specifically excludes registrars from liability and takes them out of the business of settling such disputes. The remedies available to prevailing complaining entities are limited to the cancellation of the domain-name registration of any registrant found by an arbitrator or court to be in violation of the policy.

The Uniform Domain Name Dispute Resolution Policy isn't exactly international law, but it is like a treaty between various domain-name registrars and it is likely to have far-reaching and beneficial effects. Maybe cyberspace isn't totally civilized yet, but it's on its way to being a more orderly place that is less hospitable to outlaws than it once was. You can read the entire text of the relatively short and clearly written policy on the ICANN Web site at *www.icann.org/dndr/udrp/policy. htm*. And if you think someone is using a domain name that infringes your trademark rights, see a lawyer.

SIGNING UP AND SIGNING ON

You can find a directory of accredited registrars, the countries in which they operate, and the TLD categories for which they grant registrations on the ICANN Web site at *www.icann.org/registrars/accredited-list.html*. And as soon as you become the registrant who owns a new domain name, you should consider filing for U.S. trademark registration. Just be sure that you are, indeed, using the domain name as a trademark and not just as an address for your Web site. This can be a tricky determination. Here's what the Trademark Manual of Examining Procedure, the rulebook by which trademark registration is or is not granted, has to say on the topic:

When a trademark, service mark, collective mark or certification mark is composed, in whole or in part, of a domain name, neither the beginning of the URL (http://www.) nor the TLD have any source indicating significance. Instead, those designations are merely devices that every Internet site provider must use as part of its address. Today, advertisements for all types of products and services routinely include a URL for the Web site of the advertiser. Just as the average person with no special knowledge recognizes "800" or "1–800" followed by seven digits or letters as one of the prefixes used for every toll-free phone number, the average person familiar with the Internet recognizes the format for a domain name and understands that "http," "www," and a TLD are a part of every URL.

Applications for registration of marks consisting of domain names are subject to the same requirements as all other applications for federal trademark registration.

. . .

A mark composed of a domain name is registrable as a trademark or service mark only if it functions as a source identifier. The mark as depicted on the specimens must be presented in a manner that will be perceived by potential purchasers as indicating source *and not as merely an informational indication of the domain name address used to access a web site*.

. . .

The examining attorney must review the specimens in order to determine how the proposed mark is actually used. It is the perception of the ordinary customer that determines whether the asserted mark functions as a mark, not the applicant's intent, hope, or expectation that it do so.

You can read all of what the Trademark Office has to say on this topic at *www. uspto.gov/web/offices/tac/notices/guide299.htm*. Just remember that the trademark you create for use on physical products or the services you offer must suit those uses and that the best domain names are versions of trademarks the public already knows. It doesn't work so well in reverse—naming a line of ladies' hosiery LadiesHose.com probably isn't a great marketing decision. But registering the domain name SilkyLegs.com after introducing your new Silky Legs hose works.

WORK IN PROGRESS

There are two misconceptions about cyberspace and the law. The first is that there *is* no law in cyberspace. The second is that our old, boring, existing laws don't apply in cyberspace. Neither assumption is true. There is no "cyberspace law," except for all our laws that apply to any activity that is carried out on or through the Internet. And our existing laws continue to apply. Any new activity, including marketing on the Internet, that is within the scope of existing law is regulated just like the behavior that the laws were designed to regulate. The courts must apply old laws to new activities and sometimes there is a gap between the behavior and the application, but the law is still there and new law is being written to cover gaps in existing law. This is a good thing. Sometimes individual freedom is hampered, but not much, and a society where the rule of law prevails over force or despotism or disorder is the reward for submission to the law. Like most modern innovations, the Internet can be used for good or evil ends. The growth of protocols for its use and for the protection of its users is a benign and desirable development.

32

Use of Fonts

ALLAN HALEY

Monotype Imaging

Reprinted from *AIGA Design Business and Ethics*,
"Chapter 2: Use of Fonts."

FONTS ARE CREATIVE, intellectual property, similar to designers' creative work or a proprietary business product. Since type seems so ubiquitous and fonts are so easy to share among computer users, the legal and moral issues of the simple process of using a font are often overlooked.

There are four good rules that guide ethical practice in font licensing:

If you are using a font, whether it's on your computer or that of someone else, make sure you have a license to use the font.

If you want to use a font that is not installed on your computer, you must ensure that you or your employer has a license to install the font on your computer, or else acquire a license to use it.

If you have any questions about your font license, contact the foundry or supplier of the font. (If you do not know the foundry or supplier, almost any foundry or supplier can help you identify the source.)

Don't lend or give a font to others to use. Your friends, clients, and colleagues need to acquire the rights to use them. When it comes to licensing fonts, ethical practice makes sense legally and financially. Violating the terms of a license agreement puts the designer, the client, and future business relationships at risk. An ethical approach to font use and font licenses is therefore both good business practice and good business.

Fonts are creative, intellectual property. Typefaces are collections of letterforms. They endow written communications with a character or style, which ultimately represents the character or style of the originator of the communication, whether a corporation or an individual. Typefaces are the result of extensive research, study, and experimentation, and for some designers, the creation of typefaces is a full-time occupation. The training and expertise required to develop a typeface qualifies the product as intellectual property and merits its protection under copyright law in many countries. A font is the software that describes the characters in a typeface. Digital fonts, like any software, are intellectual property and may be subject to federal copyright and trademark laws. You do not own a font. You license it for limited uses. Fonts are not bought. The right to reproduce them is licensed, and the license to use them states specific terms. The right to use a font designed by someone else for any or all communications is acquired from the foundry that created the font and is granted in the form of an end-user license agreement, or EULA. Some foundries will allow a supplier to administer the license agreements for a font, but the agreement itself is always between the licensee and the foundry that created the font. The terms of use described by an end-user license agreement vary from foundry to foundry and may vary depending on the scope of the desired use. Licenses usually grant permission for the licensee to install a given font on a certain number of computers. However, licenses can also describe use on printers, periods of exclusivity for custom typefaces and distribution rights. If you have questions about what you may or may not do with the font you are using, the best thing to do is to contact the foundry or supplier of the font.

You need permission to alter a font for use in your design. Because the software that describes a typeface is automatically subject to copyright protection upon its creation, any version of the original font is considered a "derivative work" under copyright law. It is because the adaptation is derived from copyrighted software that describes the typeface that the revision should not be considered an authorized derivative work. It cannot be used for commercial purposes without violating the copyright. Some font licenses allow the licensee to alter the characters in a font or to convert the font to other formats. Other foundries do not allow derivative works at all without permission. Therefore many designers, when asked to create a derivative work, have made it standard ethical practice to get permission from the font designer before altering any font data. If you need to find out who designed the font you want to alter, you may refer to the copyright information identified in software such as Adobe Type Manager. You may also contact the foundry or font supplier. You cannot share a font with someone who does not have his or her own license to use it. Font software may not be given or loaned to anyone who does not have a license to use it. Therefore, misuse or unauthorized copying of a font that belongs to a client or your employer is an infringement of the designer's rights and could subject you to legal action. When the client is the "end user" of the license agreement, the designer may not take the font with him or her when the project is over, even though it may mean another license must be purchased for the next job.

You can embed a font in a file to have it viewed or printed by others. A font may only be sent with a job to a service bureau, consultant, or freelancer if the contractor has a license for the font or if the license agreement makes provision for it. When necessary, it is acceptable for font data to be embedded in file formats such as EPS and PDF for printing and previewing purposes. This is an issue of ethics, respect, and law. There are tangible and intangible consequences of using a font without a license. If caught using a font without the proper license, the licensee will have to purchase the correct license for the font and in some cases pay damages to the originating foundry. More importantly, the use of a font without the proper license could prevent a professional designer from being fully compensated. It is the value of the intellectual property of a colleague that is ultimately at stake in the licensing of fonts. To purchase the proper license for a font, especially as a practicing design professional, is to recognize the value of a colleague's work, to respect the practice of another designer, and to uphold the integrity of the design profession.

Organizations
for Graphic Designers

EMILY RUTH COHEN

PROFESSIONAL ORGANIZATIONS INTERNATIONAL AND NATIONAL

The following is a list of national organizations; several have local or regional chapters. Please contact each organization for current chapter information and listings.

AIGA
164 Fifth Avenue
New York, New York 10010
(212) 807-1990
www.aiga.org

AIGA, the professional association for design, is the place design professionals turn to first to exchange ideas and information, participate in critical analysis, and research and advance education and ethical practice.

Association of Professional Design Firms (APDF)
1448 East 52nd Street, #201
Chicago, Illinois 60615
(773) 643-7052
www.apdf.org/public/index.asp

The Association of Professional Design Firms is an organization dedicated to elevating the standards of professional business practices for design consulting firms through education and the exchange of knowledge.

The Association of Registered Graphic Designers of Ontario (RGD Ontario)
96 Spadina Avenue, Suite 503
Toronto Ontario M5V 2J6 Canada (888) 274-3668
www.rgdontario.com/

The Association of Registered Graphic Designers of Ontario (RGD Ontario) represents more than 3,000 graphic designers, managers, educators, and students across Ontario. The Association's mandate is to serve the best interests of both the graphic design industry and the public in the Province of Ontario.

Center for Design and Business
169 Weybosset Street, 2nd Floor
Providence, Rhode Island 02905
(401) 454-6108
www.centerdesignbusiness.org

The Center for Design and Business (CDB) works with institutions and corporations on strategic initiatives through customized programs ranging from sponsored studios to consulting projects to executive seminars and workshops. The CDB offers catered multi-disciplinary teams in long-term relationships that offer collaboration in and outside of the classroom.

Centre for Design Innovation
ITSBIC Institute of Technology
Ballinode
Sligo Ireland
(071) 915-5496
www.designinnovation.ie

The Centre for Design Innovation is the National center of excellence for the research, understanding, and promotion of the effective use of design within business and the public sector in Ireland.

Corporate Design Foundation
20 Park Plaza, Suite 400
Boston, Massachusetts 02116
(617) 340-7676
www.cdf.org

Corporate Design Foundation, a non-profit education and research organization, was founded on the belief that design can make a major contribution both to an individual's quality of life and to a corporation's success, and that both individual and organizational interests can be served through the effective use of the design disciplines: product design, architecture, and communication design. Accordingly, our mission is to improve the quality of life and the effectiveness of organizations through design.

The Design Management Institute (DMI)
29 Temple Place, 2nd Floor
Boston, Massachusetts 02111
(617) 338-6380
www.dmi.org

The Design Management Institute (DMI) is an international nonprofit organization that seeks to heighten awareness of design as an essential part of business strategy. Founded in 1975, DMI has become the leading resource and international authority on design management. DMI has earned a reputation worldwide as a multifaceted resource, providing invaluable know-how, tools, and training through its conferences, seminars, membership program, and publications.

Graphic Artist Guild (GAG)
32 Broadway, Suite 1114
New York, New York 10004
(212) 791-3400
www.gag.org

The Graphic Artists Guild is a national union of illustrators, designers, Web creators, production artists, surface designers and other creatives who have come together to pursue common goals, share their experience, raise industry standards, and improve the ability of visual creators to achieve satisfying and rewarding careers.

The International Council of Graphic Design Associations (Icograda)
455 Saint Antoine Ouest, Suite SS
10 Montréal, Québec
Canada H2Z 1J1
(514) 448-4949
www.icograda.org

The International Council of Graphic Design Associations (Icograda) is the world body for professional graphic design and visual communication. It is a voluntary assembly of associations concerned with graphic design, visual communication, design management, design promotion, and design education. Icograda promotes graphic designers' vital role in society and commerce and unifies the voices of graphic designers and visual communicators worldwide.

Industrial Designers Society of America (IDSA)
45195 Business Court, Suite 250
Dulles, Virginia 20166-6717
(703) 707-6000
www.idsa.org

The Industrial Designers Society of America (IDSA) is the voice of the industrial design profession, advancing the quality and positive impact of design.

InSource—An Association of Corporate Creatives
PO Box 366
Pompton Plains, New Jersey 07444
www.in-source.org

To be the best resource and advocate for in-house creative management. We enhance the understanding, impact, and value of in-house design within the corporate environment. We provide expertise, tools, networking, and management support. Committed to design excellence and effective design management, InSource motivates creative thinking and promotes best practices.

International Association of Business Communicators (IABC)
1 Hallidie Plaza, #600
San Francisco, California 94102
(415) 544-4700
www.iabc.com

IABC, the International Association of Business Communicators, is the leading resource for effective communication practice. We provide products, services, activities, and networking opportunities to help people and organizations achieve excellence in public relations, employee communication, marketing communication, public affairs, and other forms of communication. People around the world—in every industry and in the public and nonprofit sectors—have taken advantage of our resources to advance their careers and meet organizational objectives.

Organization of Black Designers (OBD)
300 M Street SW, Suite #N110
Washington, DC 20024
(202) 659-3918
http://www.core77.com/OBD/welcome.html

OBD is a nonprofit national professional association dedicated to promoting the visibility, education, empowerment, and interaction of its membership and the understanding and value that diverse design perspectives contribute to world culture and commerce. OBD was founded to educate the design professions regarding the contributions of African-Americans and other people of color.

Society for Environmental Graphic Designers (SEGD)
1000 Vermont Avenue, NW Suite 400
Washington, DC 20005
(202) 638-5555
www.segd.org

SEGD is an international non-profit educational organization providing resources for design specialists in the field of environmental graphic design; architecture; and landscape, interior, and industrial design. SEGD members are leading designers of directional and attraction sign systems, destination graphics, identity programs, exhibits, and themed environments.

Society for News Design
1130 Ten Rod Road, Suite D-202
North Kingstown, Rhode Island 02852-4180
(401) 294-5233
www.snd.org

The Society for News Design encourages high standards of journalism through design. An international forum and resource for all those interested in news design, SND works to recognize excellence and strengthen visual journalism as a profession.

Society of Publication Designers (SPD)
17 East 47th Street, 6th Floor
New York, New York 10017
(212) 223-3332
www.spd.org

For over forty years, the Society of Publication Designers has been a driving force for quality and innovation in publication design. It is the one venue in which the best of the best continually strive. SPD encourages artistic excellence by judging annually the work of thousands of design professionals in the United States and abroad. The activities of SPD promote the art director's role as visual journalist and partner in the editorial process—the partner responsible for telescoping and shaping information, the one who gives tone to an editorial voice.

TDC: Type Directors Club
127 West 25th Street, 8th Floor
New York, New York 10001
(212) 633-8943
www.tdc.org

TDC is an international organization for all people who are devoted to excellence in typography, both in print and on screen. Founded in 1946, today's TDC is involved in all contemporary areas of typography and design, and welcomes graphic designers, art directors, editors, multimedia professionals, students, entrepreneurs, and all who have an interest in type including those in advertising, communications, education, marketing, and publishing.

International Webmasters Association
119 E. Union St., Suite F
Pasadena, California 91003
(626) 449-3709
www.iwanet.org/

IWA, a nonprofit professional association, is the industry's recognized leader in providing educational and certification standards for Web professionals. IWA's initiatives now support more than one hundred official chapters representing over 160,000 individual members in 106 countries. IWA's accomplishments include the industry's first guidelines for ethical and professional standards, Web certification and education programs, specialized employment resources, and technical assistance to individuals and businesses.

RELATED PROFESSIONAL ORGANIZATIONS

ACM/SIGGRAPH
www.siggraph.org

SIGGRAPH's mission is to promote the generation and dissemination of information on computer graphics and interactive techniques.

The Advertising Council
New York Office
261 Madison Avenue, 11th Floor
New York, New York 10016
(212) 922-1500
www.adcouncil.org

The Ad Council is a private, non-profit organization that marshals volunteer talent from the advertising and communications industries, the facilities of the media, and the resources of the business and non-profit communities to deliver critical messages to the American public. The Ad Council produces, distributes, and promotes thousands of public service campaigns on behalf of non-profit organizations and government agencies in issue areas such as improving the quality of life for children, preventative health, education, community well being, environmental preservation, and strengthening families.

Advertising Photographers of America (APA)
National Headquarters
PO Box 250
White Plains, New York 10605
(800) 272-6264
www.apanational.com

Since 1982, APA has worked to improve the environment for advertising photographers and clear the pathways for professional success. Promoting a spirit of mutual cooperation, sharing, and support, APA offers outstanding benefits and educational programs, while providing essential tools and resources to help members excel in business and achieve their creative goals.

The American Advertising Federation (AAF)
1101 Vermont Avenue NW, Suite 500
Washington, DC 20005
(202) 898-0089
www.aaf.org

The American Advertising Federation (AAF), headquartered in Washington, D.C., acts as the "Unifying Voice for Advertising." The AAF is the oldest national advertising trade association, representing 50,000 professionals in the advertising industry. The AAF's Web site has a comprehensive list of affiliated local federations, including local art directors' clubs (http://www.aaf.org/default.asp?id=100).

American Association of Advertising Agencies (AAAA)
405 Lexington Avenue, 18th Floor
New York, New York 10174
(212) 682-2500
www.aaaa.org/eweb/startpage.aspx

The American Association of Advertising Agencies (AAAA) is the national trade association representing the advertising agency business in the United States. It is a management-oriented association that offers its members the broadest possible services, expertise, and information regarding the advertising agency business.

American Institute of Architects (AIA)
1735 New York Avenue NW
Washington, DC 20006-5292
(202) 626-7300
www.aia.org

The AIA is the voice of the architectural profession and the resource for its members in service to society.

American Society of Interior Designers (ASID)
608 Massachusetts Avenue NE
Washington, DC 20002
(202) 546-3480
www.asid.org

ASID is a community of people—designers, industry representatives, educators, and students—committed to interior design. Through education, knowledge sharing, advocacy, community building and outreach, the Society strives to advance the interior design profession and, in the process, to demonstrate and celebrate the power of design to positively change people's lives. Its more than 38,000 members engage in a variety of professional programs and activities through a network of forty-eight chapters throughout the United States and Canada.

American Society of Landscape Architects (ASLA)
636 Eye Street, NW
Washington, DC 20001
(202) 898-2444
www.asla.org

The American Society of Landscape Architects is the national professional association representing landscape architects. ASLA promotes the landscape architecture profession and advances the practice through advocacy, education, communication, and fellowship.

American Society of Media Photographers, Inc. (ASMP)
150 North Second Street
Philadelphia, Pennsylvania 19106
(215) 451-ASMP
www.asmp.org

ASMP promotes photographers' rights, educates photographers in better business practices, produces business publications for photographers, and helps buyers find professional photographers.

Color Association of the United States (CAUS)
315 West 39th Street, Studio 507
New York, New York 10018
(212) 947-7774
www.colorassociation.com

CAUS is an international organization representing leaders in every branch of fashion, textiles, design industries, and general trade in which color is a factor. The Association serves as the authority and arbiter of commercial colors in the United States and in this role exerts great influence on American production and businesses worldwide.

Color Marketing Group (CMG)
5845 Richmond Hwy., #410
Alexandria, Virginia 22303
(703) 329-8500
www.colormarketing.org

Color Marketing Group is the premier international association for color design professionals. Our mission is to create color forecast information for professionals who design and market color. We are "the" place for color info exchange.

IDEAlliance
1421 Prince St., Suite 230
Alexandria, Virginia 22314-2805
(703) 837-1070
www.idealliance.org

IDEAlliance is an established industry organization with a diverse and impressive membership that has been developing, educating, and validating best practices in publishing and information technology for forty years.

International Interior Design Association (IIDA)
222 Merchandise Mart
Chicago, Illinois 60654-1104
(312) 467-1950
www.iida.com

The International Interior Design Association (IIDA) works to enhance quality of life through excellence in interior design and to advance interior design through knowledge, value, and community.

National Association of Schools of Art and Design (NASAD)
11250 Roger Bacon Drive, Suite 21
Reston, Virginia 20190
(703) 437-0700
nasad.arts-accredit.org

NASAD is an association of approximately 248 schools of art and design, primarily at the collegiate level but also including precollegiate and community schools for the visual arts disciplines. It is the national accrediting agency for art and design and art- and design-related disciplines.

The One Club for Art and Copy
21 East 26th Street
New York, New York 10010
(212) 979-1900
www.oneclub.com

The One Club is the world's foremost nonprofit organization for the recognition and promotion of excellence in advertising.

Picture Agency Council of America (PACA)
23046 Avenida de la Carlota, Suite 600
Laguna Hills, California 92653-1537
(949) 282-5065
www.pacaoffice.org

PACA, the Picture Archive Council of America, is the trade organization in North America that represents the vital interests of stock archives of every size, from individual photographers to large corporations, who license images for commercial reproduction.

Printing Industries of America/Graphic Arts Technical Foundation (PIA/GATF)
200 Deer Run Road
Sewickley, Pennsylvania 15143
(412) 741-686
www.gain.net/eweb/StartPage.aspx

Printing Industries of America/Graphic Arts Technical Foundation (PIA/GATF) is the world's largest graphic arts trade association, representing an industry with more than $171.5 billion in revenue and 1.08 million employees.

Society of Illustrators (SI)

128 East 63rd Street
New York, New York 10021
(212) 838-2560
www.societyillustrators.org/index.cms

The mission of the Society is to promote the art and appreciation of illustration, as well as its history and evolving nature, and to encourage high ideals through exhibitions, lectures, education, and by fostering a sense of community and open discussion.

Society of Photographers and Artists Representatives (SPAR)

60 East 42nd Street, Suite 1166
New York, New York 10165
(212) 779-7464
www.spar.org/

SPAR provides leadership, and through its programs and publications, promotes the advancement of the profession.

University and College Designers Association (UCDA)

199 W. Enon Springs Road, Suite 300
Smyrna, Tennessee 37167
(615) 459-4559
www.ucda.com

The University and College Designers Association (UCDA) exists to promote excellence in visual communications for educational institutions.

Volunteer Lawyers for the Arts (VLA)

1 East 53rd Street, 6th Floor
New York, New York 10022
(212) 319-2910
www.vlany.org/

Volunteer Lawyers for the Arts has been the leading provider of pro bono legal services, mediation services, educational programs and publications, and advocacy to the arts community in the New York area.

BIBLIOGRAPHY

BOOKS

2007 Artist's & Graphic Designer's Market, by Mary Cox. Cincinnati, OH: North Light Books, 2006.

Branding for Nonprofits: Developing Identity with Integrity, by DK Holland. New York: Allworth Press, 2006.

Breaking Into Graphic Design: Tips from the Pros on Finding the Right Position for You, by Michael Jefferson. New York: Allworth Press, 2005.

Business and Legal Forms for Graphic Designers, Third Edition, by Tad Crawford and Eva Doman Bruck. New York: Allworth Press, 2003.

The Business Side of Creativity, by Cameron S. Foote. New York: W. W. Norton & Company, 2002.

Careers by Design: A Headhunter's Secrets for Success and Survival in Graphic Design, by Roz Goldfarb. New York: Allworth Press, 1993.

Communication Design: Principles, Methods, and Practices, by Jorge Frascara. New York: Allworth Press, 2004.

The Complete Guide to Eco-Friendly Design, by Poppy Evans. Cincinnati, OH: North Light Books, 1997.

Creating the Perfect Design Brief: How to Manage Design for Strategic Advantage, by Peter L. Phillips. New York: Allworth Press, 2004.

The Creative Business Guide to Running a Graphic Design Business, by Cameron S. Foote. New York: W. W. Norton & Company, 2001.

Design Management: Using Design to Build Brand Value and Corporate Innovation, by Brigitte Borja de Mozota. New York: Allworth Press, 2003.

Design Management: Managing Design Strategy, Process and Implementation, by Kathryn Best. Lausanne, Switzerland: AVA Publishing, 2007.

The Designer's Commonsense Business Book, by Barbara Ganim. Cincinnati, OH: North Light Books, 1995.

GOOD: An Introduction to Ethics in Graphic Design, by Lucienne Roberts. Lausanne, Switzerland: AVA Publishing, 2006.

Graphic Artist's Guild Handbook of Pricing and Ethical Guidelines, Tenth Edition, by The Graphic Artist's Guild. Cincinnati, OH: North Light Books, 2001.

The Graphic Design Business Book, by Tad Crawford. New York: Allworth Press, 2005.

The Graphic Designer's Guide to Better Business Writing, by Barbara Janoff and Ruth Cash-Smith. New York: Allworth Press, 2007.

The Graphic Designer's and Illustrator's Guide to Marketing and Self-Promotion, by Maria Piscopo. New York: Allworth Press, 2004.

Graphic Designer's Guide to Clients: How to Make Clients Happy and Do Great Work, by Ellen M. Shapiro. New York: Allworth Press, 2003.

Graphically Speaking: A Visual Lexicon for Achieving Better Designer-Client Communication, by Lisa Buchanan. Cincinnati, OH: F & W Publications, 2002.

Inside the Business of Graphic Design: 60 Leaders Share Their Secrets of Success, by Catharine Fishel. New York: Allworth Press, 2003.

Orbiting the Giant Hairball: A Corporate Fool's Guide to Surviving with Grace, by Gordon Mackenzie. New York: Viking Adult, 1998.

The Graphic Designer's Guide to Pricing, Estimating & Budgeting, by Theo Stephan Williams. New York: Allworth Press, 2001.

Selling Graphic and Web Design: Third Edition, by Donald Sparkman. New York: Allworth Press, 2006.

Starting Your Career as a Freelance Illustrator or Graphic Designer, Revised Edition, by Michael Fleishman. New York: Allworth Press, 2001.

Talent Is Not Enough: Business Secrets For Designers, by Shel Perkins. Berkeley, CA: Peachpit Press, 2006.

The Trademark Guide: The Friendly Handbook for Protecting & Profiting from Trademarks, by Lee Wilson. New York: Allworth Press, 2004.

Visual Research: An Introduction to Research Methodologies in Graphic Design, by Ian Noble and Russell Bestley. Lausanne, Switzerland: AVA Publishing, 2005.

MAGAZINES

@Issue: The Journal of Business and Design
Corporate Design Foundation, 20 Park Plaza Suite 400, Boston, MA 02116–4303; (617) 566–7676; *www.cdf.org*

Communication Arts
110 Constitution Drive, Menlo Park, CA 94025; (650) 326–6040; *www.commarts.com*

Creative Business
29 Temple Place, Boston, MA 02111; (617) 451–0041; *www.creativebusiness.com*

Design Issues
c/o The MIT Press
238 Main St., Suite 500, Cambridge, MA 02142–1406; (617) 253–2889; *www.mitpressjournals.org/loi/desi*

Design Tools Monthly
766 Quince Circle, Boulder, CO 80304; (303) 543–8400; *www.design-tools.com/*

Emigre
1700 Shattuck Ave., #307 Berkeley, CA 94709; (530) 756–2900; *www.emigre.com*

Eye
Haymarket Publishing; 174 Hammersmith Road, London W6 7JP; +44 (0) 20 8 267 5000; *www.eyemagazine.com/home.php*

GD USA
79 Madison Avenue, Suite 1202, New York, NY 10016; (212) 696–4380; *www.gdusa.com*

Graphis
Graphis Inc. 307 Fifth Avenue, 10th Floor, New York, NY 10016; (212) 213–3229; *www.graphis.com*

How Magazine
F+W Publications, Inc. 4700 E. Galbraith Rd. Cincinnati, OH 45236; (513) 531–2690; *www.howdesign.com*

I.D.
38 East 29th Street, Floor 3, New York, NY 10016; (212) 447–1400; *www.idonline.com*

Layers Magazine
333 Douglas Road East, Oldsmar, FL 34677; (813) 433–5010; *www.layersmagazine.com*

Metropolis
61 W. 23rd St., 4th Floor, New York, NY 10010; (212) 627–9977; *www.metropolismag.com/cda*

Print
P.O. Box 420235, Palm Coast, FL 32142–0235; (877) 860–9145; *www.printmag.com*

Step Inside Design
6000 N. Forest Park Drive, Peoria, IL 61614; (888) 698–8543; *www.stepinsidedesign.com*

Dynamic Graphics Magazine
6000 N. Forest Park Drive, Peoria, IL 61614; (888) 698–8542; *www.dynamicgraphics.com*

Wired
520 Third Street, 4th Floor, San Francisco, CA 94107; (415) 276–5000; *www.wired.com*

ONLINE MAGAZINES

A List Apart—www.alistapart.com

Corporate Identity Documentation—www.cidoc.net

Design Boom—www.designboom.com/eng

Digital Media World—www.dmw.com.au

Graphic Define Magazine—www.graphicdefine.org

Digital Web Magazine—www.digital-web.com

Netdiver Magazine—www.netdiver.net

PingMag—www.pingmag.jp

U&lc Magazine—www.itcfonts.com/Ulc/4012

Typographica—www.typographica.org

Voice: AIGA Journal of Design—www.aiga.org/content.cfm/voice

BLOGS

A List Apart—*www.alistapart.com*

Be A Design Group—*www.beadesigngroup.com*

Coudal Partners—*www.coudal.com*

Design Inspiration—*www.diinterviews.com*

Design Melt Down—*http://designmeltdown.com*

Design Observer—*www.designobserver.com*

Signal vs. Noise—*http://37signals.com/svn*

Speak Up—*www.underconsideration.com/speakup*

UnBeige—*www.mediabistro.com/unbeige*

AN ENDNOTE

BY RICHARD GREFÉ,
EXECUTIVE DIRECTOR, AIGA,
THE PROFESSIONAL ASSOCIATION FOR DESIGN

AIGA, THE PROFESSIONAL association for design, has developed standards of conduct for designers as a model for professional performance. The intent is to establish a clear set of principles for designers as professionals, detailing the relationship between the designer and clients, audiences, society, the environment, intellectual property, and other designers.

Only as designers reflect a high level of integrity in their performance as professionals, reinforced through wide acceptance and consistent adherence of published standards, will an established ethos be associated with the profession. This ethos will, in turn, define the expectations others have of the profession and will earn a level of respect and trust for the profession.

As the oldest and largest professional association of communication designers, AIGA's standards provide both direction for the profession and explanation of practices for clients.

The AIGA standards, in their entirety, appear in chapter 2.

The standards are consistent with model codes developed by other professions and, at their core, are based on the *Code of Ethics and Professional Conduct* published by the International Council of Graphic Design Associations (Icograda) and have been refined to reflect practices within the United States. AIGA is confident that they form the basis for designers' work anywhere in the global design economy.

AIGA has published *Design Business and Ethics*, a series of publications that are available for designers to share with clients and others, documenting appropriate practices and standards (*www.aiga.org/design-business-ethics*). The professional standards are included in this series.

To the extent that designers use the initials "AIGA" after their name or acknowledge membership in AIGA, they are making a commitment to uphold the professional standards. Some designers also include language at the bottom of each invoice that acknowledges that the firm's practice is governed by the AIGA standards for professional practice. Every effort should be made by each designer to advance these standards in order to reinforce their authority.

An Endnote on Compensation for Work and the Troublesome Issue of Speculative Work

Designers regularly receive requests for *pro bono* work and are sometimes naively asked for casual assistance on design problems. The expectation that designers will undertake speculative projects fails to respect the value of their work. Accepting such projects reflects a lack of confidence in the value of one's own work. Every designer will be challenged on this practice and will make individual decisions on a case-by-case basis. Only if the profession as a whole acts consistently on the issue, however, will a new norm regarding this troublesome practice be established.

A prohibition on speculative work is not part of the standards *per se*, but is consistent with the pursuit of professionalism contained in the standards. There are two implicit restrictions that are widely accepted within the profession:

- ❑ A designer shall not undertake any work for a client without adequate compensation, except with respect to work for charitable or nonprofit organizations; and

- ❑ A designer shall not undertake any speculative projects either alone or in competition with other designers for which compensation will only be received if a design is accepted or used. This applies not only to entire projects but also to preliminary schematic proposals.

Speculative work is not an ethical issue in the sense of a moral or natural right or wrong. Speculative work represents an approach toward problem solving, which few in the profession should sanction. It suggests that effective design outcomes can be achieved by developing visual representations without critical research and problem analysis. To this extent, it actually compromises the value the client receives and marginalizes the profession, relegating it to decoration. This is not in the best interest of the client, the designer, or the profession.

BIOGRAPHIES

Daniel Abraham is an attorney in private practice, serving the creative community in copyright, licensing, and trademark matters. Prior to entering full-time legal practice, Abraham worked as a professional illustrator; his work appeared in newspapers, magazines, and corporate publications around the country. Abraham currently teaches copyrights and contracts to illustration students at the Fashion Institute of Technology; formerly, he instructed students at Parsons the New School for Design. He has spoken on copyright issues for the Society of Illustrators, the Graphic Artists Guild, the Society of Scribes and the School of Visual Arts. As national vice president for Legislation of the Graphic Artists Guild from 1987 to 1998, Abraham co-directed the national Artists for Tax Equity lobbying effort, which in 1988 won artists exemption from the tax capitalization requirements of the Tax Reform Act of 1986, and coordinated the Guild's campaign in the mid-1990s which exempted rights transfers by California artists from state sales tax. Mr. Abraham's law office is in Brooklyn, New York.

Marci Barbey is the director of finance and human resources for Carbone Smolan Agency. In this capacity, she oversees the agency's financial and accounting needs, and fulfills the agency's legal and administrative HR functions as well.

Author of the forthcoming RockBench Press title *Managing (Right) for the First Time*, **David C. Baker** is the leading management consultant for the creative services field (advertising, design, public relations, and interactive). Through ReCourses, Inc., he has guided hundreds of firms through management issues, difficult transitions, and growth. He has written for nearly every publication and spoken for nearly every conference in the industry and conducts a dozen yearly seminars on management.

Eva Doman Bruck served as business manager for Milton Glaser, taught at the School of Visual Arts, and co-authored *Business and Legal Forms for Graphic Designers, Business and Legal Forms for Interior Designers*, and *Business and Legal Forms for Industrial Designers*.

Don Brunsten (A.B., J.D., Stanford University) is an attorney specializing in intellectual property, contracts, and business organization. He is based in Los Angeles and is a principal of Brunsten and Associates (*www.brunsten.com*), a law firm focused on representing companies and individuals in all branches of design. A founder of the Design Coalition, he is co-author of the *AIGA Standard Form of Agreement for Design Services*.

As a consultant to creative professionals, **Emily Cohen** provides confidential, experienced, and objective advice to both established, creative firms and in-house creative departments. She offers expertise on implementing effective staff, project, and studio management strategies; approaching client and vendor relationships; conducting client surveys; and writing winning proposals, creative briefs, and contracts. She currently serves on the board of advisors of InSource; served as secretary for the AIGA/NY board of directors; and has taught classes and conducted seminars for many leading design schools, industry conferences, and organizations. Additional information is available at *www.emilycohen.com*.

Donald Carli is a senior research fellow at the Institute for Sustainable Communication (ISC), sustainability and technology editor for *Graphic Arts Monthly* magazine, and CEO of the consulting firm Nima Hunter, Inc. He has written for and been quoted in numerous articles on trends and technologies related to design, print, and sustainability in publications such as *Graphis, Step by Step, Graphic Arts Monthly, Printing Impressions, Graphic Communications World, Ethical Corporation, Aktuell Grafisk Information, The New York Times Magazine*, and *Fortune* magazine. Author of the AIGA *Design Business and Ethics* series guide "Print Design and Environmental Responsibility," he is an AIGA student chapter faculty advisor at New York City College of Technology of the City University of New York. He recently led an ISC Responsible Enterprise Print assessment of AIGA's printing and publishing activities, and is senior consultant to the ISC Sustainable Advertising Partnership (*www.SustainableAds.org*).

Tad Crawford served as general counsel for the Graphic Artist Guild. Currently president of Allworth Press, he is the author of *Legal Guide for the Visual Artist* and *The Graphic Design Business Book* and the coauthor of *Business and Legal Forms for Graphic Designers*.

Leonard DuBoff, founder of The DuBoff Law Group, LLC, in Portland, Oregon, specializes in representing creative people. He taught law for more than twenty-five years and has written numerous books and scholarly articles. He also contributes to nonlegal publications such as *Communication Arts*. He has received many honors and awards, including the Oregon Governor's Arts Award.

Cameron S. Foote is the editor of *Creative Business*, a newsletter that addresses the business concerns of freelancers and principals of small to medium-size design firms. He is the author of the best sellers *The Business Side of Creativity* and *The Creative Business Guide to Running a Graphic Design Business*. He can be reached at: mail@creativebusiness.com.

Jim Faris is an independent design consultant based in Santa Cruz, California. He has worked on a wide range of branding, product design, and design management projects with a diverse clientele including Apple, Toyota, NYTimes.com, and the Australian Taxation Office. Between 1985 and 2000, he was a principal at AlbenFaris, one of the first generation graphic design firms to specialize in interactive media. While at AlbenFaris, he created the brand identity for Apple's Macintosh operating system, his best-known design. Earlier, he was director of graphic design for the Museum of Modern Art, New York, and was a senior designer at Ciba-Geigy Corporation (now Novartis).

In 1962, **Colin Forbes** was a founding partner of Fletcher/Forbes/Gill in London and of Pentagram in 1972. He established the first Pentagram office in New York in 1978. He served as national president of AIGA from 1984 to 1986, chairing its first national conference in 1985, and was awarded the AIGA Medal in 1991.

Milton Glaser is among the most celebrated graphic designers in the United States. He has had the distinction of one-man shows at the Museum of Modern Art and the Georges Pompidou Center. He was selected for the lifetime achievement award of the Cooper-Hewitt, National Design Museum. A Fulbright Scholar, Glaser is an articulate spokesman for the ethical practice of design. He continues to produce an astounding amount of work in many fields of design.

Ed Gold is the author of *The Business of Graphic Design*. He currently teaches at the University of Baltimore, where he also serves as the director of the Ampersand Institute for Words and Images, the associate director of the School of Communications Design, and the director of the MFA in integrated design.

Jessica Eve Goldfarb is managing partner, counsel, and recruiter at Roz Goldfarb Associates. She served in the Clinton administration as an employment and technology specialist for Vice President Gore, the Labor Department, and the National Commission for Employment Policy. She also practiced employment law at a firm and holds a J.D. from NYU.

Roz Goldfarb founded Roz Goldfarb Associates in 1985 on the precepts of "civilized headhunting" and career management. She has recruited for creative and business positions in every area of design. Holding an MFA from Pratt, she is an author, educator, and respected advisor to many leaders in these industries.

Steven Heller is a columnist for *The New York Times Book Review*. Heller is also the co-founder and co-chair (with Lita Talarico) of the MFA Design Department and co-founder (with Alice Twemlow) of the MFA Design Criticism Department at the School of Visual Arts, New York. He is editor of *Voice: AIGA Online Journal of Design*, and author of well over one hundred books on design and popular culture, including over thirty for Allworth Press.

Richard Grefé is the executive director of AIGA, the professional association for design, and IDCA, the International Design Conference in Aspen. He is also a vice president of Icograda. Since 1995, he has developed programs at AIGA that reinforce the relevance of design as an extraordinary creative gift and a critical element of business strategy.

Michael Jefferson, author of *Breaking Into Graphic Design: Tips from the Pros on Finding the Right Position for You*, is a graduate of Pratt Institute. Using his expert knowledge of the application process, Michael found a rewarding, full-time position as a graphic designer. He lives in Washington, D.C.

Steve Liska founded Liska+Associates, Inc., in 1980. His design work has received distinguished awards and has been featured in every leading design journal. He is presently chairman of the board of directors of the nonprofit organization Make A Better Place (MABP). Liska frequently contributes his time to AIGA, and is a founding member of the AIGA Center for Brand. Prior positions at AIGA include serving on the national board of directors and as president of the Chicago chapter. A frequent design judge and lecturer, Liska has taught master's courses at the School of the Art Institute of Chicago, Kent State University, and Syracuse University.

Shel Perkins is a graphic designer, management consultant, and educator with twenty years of experience in managing the operations of leading design firms in the U.S. and the U.K. He currently provides management consulting services to a range of creative firms in both traditional and new media. He writes the "Professional Practice" column for *STEP* magazine, the *Design: Business* newsletter for AIGA, and the "Design Firm Management" column for Graphics.com. Author of *Talent Is Not Enough: Business Secrets For Designers*, Perkins has given presentations and workshops for many organizations, including IDSA, SEGD, HOW, *Dynamic Graphics, STEP*, and the Graphic Artists Guild. He teaches courses in professional practices at the California College of the Arts, the Academy of Art in San Francisco, and the University of California. He has served on the national board of the Association of Professional Design Firms and has been honored as an AIGA Fellow.

Peter L. Phillips is an internationally recognized expert in developing corporate design management strategies and programs. He has had more than thirty years experience as a senior corporate design manager, consultant, author, and lecturer. Author of *Creating the Perfect Design Brief: How to Manage Design for Strategic Advantage*, Phillips also serves on the advisory board and is an adjunct professor in design management for the Suffolk University Executive MBA Program in Innovation and Design Management.

Maria Piscopo is an art/photo rep, professional speaker, and author specializing in marketing creative services. Information about her workshops for AIGA chapters and the AIGA San Diego Y Conference can be found on her Web site, *www. mpiscopo.com*. Piscopo is also a contributing writer to *Communication Arts* magazine and *Dynamic Graphics* magazine. She is the author of *Graphic Designer's and Illustrator's Guide to Marketing and Promotion*.

Monona Rossol is a chemist, artist, and industrial hygienist. She is the founder and president of ACTS (Arts, Crafts and Theater Safety), a nonprofit corporation based in New York City, and is dedicated to providing health and safety services to the arts world. She is also the author of *The Health and Safety Guide for Film, TV, and Theater* and *The Artist's Complete Health and Safety Guide*.

Don Sparkman is the president of Sparkman+Associates, Inc. He is also the creative director for S+A's national accounts such as AT&T, Black & Decker, COMSAT, Eckerd Drugs, Head Sportswear, ICF Kaiser, IRS, LCI International, Marriott Corporation, MCI, NASA, OSHA, Rubbermaid, Sallie Mae, and the U.S. Postal Service. He has won numerous awards for design excellence, nationally and internationally, and his design work has been featured in many national design publications, including *Graphis*. He has written two books, *The Design and Printing Buyer's Survival Guide* and *Selling Graphic and Web Design*. He has lectured at George Washington University, Corcoran School of Art, Northern Virginia Community College, the Design Management Institute, the Art Directors Club of Metropolitan Washington, AIGA, and in many other venues.

Ray Taylor is an insurance broker working with artists, graphic designers, and photographers. He is a principal of Taylor & Taylor.

Scott Taylor is a member of the New York State Bar and has been an insurance broker for twenty-five years. He works with photographers, commercial producers, equipment rental companies, and others in the film industry. He is a principal of Taylor & Taylor.

A lawyer for more than twenty years, **Lee Wilson** has written several books on intellectual property law topics. Her most recent book is *Fair Use, Free Use, and Use By Permission*. She lives and writes in the woods north of Nashville.

INDEX

Books from Allworth Press

Allworth Press is an imprint of Allworth Communications, Inc. Selected titles are listed below.

How to Think Like a Great Graphic Designer
by Debbie Millman (6 × 9, 256 pages, paperback, $24.95)

Creating the Perfect Design Brief: How to Manage Design for Strategic Advantage
by Peter L. Phillips (6 × 9, 224 pages, paperback, $19.95)

Designing Logos: The Process of Creating Logos That Endure
by Jack Gernsheimer (8 1/2 × 10, 208 pages, paperback, $35.00)

Advertising Design & Typography
By Alex W. White (8 3/4 × 11 1/4, 224 pages, hardcover, $50.00)

The Graphic Designer's Guide to Better Business Writing
by Barbara Janoff and Ruth Cash-Smith (6 × 9, 256 pages, paperback, $19.95)

The Graphic Design Business Book
by Tad Crawford (6 × 9, 256 pages, paperback, $24.95)

Business and Legal Forms for Graphic Designers, Third Edition
by Tad Crawford and Eva Doman Bruck (8 1/2 × 11, 208 pages, paperback, includes CD-ROM, $29.95)

The Graphic Designer's Guide to Pricing, Estimating, and Budgeting, Revised Edition
by Theo Stephan Williams (6 3/4 × 9 7/8, 208 pages, paperback, $19.95)

Inside the Business of Graphic Design: 60 Leaders Share Their Secrets of Success
by Catharine Fishel (6 × 9, 288 pages, paperback, $19.95)

The Graphic Designer's Guide to Clients: How to Make Clients Happy and Do Great Work
by Ellen Shapiro (6 × 9, 256 pages, paperback, $19.95)

Editing by Design: For Designers, Art Directors, and Editors
by Jan V. White (8 1/2 × 11, 256 pages, paperback, $29.95)

How to Grow as a Graphic Designer
by Catharine Fishel (6 × 9, 256 pages, paperback, $19.95)

Selling Graphic and Web Design, Third Edition
by Donald Sparkman (6 × 9, 224 pages, paperback, $24.95)

Design Management: Using Design to Build Brand Value and Corporate Innovation
by Brigitte Borja de Mozota (6 × 9, 256 pages, paperback, $24.95)

The Real Business of Web Design
by John Waters (6 × 9, 256 pages, paperback, $19.95)

To request a free catalog or order books by credit card, call 1-800-491-2808. To see our complete catalog on the World Wide Web, or to order online for a 20 percent discount, you can find us at ***www.allworth.com.***